Der Welsche Gast
(The Italian Guest)

MEDIEVAL GERMAN TEXTS IN BILINGUAL EDITIONS

GENERAL EDITOR

Michael Curschmann
Princeton University

ADVISORY BOARD

Maria Dobozy
University of Utah

Ann Marie Rasmussen
Duke University

James Schultz
University of California, Los Angeles

A list of books in the series appears at the end of this book.

Medieval Institute Publications is a program of
The Medieval Institute, College of Arts and Sciences

 WESTERN MICHIGAN UNIVERSITY

Der Welsche Gast
(The Italian Guest)

Thomasin von Zirclaria

Translated with Introduction and Notes
by Marion Gibbs and Winder McConnell

TEAMS • Medieval German Texts in Bilingual Editions IV

MEDIEVAL INSTITUTE PUBLICATIONS
Western Michigan University
Kalamazoo

Library of Congress Cataloging-in-Publication Data

Thomasin, von Zerclaere, ca. 1186-ca. 1235.
 [Wälsche Gast. English]
 Der Welsche Gast = The Italian guest / Thomasin von Zirclaria ; translated
with introduction and notes by Marion Gibbs and Winder McConnell.
    p. cm. -- (Medieval German texts in bilingual editions ; IV)
 Includes bibliographical references.
 ISBN 978-1-58044-145-2 (paperbound : alk. paper)
 1. Thomasin, von Zerclaere, ca. 1186-ca. 1235. Wälsche Gast. 2. Virtue
--Poetry. 3. Didactic poetry, German--Translations into English. I. Gibbs,
Marion E. (Marion Elizabeth), 1940- II. McConnell, Winder. III. Title. IV.
Title: Italian guest.
 PT1658.T4A25 2010
 831'.2--dc22
                                2009040821

Manufactured in the United States of America

P 5 4 3 2 1

CONTENTS

A Note from the Editor   vii

Acknowledgments   ix

Introduction   1

Selected Bibliography   33

The Italian Guest

    Thomasin von Zirclaria's Prose Foreword   43

    Preface to Book I   56

    Book I   57

    Book II   76

    Book III   86

    Book IV   105

    Book V   123

    Book VI   135

    Book VII   155

    Book VIII   171

    Book IX   197

    Book X   212

    Notes   227

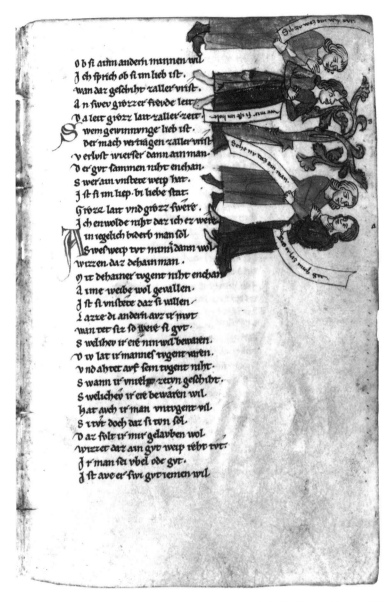

Figure 1. Thomasin von Zirclaria, "The Italian Guest." Heidelberg, Universitätsbibliothek, Cpg. 389, fol. 63r. The scene in the right margin dramatizes lines in the text to the left that deplore the unfortunate lot of a man whose wife loves another. To the left of the tree, a "friend" alerts the cuckold to what his wife is doing ("sih zv waz din wip tvt"), causing him to exclaim, 'Woe is me, she loves him' ("we mir si ist im holt"). On the other side, her lover chin-chucks the wife and crows, 'what if your husband saw this' ("sehe nu daz din man"). 'God forbid,' she replies ("des erlaz mich got"). Photo: Universitätsbibliothek Heidelberg.

A NOTE FROM THE EDITOR

Volume 4 of the Medieval German Texts in Bilingual Editions series should not go out without a word of explanation on two accounts.

The reader will notice that, contrary to our own editorial policy, the Thomasin translation appears here without the original text on facing pages. The decision to dispense with the original was not made lightly. Indeed, the publisher of the Middle High German text, Walter de Gruyter, Berlin, generously agreed to waive the permissions fee. We decided to deviate here from the policy to which future volumes will return for two reasons. First, *Der Welsche Gast* is a long text that has much to interest scholars and readers from many different disciplines. This meant that abridging it was out of the question. Including the original German would have necessitated breaking it up into two volumes, an impractical and cumbersome solution. Second, including the original German would have substantially delayed the publication of the volume, because this translation was begun without such an arrangement in mind and was well advanced by the time the series editors were able to persuade the translators that ours was the right series for them. At that stage, it would have been difficult and counterproductive to go back and reconcile line count and subdivisions in the translation with those of the original so that they could be presented on facing pages. In the end, the series editors decided that dispensing with the original (which is otherwise readily available) would facilitate the timely publication of an excellent translation in an accessible format, making this important and unjustly neglected work available to an interdisciplinary audience for the first time.

A second feature that deserves brief comment is illustration, or rather, the lack of it. To provide at least a glimpse of the medieval reality we have included two pictures from the Heidelberg manuscript on which the still-current nineteenth-century edition and hence the translation are based. *Der Welsche Gast* is one of those relatively rare cases in which systematic illustration of the text was not an afterthought but part of the original concept. Unfortunately, the book as it was composed around 1215/16 has not survived, but the Heidelberg manuscript gives us a fairly clear idea of the general layout and the topics covered by illustrations. These illustrations are not inserted into the text, but arranged around the margins—mostly left or right and occasionally at the bottom. They provide a second line of approach to the text—not independent of it but evocative and sometimes explanatory in ways in which the text alone is not. Medieval audiences fully recognized their importance as an integral part of Thomasin's composition, hence almost all of the surviving manuscripts carry some version of the original set of illustrations, although the layout changed to a more traditional format. In other words, the modern reader who does not have access to the original or a facsimile must be content with a severely curtailed version of the medieval work. To be aware of this limitation is extremely important, and it is hoped that readers will have occasion to look at the missing pictures in the facsimile of the Heidelberg manuscript or under the URL <http://digi.ub.uni-heidelberg.de/cpg389>, where the same manuscript appears in digitized form. In addition, the edition by F. W. von Kries includes reproductions of all the pictures in all of the manuscripts.

ACKNOWLEDGMENTS

We would like to thank Father Daniel A. Looney and Father Richard Blinn, S.J. for their assistance with several of the biblical references contained within *Der Welsche Gast*. We are also grateful to the editorial board of Medieval German Texts in Bilingual Editions for accepting this translation of Thomasin's primer on etiquette and ethics for publication in the series. We owe a special debt of thanks to Professor Michael Curschmann of Princeton University, general editor of the series, for his careful attention to our work. Finally, our sincere thanks to Patricia Hollahan, managing editor of Medieval Institute Publications at Western Michigan University, for her indispensable assistance in bringing this project to a successful completion.

INTRODUCTION

Factual knowledge regarding the life of the Italian Thomasin von Zir-claria[1] (ca. 1186–ca. 1259) is not abundant, but we are fortunate to have some written evidence of his existence. A document from 1217 in the Bib-liotheca Civica Cividale in Friuli in northeastern Italy contains a reference to a certain "Thomasinus canonicus Aquilegensis." In a necrology of the "Ecclesia," or patriarchate, of Aquileja, a town in the Italian province of Udine, the death of a canon by the name of "Thomasinus de Cerclara" is noted.[2] In the one literary work of the author that has been handed down to posterity, *Der Welsche Gast* (*The Italian Guest*),[3] Thomasin informs us in

---

[1] "Thomasîn von Zerclære," as the author identifies himself in verse 75, is a Germanized form of the Italian Tommasino dei Cerchiari. We have adhered to the common spelling of Thomasin's name to be found in most of the English-language secondary literature: "Thomasin von Zirclaria." In 14681, Thomasin states: "Mîn buoch heist der welhisch gast" and we have used the normalized New High German form of the title, namely, *Der Welsche Gast*, when referring to the work in our introduction and in the notes, although it should be mentioned that the variant *Der Wälsche Gast* is used frequently in German publications.

[2] Friedrich Neumann, "Einführung in Thomasins Verswerk," in *Der Welsche Gast des Thomasîn von Zerclaere. Codex Palatinus Germanicus 389 der Universitätsbibliothek Heidelberg*, ed. Friedrich Neumann and Ewald Vetter (Wiesbaden: Dr. Ludwig Reichert Verlag, 1974), p. 9.

[3] The epithet "welsch" (cognate with "walhisch, welhisch, walsch") may also refer to someone or something whose origins are to be sought in the French or Romanic sphere. Nigel Harris translates *Der Welsche Gast* as "The Visitor from the Romance Lands," but it is more likely that Thomasin is thinking specifically of his Friuli home-land when he uses the term. See Nigel Harris, "Didactic Poetry," in Will Hasty, ed., *German Literature of the High Middle Ages*, The Camden House History of German Literature, vol. 3 (Rochester: Camden House, 2006), pp. 123–40, esp. p. 133.

verses 71ff. that he was born Thomasîn von Zerclære in "Frîule," that is, the region of Friuli/Lombardy, in northern Italy. His primer on etiquette and ethics can be dated from internal evidence to spring 1216, as he intimates in verses 11717–22 that the grave of Christ has been lost (to the Muslims) for twenty-eight years, a reference to the taking of Jerusalem by Saladin in July 1187. He had not yet turned thirty by the time the work was completed (verse 2445), but, given life expectancy for male members of the nobility about the year 1200, Thomasin would have been, as Friedrich Neumann has noted, "auf der Höhe seines Lebens,"[4] and was quite likely born about 1186. More specific details concerning his life have eluded scholars and even the most recent scholarship concerning Thomasin's status within society remains inconclusive. Although he is generally acknowledged to be a cleric who *may* have stood in close proximity to Wolfger, bishop of Passau,[5] these presumptions have also been questioned of late.[6] As Willms has pointed out, *Der Welsche Gast* lacks any form of dedication to the bishop,[7] something that one would have expected had Wolfger, in fact, been Thomasin's benefactor. Moreover, Thomasin is unsparing in his criticism of the religious nobility (6521–80), and, in Book VIII of *Der Welsche Gast*, what we might designate as his "political" manifesto, clearly, in opposition to Wolfger, champions the cause of Frederick II over Otto of Brunswick, who was crowned Emperor Otto IV in October, 1209, by Pope Innocent III. Thomasin appears, nonetheless, to have accompanied Wolfger to Rome for the coronation. Whatever he may have felt about Otto of Brunswick, Thomasin had nothing but veneration for Pope Innocent III, if we are to judge by his spirited panegyric to the Holy Father in Book VIII (11091ff.) and his reproach of anyone who, without actually knowing the pope, voiced criticism of his actions and accused him of greed, treachery, and complicity with the devil. Although he does not name Walther von der Vogelweide, Thomasin clearly has him in mind, particularly in 11191ff.

---

[4] Neumann, "Einführung in Thomasins Verswerk," p. 7.

[5] Wolfger von Erla, bishop of Passau (1191–1204) and patron of, among others, Walther von der Vogelweide, was patriarch of Aquileja between 1204 and 1218.

[6] See Eva Willms, ed. and trans., *Thomasin von Zerklaere. Der Welsche Gast. Text (Auswahl), Übersetzung. Stellenkommentar* (Berlin: Walter de Gruyter, 2004), p. 4. Internal "evidence" from the beginning of Book IX of *Der Welsche Gast* would seem to indicate that Thomasin had earlier devoted himself to a more secular occupation, given the reference, made by his pen in a sort of admonishment to the author, to his having watched jousts, danced with ladies, but apparently now turned his back on the world of the court.

[7] Willms, *Thomasin von Zerklaere*, p. 3.

Thomasin's erudition is without question. Counted among the theological and philosophical influences to be found in *Der Welsche Gast* are the Bible, Boethius, Cicero, Seneca, Horace, St. Augustine, John of Salisbury, Isidore of Seville, Ambrose of Milan, and Pope Gregory I.[8] Thomasin draws upon a wealth of examples from biblical and classical sources to illustrate the virtues, or vices, that he discusses in detail in his treatise. As such, one would assume that *Der Welsche Gast* was directed at a relatively well-educated audience, although in Book VII he makes it abundantly clear that his age was certainly not a golden one for education.

While no other works of Thomasin are extant, he does make reference in verses 1173ff. to a "buoch von der hüfscheit" ('book on courtesy') that he had earlier composed in Italian. Presumably, his later reference in 1551ff. to earlier commentaries on "valscheit" ('falsity, duplicity') that he had formulated in Italian "einer vrouwen ze êre" ('to the honor of a woman'), as well as to those on virtue (1677ff.), are allusions to the same book. Thus, while this cannot be claimed definitely, it is not at all unlikely that Thomasin is regurgitating in *Der Welsche Gast* many of the ethical concepts that he had previously imparted to an Italian audience.

Over three decades ago, Friedrich Neumann described Thomasin's *Der Welsche Gast* as a linguistic phenomenon without comparison within the corpus of German literature of the Hohenstaufen period.[9] In the didactic literature of the time, *Der Welsche Gast* does indeed occupy a unique position. Nigel Harris has not exaggerated with his designation of the work as a "monumental moral compendium" that demonstrates "the ultimate indivisibility of religious and ethical perspectives."[10] While it may certainly be claimed that works of other genres, such as courtly romances, heroic epics, *bîspele, sprüche* (including *Sangsprüche*), as well as the *mæren* of Hartmann von Aue (*Der arme Heinrich, Gregorius*), evince obvious didactic moments, Thomasin's *Der Welsche Gast* dispenses with any narrative framework which could possibly divert his audience's attention from the moral lesson at hand. The work betrays the heavy hand of the clerical moralist who moves from providing the younger members of his audience with a primer for proper social etiquette in his early verses to a meticulous analysis of what he

---

[8] See the extensive list provided by Michael Resler in his entry, "Thomasîn von Zerclære," in James Hardin and Will Hasty, eds., *German Writers and Works of the High Middle Ages: 1170–1280*, Dictionary of Literary Biography, vol. 138 (Detroit: Gale Research Inc., 1994), pp. 133–40, esp. p. 136.

[9] Neumann, "Einführung in Thomasins Verswerk," p. 2: "als Sprachwerk eine Merkwürdigkeit, der nichts Vergleichbares zur Seite steht."

[10] Harris, "Didactic Poetry," p. 133.

clearly viewed as the appropriate ethical code for the nobility of his time, often presented against the backdrop of a thundering condemnation of the state of contemporary affairs. Thomasin directs his words at the representatives of both the lay and religious nobility of Germany. He exhorts them to adhere to the *bîspele* ('examples') that he provides and to take their *bilde* ('models') as the basis for their own behavior. His book, as he clearly indicates at the conclusion, is not intended for dullards, but for the man imbued "mit stæte" ('with constancy' [14743]).

We have taken as our text the 1852 edition by Heinrich Rückert, reprinted in 1965 with a foreword by Friedrich Neumann and based on MS A, the Gotha Pergament Codex (MS G, dated to 1340), the paper manuscript from Dresden (MS D) from the middle of the fifteenth century and related to A, and Gr, the parchment manuscript once owned by Wilhelm Grimm and dating from the thirteenth century. Given the "quite excellent text" of MS A,[11] and for technical reasons, we chose Rückert's edition in preference to the later edition by F. W. von Kries (1984–85). The most recent edition, by Raffaele Disanto (2002), also follows MS A, but without normalization and many of Rückert's emendations. This edition will nevertheless be found useful for the reader who wishes to compare our translation with the original.

In his introduction to Rückert's edition of *Der Welsche Gast*,[12] Friedrich Neumann lists twelve manuscripts that were known to the editor: A (Heidelberg), G (Gotha), E (Erbach), S (Stuttgart), Gr, D (Dresden), M (Munich), U (Munich, previously Ulm), W (Wolfenbüttel), a (Heidelberg), b (Heidelberg), c (Heidelberg). To these, Neumann adds six further manuscripts cited by Konrad Burdach in his *Die illustrierten Handschriften des Welschen Gastes*, that are located in Büdingen, Budapest, the duke of Hamilton's collection, Wolfenbüttel, Karlsruhe, and Königsberg, while another manuscript, the Watzendorf, is to be found in Coburg. Based on the dates indicated on illustration 35 of MS A, Neumann assumes that five or six manuscripts may have been lost. Since Neumann offered his overview of the manuscript tradition over forty years ago, a total of twenty-four manuscripts—thirteen on parchment, eleven on paper—have been identified, of which fifteen are more

---

[11] Willms, *Thomasin von Zerklaere*, p. 16. The four-volume edition by F. W. von Kries (*Thomasin von Zerclaere. Der Welsche Gast* [Göppingen: Kümmerle-Verlag, 1984–85]) has come under fire for its less than ideal editing (e.g., Willms, *Thomasin von Zerklaere*, p. 18).

[12] Heinrich Rückert, ed., *Der Wälsche Gast des Thomasin von Zirclaria*, mit einer Einleitung und einem Register von Friedrich Neumann, Deutsche Neudrucke, Reihe: Texte des Mittelalters (1852; rpt. Berlin: Walter de Gruyter & Co, 1965; Neumann: pp. v–li, here. See pp. xlvi–li for an account of the manuscript tradition).

or less complete.[13] The oldest manuscript, considered to be closest to the original, is the Heidelberg manuscript Cpg. 389, which dates from shortly after the middle of the thirteenth century. A comparison of all extant manuscripts by Willms has determined their essential independence of each other, with only one, W, having been copied from another (U). There are two major strands comprising the manuscript tradition. The first strand, considered closest to the original text, is represented by A and F (Schlierbach), the latter identified as late as 1968, and a fragment. The Gotha manuscript (G) and some fragments represent the second strand and are viewed as a moderately revised version of A. The relationship of the manuscripts to one another is, however, somewhat enigmatic, given the tendency of scribes to use versions that belonged to different strands when composing their individual versions.

The number of extant manuscripts of *Der Welsche Gast* suggests that it was a popular work, "well received and widely read not only during its own age but by later generations as well."[14] This was probably in no small way due to the fact that most of the manuscripts were prolifically illustrated. One hundred and twenty illustrations are to be found, either in part or in their entirety, in all of the complete manuscripts other than M. They were clearly intended as an integral part of Thomasin's work, and the author himself alludes to the illustrated portrayal of the perjurer on the stairway leading to hell in verses 11970–71. Unlike illustrations in other medieval manuscripts, such as those contained in the Nibelungen Hundeshagen Codex, which, in themselves, provide an illiterate contemporary with an optical synopsis of major "stations" in the plot of the *Nibelungenlied*, the illustrations in Thomasin's *Der Welsche Gast* sometimes seem to presume a certain literacy on the part of the viewer, especially with respect to those that complement the author's discourse on the virtues. The names of the latter are to be seen, for example, above the heads of the figures in illustration 78, depicting the specific virtues such as modesty and generosity, and each carries a banner with a specific declaration. Nor are banners with texts solely confined to the virtues; they are to be found in copious numbers throughout the illustrations. Thomasin's remarks in Book I (especially 1103–6) concerning the uneducated who should look to pictures for instruction must be

---

[13] Willms, *Thomasin von Zerklaere*, p. 15. See also Horst Wenzel and Christina Lechtermann, eds., *Beweglichkeit der Bilder. Text und Imagination in den illustrierten Handschriften des "Welschen Gastes" von Thomasin von Zerclaere* (Cologne: Böhlau Verlag, 2002), pp. 257–65. Note also Michael Curschmann, "Interdisziplinäre Beweglichkeit—Wie weit reicht sie?" *Zeitschrift für Deutsche Philologie*, 123, no. 1 (2004): 109–17. Also von Kries, *Thomasin von Zerclaere*, vol. 1, pp. 48–56.

[14] Resler, "Thomasîn von Zerclaere," p. 139.

understood in that context. Pictures generate conversation, projecting the text into the realm of informal orality where the debate or rumination takes place that is meant to follow.[15] Thus, while the illustrations of *Der Welsche Gast* may not be accorded any great artistic merit in all but one or two of the extant manuscripts, they obviously fulfill an extremely important didactic function.[16] It is generally assumed nowadays that these illustrations were part of Thomasin's original conception of the book, and he may even have played an active role in their selection and placement.

Thirteen of the extant manuscripts and fragments contain the basic compendium of illustrations, although the actual number in each manuscript may vary considerably, given the diverse degree of completeness among the manuscripts. Based on the empty spaces contained therein, four manuscripts were intended to include illustrations, but these were never added. Three fragments have no illustrations and no indication that any were to be added at a later date.

Thomasin's *Der Welsche Gast* consists of 14,742 verses. They were miscounted as 14,752 by Rückert,[17] but to avoid confusion for readers who wish to reach for the MHG original we have retained the incorrect numbering, as has Disanto in his new edition. The four-beat lines are composed in rhyming couplets and divided among ten books (*teil* or *tail*). To these must be added the extensive foreword in which Thomasin provides a prose synopsis of the contents of each of the ten books contained within the work. As was customary in many medieval works, the author identifies himself and sets out in a brief prologue the reasons for having decided to write his book. His objective is first and foremost to instruct, to serve as a mentor, not only to

[15] On this point see Michael Curschmann, "Volkssprache und Bildsprache," in Eckart C. Lutz et al., eds., *Literatur und Wandmalerei*, vol. 1: *Erscheinungsformen höfischer Kultur und ihre Träger im Mittelalter* (Tübingen: Max Niemeyer, 2002), pp. 9–46, esp. pp. 15–17. Rpt. in Curschmann, *Wort—Bild—Text. Studien zur Medialität des Literarischen in Hochmittelalter und früher Neuzeit*, 2 vols., Saecula spiritalia 44 (Baden-Baden: Valentin Koener, 2007), vol. 2, pp. 801–38.

[16] See the detailed analysis of each illustration in F. W. von Kries, ed., *Thomasin von Zerclaere. Der Welsche Gast*, vol. 4: *Die Illustrationen des Welschen Gasts: Kommentar mit Analyse der Bildinhalte und den Varianten der Schriftbandtexte. Verzeichnisse, Namenregister, Bibliographie*, Göppinger Arbeiten zur Germanistik 425 IV (Göppingen: Kümmerle-Verlag, 1985). Note particularly also the facsimile edition of the Heidelberg manuscript (A), as listed in the bibliography below, and the prolific illustrations reproduced in Wenzel and Lechtermann, *Beweglichkeit der Bilder*, particularly those in full color between pp. 138 and 139.

[17] On p. 36, the jump from verse 1290 to 1300 (skipping over 1295) is clear, as is the jump from 1490 to 1500 (skipping over 1495) on p. 41. Note as well that verse 3635 on p. 99 in Rückert is numbered incorrectly as 2635.

the young but also to the higher lay and ecclesiastical nobility of his time. It is fascinating to note how Thomasin moves from offering some rather banal comments on appropriate etiquette for young noblemen and noblewomen in the earlier part of his work to composing a remarkably intense treatise addressing major concepts of medieval ethics such as virtue, constancy, justice, moderation, and generosity that constitutes the core of his text.

Book I is directed at young noblemen and noblewomen and not only provides the reader with an overview of the secular literature, particularly the romance literature, of Thomasin's age but also presents the author's audience with a compendium of male and female figures from secular literature that those young squires and maidens might take as their "models" in the attempt to adhere to a virtuous and worthy life. The reader is not at all surprised to find King Arthur,[18] Charlemagne, and Gawain, Erec, Cligès, and other knights of the Round Table included in Thomasin's list of prominent figures, but is given reason to pause when he or she encounters in verse 1051 the name of a "hero" who could hardly be considered the epitome of Christian virtue to a poet who, whatever his actual rank, was undoubtedly a cleric: "an gevuoc volgt ir Tristande" ('copy Tristan in behaving correctly' [1051]). Assuming that this is the Tristan of Gottfried von Strassburg (or one of Gottfried's sources), it is nothing short of paradoxical that a cleric would admonish his young readers to take as a model a man who, his qualities as a knight and artist notwithstanding, was engaged in a highly illicit, adulterous relationship with his uncle's spouse. One gains the distinct impression that Thomasin, and perhaps others among his contemporaries, were fully capable of distinguishing between the noble and courageous Tristan the knight and Tristan the adulterer.

Book II focuses on the "princes and noble gentlemen" of chivalrous society as the individuals most suited to provide a good example for young and old alike. Early on in this book, Thomasin emphasizes the need for the lord to be "ganz an stætekeit" ('the epitome of constancy' [1789]), a virtue to which he will repeatedly return throughout his book, as it is *the* virtue on which all others depend. It is here that he offers a vigorous condemnation of inconstancy, of which all mankind is guilty, and the vice of lying, "der helle port" ('the gateway to hell' [2122]), maintaining that there is nothing that he abhors more in a nobleman than the latter. Thomasin goes on to discuss why the four elements (fire, air, water, earth) are at variance

[18] It is, however, intriguing to note that, in his criticism of worldly power and authority, Thomasin conveys a much more critical stance towards Arthur (3535ff.). While the head of the Round Table may well be known today as much as he was in former times, "waz hilft in daz" ('how does that help him?' [3537]). Thomasin even suggests that Arthur would be better served through a "pâter noster" (3538).

with one another, suggesting that this is why there is no constancy here on earth (2405) and linking such inconstancy to the discord to be found in his own time among the Italian cities, but also to the treachery to be found in other lands. The book ends on an apocalyptic note: "ir seht wol der unstæte maht: / vil grôziu zeichn gît uns ir kraft / daz diu werlt welle schier/nemen end"('You can clearly see the power of inconstancy; its power gives us so many clear signs that the world is soon coming to an end' [2501–4]).

In Book III, Thomasin continues his discourse on inconstancy, which he views as married to other vices. He is particularly perturbed over the propensity of man to defy the natural (and ordained) *ordo* of things, pointing to the squire who would like to exchange his life for that of a peasant, whereas the priest would like to become a knight and the knight a priest, while the craftsman and the merchant would similarly like to exchange professions. Thomasin also emphasizes that wealth is not a panacea for all concerns and it, as well as we ourselves, is, after all, transitory and ultimately useless. His admonishments in this book constitute a variation on the biblical theme of a rich man's difficulty getting into heaven. Moreover, authority, power, and fame constitute a burden and are not worth pursuing. The appropriate aim for man is to acquire *summum bonum*, "gotes huld" ('the grace of God' [2838]). Thomasin concludes this book with some critical remarks on "desire" and, in particular, the decidedly deleterious effect it can have on the relationship between a man and a woman, a discourse that allows him to reaffirm the medieval belief so common to other works that joy was never without sorrow.

In Book IV, Thomasin turns his attention to vice and underscores how important it is, particularly for a nobleman, to disdain wealth, authority, fame, power, nobility, and desire. "Nobility" in the sense intended here by Thomasin can hardly refer to "inner" nobility, but rather to the idea of relying entirely on one's status within society, making no attempt to better oneself. He links wealth to avarice, authority to pride, power to arrogance and shame, fame to extravagance, nobility to foolishness, desire to sloth, gluttony, lasciviousness, and drunkenness. The book is also dedicated to a discourse on virtue and constancy, with Thomasin emphasizing that virtue is nothing without constancy. Within the context of a discussion of justice and injustice, he also takes up the perennial question of why evil can flourish in the world while good men suffer. His response is the usual one offered by the Church that continues even to the present day: each will receive according to his due in the next world and no mortal can fathom the depth of God's wisdom. It is a call to accept the decisions of God, as being, while mysterious, innately good and just.

Book V of *Der Welsche Gast* is devoted to a discussion of the dichotomy between the highest good (God) and the greatest evil (the devil), between virtue and vice. In a sense, the world has been stood on its head. Thomasin notes the manner in which the six attributes— nobility, power, desire, reputation, wealth, and authority—can be employed for good or evil, depending on the individual who obtains them. Thomasin uses the illustration of two stairways, whereby the steps of the first, which leads to God and heaven, are represented by the virtues, while the second is composed of steps representing vices that lead down to the infernal regions. It is an illusion to believe that the six aforementioned attributes can be used as a springboard to heaven. Wealth can never replace virtue as a prerequisite for admission to the heavenly kingdom, as Thomasin appropriately describes through numerous examples from both history and the Bible. He employs here the *in illo tempore* motif to underscore the dichotomy between the happier times of the past, when virtue was recognized and accorded its proper due, and the paucity of virtuous people to be found in the world in his time, a time in which not only figures of the stature of Arthur, Erec, Gawain, Parzival, and Iwein but also classical philosophers such as Aristotle, Zeno, Parmenides, Pythagorus, and Anaxagorus are sorely missed. The book also contains an intriguing—and one wonders whether it is not an autobiographical—diatribe against the bishop who will not support his priests in their schooling and against the generally negative attitude prevailing within society towards those who have been well educated. By the conclusion of this book, Thomasin has, in fact, shunned all six of the attributes listed at the outset as being promoters of vice both in youth and old age.

Thomasin continues his *laudatio* on virtue in Book VI, demonstrating the benefits it brought, even in this world, to biblical figures such as Job, Moses, David, and Joseph. He has particularly harsh words here for moneylenders and warns, in true clerical fashion, that the sins of the fathers may be visited upon their sons. He offers a formula for a good life on this earth: be humble and avoid arrogance, envy, anger, and salacious living. Be just in one's dealings with others. Avoid sloth; do not succumb to larceny, thieving, vanity, fame, deceit, perjury, frivolity, lechery, gluttony, drunkenness, and avarice. Adhere to the truth in all things. Intriguing in this book is Thomasin's extension of the idea of "chivalry" to embrace not just the knight who "breaks a lance" in the service of what is good but anyone who wages a campaign against vice on this earth, the contemporary ideal of the *miles christianus*. He refers to a "host of vices" whose four "commanders" are Arrogance, Impurity, Malevolence, and Sloth. On the side of virtue are to be found in this struggle Good Sense, Justice, Prudence, Security, Faith, Hope, Courage, Chastity, Constancy, and Humility. Thomasin once again proves to be a keen observer of the human condition, for he cautions that the one who vanquishes the vices should take care not to fall victim himself to arrogance. He underscores the significance of "gotes gnâde" ('the grace of God'), claiming that the person who does not enjoy it is the scion of evil. As elsewhere, he extends his advice to members of both the knighthood and the priesthood. Representatives of both bodies must live by example and must accept their place in the world. He despairs of those who abuse their authority, lords who order their vassals to sin and thus bring both themselves and those beholden to them to the gates of hell. Nobility of virtue is to be observed, nobility of wealth to be rejected. Yet, like Hart-mann von Aue in *Der arme Heinrich*, Thomasin does not see a contradic-tion between wealth and enjoying God's grace, provided that the man who enjoys wealth and honor is a virtuous man and, as he indicates in Book VII of his work, directs his mind to the ultimate origin of these benefits. If, however, it is God's will that a man live his life in poverty, he should do so without complaint and in the belief that a loving God is always at his side. Thomasin closes this book with an admonition to his readers to confess their sins and do penance before departing this world.

In Book VII of *Der Welsche Gast*, Thomasin turns his attention to the properties of the soul. As its "qualities" are the virtues, the soul is to be accorded more worth than the body. The soul must hold dominion over five external (nobility, power, wealth, reputation, authority) and five inter-nal attributes (strength, speed, desire, beauty, agility) of man, as well as over speech, which is considered both an external and internal attribute. Thomasin places particular emphasis here on the significance of intellect, common sense, and reasoning, gifts of the Almighty, which, were it not for the sins of man, would elevate him to the same level as angels. Here again, Thomasin points to a topsy-turvy world: priests and knights are no longer the models of exemplary lives that should be provided for others in society. The priest wishes to use the sword of the knight to acquire wealth, while the knight's purpose in learning how to read is to be able to record the interest owed to him by debtors. Thomasin urges his readers to heed the advice of four qualities: Imagination, Reason, Memory, and Intellect. He also underscores the value of the seven liberal arts, the trivium and qua-drivium: Grammar, Dialectic, Rhetoric; Arithmetic, Geometry, Music, and Astronomy, which, although impossible to master completely, should be a source of peace and richness in a person's life. Yet, there are two other arts that are superior to all the rest, namely, Divinity, "mistress of all the arts," which instructs a person in the protection of his soul, and Physic, which shows how one can remain healthy in body. Undoubtedly reflecting his own erudite background, Thomasin, somewhat wistfully, casts an eye back to a time when more store was set by education and the importance accorded the latter in the upbringing of one's progeny.

Book VIII is the longest in *Der Welsche Gast*. Thomasin begins with a discourse on the malevolent "sisters," inconstancy and immoderation, and contrasts immoderation with its antonym, moderation, "des sinnes wâge zaller vrist" ('always the measure of the intellect' [9936]). Moderation is, of course, a key concept in medieval life and philosophy and the very *ordo* of society depends upon its maintenance. Anything taken to excess, even virtues such as humility, generosity, mercy, and tolerance, can be transformed through immoderation into vices, while the practice of moderation may well turn vices such as anger, arrogance, and spitefulness into virtues. It is also in this book that Thomasin reaffirms a major tenet of medieval culture and civilization, one that separates that age so radically from our own, namely, the belief in the correspondence of the inner and the outer. He declares in verses 10437–40 that "what one sees on the outside is not without significance, for it always signifies what is on the inside, too." Returning to his major theme of moderation/immoderation, Thomasin alludes to political developments, namely, the arrogance he associates with the unsuccessful candidate for the imperial throne, Otto of Brunswick, who had three lions (two too many, a sign of arrogance) and a demi-eagle (lacking a half, thus, unable to fly to lofty heights and so symbolizing a diminution of honor) emblazoned on his shield. He augments this with examples from biblical history, citing numerous examples of rulers who fell prey to arrogance and suffered accordingly.

Thomasin also voices his belief that man should accept the hierarchical order in which he finds himself and humbly and dutifully obey his master. He is particularly adamant on this point with respect to the pope's position in the world and unrelenting in his condemnation of the latter's critics, notably among them the poet Walther von der Vogelweide, the only one actually named. The modern reader will marvel over Thomasin's logic when explaining the dichotomy between rich and poor in the world: "diu milte diuhte gar enwiht, / wære dehein arme niht" ('generosity would be worthless if there were no poor people' [11523–24]). His ecclesiastical stance on the proper attitude of the nobility in the matter of war is thoroughly orthodox and echoes much of what Christian Europe had heard since Pope Urban II had called for a crusade to the Holy Land at the end of the eleventh century: it is arrogance and vanity that cause Western chivalry to turn on its own when God and Christianity are best served by fighting to liberate the Holy Land. In this respect, Thomasin exhorts Frederick II to follow the tradition of his forebears and lead a crusade to the Middle East. He attributes great significance to the fact that Frederick II will be the third in line of his dynasty to undertake such a campaign as he associates the number three with perfection and thus with the inevitable success of the mission. Thomasin returns to the theme of arrogance towards the close of this book, intimating that arrogance leads to guilt which brings with it a fall from God's grace.

Book IX of Thomasin's *Der Welsche Gast* opens with a remarkable chastisement of the author proffered by his pen, which appears indignant at having been abused throughout the previous eight months devoted to the writing of the volume. Striking is the allusion by the quill to what appears to be Thomasin's (past) life at court, a time when he enjoyed dancing and attending jousts. The narrator retorts that this was not simply a labor of love, conceived for the delight of his readers, but an absolute necessity because "man nien tuot daz man sol" ('people never behave as they ought to' [12290]). Thomasin focuses on the theme of justice in this book and links it early on with the concept of moderation. Justice is to be dispensed equally among all, whether rich or poor, and both rich and poor should enjoy equal representation before a court of law. Justice must be based not on gain, favoritism, patronage, the desire for fame, or the various passions, but on sound advice from trustworthy counselors. Thomasin criticizes the tendency to allow undue compassion to compromise justice; here, again, a fine balance needs to be struck between dispensing justice and demonstrating pity for the condemned. A significant point to be noted in this book is Thomasin's linking of spiritual and worldly justice. He attributes the sundering of this bond as detrimental to the dispensing of justice, to the point that even the threat of excommunication does not instill fear in the heart of a transgressor. Thomasin demonstrates here his unequivocal alignment with orthodox Catholicism, heaping lavish praise on Leopold VI of Austria for his harsh treatment of heretics. Also at the core of Book IX is the biblical exhortation: "Judge not, lest ye be judged." A lord should place absolute faith in God, for, in doing so, and adhering to His commandments, he will certainly prevail. Thomasin also offers sage words on the value of accepting sound advice, regardless of the source, although a lord should always be wary of accepting unsolicited advice. The book concludes with an admonishment directed against those who commit injustice out of ignorance, those who commit an injustice intentionally, and, in a tone that rings thoroughly "modern," those who do not act to prevent an injustice from befalling another out of idleness, because they simply do not want to "become involved."[19]

The final book of Thomasin's *Der Welsche Gast* opens with an assurance on the part of the author to his pen that he will soon conclude his work, but that he feels compelled to hold forth at this point on the "mirror of virtues," the "child of justice," namely, generosity. Noteworthy in this book is Thomasin's comparison of justice and generosity, his claim that, while justice both gives and takes (13615), generosity only gives, and, while justice dispenses

---

[19] Thomasin echoes here the same admonishment to be found in Book 1 of Cicero's *De Officiis*.

both joy and sorrow, generosity always provides a man only with what will give him joy (13623ff.). It is scarcely surprising that Thomasin declares generosity to be the virtue that pleases him above all others (13741–42). Wickedness is associated with avarice, nobility with generosity. Thomasin appears again to counter the tenor of his age when he claims that it is foolish to deem the man who has nothing to give lacking in generosity. His claim that "wir erahten niwan daz / daz wir mugen gesehen baz" ('we only value what we are more likely to see clearly' [13989–90]) reflects the medieval idea of the inner corresponding with the outer,[20] a tenet that Thomasin, in contradistinction to what he has already stated in Book VIII, verses 10437–40, now appears to reject: "man merket niht waz in dem muot / sî" ('People do not notice what is in the heart' [13991–92]). He rails against those who are generous with ill-gotten gains and against those who are only too ready to accept such gifts. True generosity is the antithesis of avarice. Timing is also important, according to Thomasin, and anyone who wishes to give out of generosity should not let the one to be benefited wait until he is virtually forced to beg for aid. The recipient should never gain any impression other than that his benefactor is acting willingly and with a glad heart. The emphasis must be on the giving itself and not on recompense, thanks received, or how one might otherwise stand to gain from having provided gifts. Thomasin addresses when it is appropriate to give publicly, when clandestinely, what to give, to whom, and how a gift can be given in a manner destined to bring joy rather than embarrassment to the one receiving it. The aristocratic bias against the mercantile class is made abundantly clear in this book as he admonishes his audience to avoid ever appearing as a merchant, a "bad trait." Thomasin concludes Book X, and his work, with some comments on the appropriate recipient of *Der Welsche Gast*. It is intended for the person who knows courtesy and who is virtuous. His "Italian Guest" is not to seek lodging with some scoundrel, for it will soon find itself cast aside and neglected. His book is meant to improve, but also to be improved upon, for, as he claims, "der vrum man sol tuon baz / dan du lêrest" ('the good man must perform even better deeds than you teach' [14747–48]).

[20] See Walter Haug's splendid article, "Montage und Individualität im *Nibelungenlied*," in Fritz Peter Knapp, ed., *Nibelungenlied und Klage. Sage und Geschichte, Struktur und Gattung. Passauer Nibelungengespräche 1985* (Heidelberg: Carl Winter Universitätsverlag, 1987), pp. 277–93. Rpt. in Haug, *Strukturen als Schlüssel zur Welt. Kleine Schriften zur Erzählliteratur des Mittelalters* (Tübingen: Max Niemeyer, 1989), pp. 326–38. Haug's elucidation of the manner in which this tenet is defied by the poet of the heroic epic could justifiably be viewed—despite the relative brevity of the article—as one of the most significant contributions to medieval studies to have appeared over the past half-century.

Medieval literature offers a plethora of abstract concepts that are to be found in every genre, for which modern cognates may exist but the meaning of which may often have shifted, or changed completely, in the intervening centuries. Whether the work in question was intended chiefly for entertainment, or, as in the case of Thomasin's *Der Welsche Gast,* composed primarily for didactic purposes, the translator often confronts the formidable challenge of rendering such abstract terms into the target language in a way that adequately conveys to a modern audience the semantics of the original. This challenge is heightened by the fact that an individual concept may mean different things in different contexts. We have, therefore, felt it prudent to offer in this introduction some comments on key terms to be found in Thomasin's *Der Welsche Gast* and, where appropriate, to indicate the reasoning behind our choice of an English "equivalent." We remain fully aware, of course, that other renderings may be equally acceptable. Medieval terms such as *êre, list, sin, bescheidenheit, erge, zuht, muot, reht, tugent, sælde, mâze,* and *stæte,* for example, are, more often than not, difficult, if not impossible, to render into English using a single word. By no means would we contend that we have everywhere through our renderings captured the meaning of the original as Thomasin understood it, and there remain several instances when we feel a particular word or turn of phrase has eluded our understanding of what Thomasin intended to convey.

One of the most frequently used abstract terms throughout *Der Welsche Gast* is *sin,* which Lexer defines as "körperlicher, wahrnehmender sinn . . . der innere sinn . . . der denkende geist, verstand . . . bewusstsein, besinnung; weisheit, kunst . . . verständige handlung, kunstgriff; gesinnung."[21] When Thomasin initially uses the word in 50, it is to describe the motivation behind his composing of the work: "ich hân einn andern sin erkorn" ('I have something else in mind' or 'I have a different intention'). The application of *sin* in this context is clearly quite different from its use in other parts of the book. When we encounter it within 100–101, *sin* conveys a very different meaning: "des vlîzet er sich gern mit allem / sînem sinne und sînem muot." The latter part of this sentence would appear, in this context, to be the Middle High German equivalent of the contemporary English idiom '[with all of] his heart and soul.' However, when once again used in combination with "muot" in 6314–15 ("ich muoz kêren an gewin / mînen sin und mînen muot" = 'I must turn my thoughts and my heart towards profit'), the aforementioned English idiomatic expression would appear somewhat

---

[21] Matthias Lexer, *Mittelhochdeutsches Handwörterbuch,* vol. 2 (1876; rpt. Stuttgart: S. Hirzel Verlag, 1974), cols. 926–27.

out of place. In this instance, we felt that *sin* was more appropriately rendered as 'thoughts.' When Thomasin concludes the preface to *Der Welsche Gast* with the declaration that he desires to have God grant him *sinne* (139) as he begins the task of writing his book, the word must be understood in the sense of 'know-how' or 'ability' (to perform the task at hand), a concept we have rendered into English as 'wit.' A different nuance attaches to *sin* in 150: "man habe den sin und ouch den rât." While *sin* in this context might arguably be associated semantically with the earlier occurrence of *sinne* in 139, we have elected to use the formulation 'good sense,' not least of all because of the combination of *sin* and *rât*, whereby we understand *rât* in this context to convey the idea of 'intelligence' or 'wisdom,' thus: 'one should have the good sense and wisdom.' This is not dissimilar to what we find in 2602, where Thomasin says that anyone who might wish to show good sense should note that evil acts are a transgression against God: "daz merke swer wil haben sin" = 'Let anyone who cares to have good sense take note of that.' *Sin* is capitalized by Rückert in 7470 and conveys the idea of 'good sense' as a prerequisite for sound military leadership (note also *sinne* in 7557). *Sinne* may also be used to denote the idea of 'mind,' as in 188, where Thomasin refers to young people who can obtain more of his good advice "ob si sichs vlîzent von ir sinnen" ('if they put their minds to it').[22] An even more poignant example of how *sin* is used to depict the idea of 'mind' is to be found in 1961 where Thomasin claims rather pessimistically: "swer vil gedenket, krenkt den sin" ('Anyone who thinks too much damages the mind'). The behavior of noblemen and priests who grow hostile towards one another and act in an uncouth manner is viewed as having derived "von krankem sin" (12756) or "von swachem sinne" (12760), which we have rendered as a 'feeble mind.' In his description of the uncouth behavior of young noblemen during drinking bouts at the inn, Thomasin contrasts such antics with someone who "dâ hât schœnen sin" (327) and who, precisely because of his "schœnen sin," is unwelcome among these fellows. "Sin" in this instance, combined with the epithet "schœn," conveys the idea of 'finer feeling' or 'demeanor.' *Sin* may also convey the concept of 'common sense, intellect,' as is the case when it occurs, for example, in combination with the term "bescheidenheit" in verse 8559 or 8592 (see also 9821 and 9844), a concept to which it can stand in close semantic proximity. In 8603, *sin* is 'intellect, reason' and it is granted by God, a sentiment that is echoed in 8759 ("Von got kumt aller sin" = 'All reason derives from God'). The word is also used in a very specific context in "vümf sin" ('the five senses' [9473 and throughout]).

---

[22] Note also Otfrid Ehrismann's pertinent remarks on the phrase *herze unde sin* in Ehrismann et al., *Ehre und Mut, Aventiure und Minne. Höfische Wortgeschichten aus dem Mittelalter* (Munich: Verlag C. H. Beck, 1995), p. 87.

Even more prolific than *sin* is the term *muot* (Lexer: "kraft des denkens, empfindens, wollens, sinn, seele, geist; gemüt, gemützustand, stimmung, gesinnung").[23] *Muot* can be semantically related to *sin* (which Lexer, as noted above, even lists as one of its synonyms). Here again, it is impossible to render the term into English by adhering to a single equivalent concept. We need to distinguish, for example, between *muot* in the sense of 'heart,' as in 783 ("swa ein wîp hât einn reinen muot" = 'If a woman has a pure heart') and *muot* with the meaning of 'intention,' as in 6168 ("wan got siht niwan an den muot" = 'for God sees only the intention that is behind it') and in 6199–6200 ("unser herre siht ze dem muote / baz dan ze deheinem guote" = 'Our Lord looks more closely at the intention than at any riches').[24] In a number of instances, we have elected to avoid a translation of *muot* per se and have concentrated on the preceding adjective, as in 1327: "vrœlîchen muot" = 'great happiness'; 1349: where a woman who would value material things more than her friend is labeled as having "valschen muot," which we have rendered as her being 'a false woman'; 1986: "stæten muot" = 'constancy'; 5020: "tœrschen muot" = 'a foolish man'; 6882: "nîdigen muot" = 'jealousy'; 10003: "blœden muot" = 'foolish'; 11344: "seltsænen muot" = 'strange'; 13432: "mit gewizzem muot" = 'with certainty'; or 13603: "von miltem muot" = 'from generosity.' In the case of 713–14, where a child is admonished not to have "sô ringen muot," the context makes it abundantly clear that Thomasin is referring here to the lack of common sense, which we have understood to intimate that the child should not be 'so foolish' [as not to hold his tongue]. Substitution of a verbal construction for the noun and its accompanying adjective may also be suitable, as in 12998 with its reference to the regret often felt by a man who likes to act without think-

---

[23] Lexer, *Mittelhochdeutsches Handwörterbuch*, vol. 1, cols. 2241–42.

[24] *Muot* is associated throughout *Der Welsche Gast* with a myriad of epithets, such as "reinen muot" ('a pure heart' [783]), "kiuschem muot" ('modest demeanor' [840]), "senfter muot" ('gentle disposition' [1013]), "tugenthaften muot" ('virtuous heart' [1272]), "zwivalter muot" ('ambivalent heart' [2019]), "bœsen muot" ('bad heart' [2881]), "unrehten muot" ('false disposition' [3904]), "edelem muot" ('noble spirit' [4417]), "gireschen muot" ('greedy disposition' [7358]), "guoten muot" ('good intentions' [7670]), "unriterlîchen muot" ('unknightly disposition' [7768]), "vrîen muot" ('free spirit' [7851]), "listigen muot" ('sly disposition' [8074]), "hohen muot" ('high-spirited' [8722]), "willigen muot" ('willing spirit' [11512]), "wîsen muot" ('wise mind' [11987]), "mannes muot" ('mentality of a man' [12048]), "rehten muot" ('the right idea' [12547]), "vrevelen muot" ('reckless disposition' [13400]), "zagehaften muot" ('cowardly disposition' [13504]), "swachem muot" ('feeble spirit' [13532]), "argen muot" ('greedy heart' [13886]), "rîchem muot" ('noble spirit' [13952]).

ing: "der treit dicke riwegen muot" ('he often regrets it'). On occasion, the application of a modern English idiom appeared to be the most appropriate manner to deal with the Middle High German original, as in the case of 7533 where a man who has been successful combating vices is admonished never to have "rüemigen muot," which we feel is accurately captured in the rendering that the man should take care never 'to become too full of himself.'

The term *bescheidenheit* cannot be rendered into NHG as "Bescheidenheit" ('modesty, unpretentiousness'). Etymologically it carries the basic idea of discernment, the ability to make (meaningful) distinctions. In Thomasin's work it has to do with the idea of caution, good sense, or prudence that would come from understanding a situation, as in the modern "Bescheid wissen" ('to be informed'). Thus, when Thomasin maintains: "den schilt gît dir Bescheidenheit" ('Prudence gives you her shield' [7474]), we take this to mean that prudence (or caution/common sense) is a man's best defense, and Thomasin appears to support such a view in 7477–88 ("wan swelich man bescheiden ist, / der ist ouch sicher zaller vrist" = 'for the man who is prudent [i.e., from understanding the situation] is also always secure').

One of the most common terms associated with medieval chivalrous society is *zuht* (which often appears in connection with *tugent*). It occurs for the first time in *Der Welsche Gast* in 25 (with *tugende* appearing initially in 26) as the narrator declares that it is time for him to indicate "waz zuht sî" ('what courtesy is'). We understand 'courtesy' to convey all forms of refinement that a young nobleman or noblewoman would be expected to acquire and demonstrate at court, similar to what one finds in Lexer: "bildung des innern u. äussern menschen, wolgezogenheit, feine sitte u. lebensart, sittsamkeit, höflichkeit, liebenswürdigkeit, anstand."[25] In Thomasin, the word means 'correct behavior' and specifically behavior that conforms to the standards of chivalry. In some contexts it can correspond to 'discipline' or 'teaching.' At this first occurrence in *Der Welsche Gast* we render it as 'courtesy,' but that was not always the most appropriate translation. We note that Eva Willms translates the phrase here more generally as "die Lehre einer guten Erziehung." A common formulation is the combination *zühte lêre* ('courtesy's lesson,' for example, 30, 37). In the case of 268: "ez ist gar wider zühte lêre," we have opted for the euphemistic 'It goes completely against the dictates of propriety,' while for the same formulation in 338, we have chosen 'correct behavior.' The *semantic* word-field around *zuht* appears to be relatively more homogenous than is the case with other

---

[25] Lexer, *Mittelhochdeutsches Handwörterbuch*, vol. 3, cols. 1169–71. See also Ehrismann, *Ehre und Mut*, pp. 248–53, in particular p. 252.

abstract concepts, notably *sin*. Thomasin uses *zuht* prolifically throughout Book I of *Der Welsche Gast*, in fact, more than twice the number of times as in all other books combined. *Zuht* does not appear at all in Books V and VI, indicative of Thomasin's switch in focus from courtly etiquette to medieval ethics.

The concepts of *stæte* or *stætekeit* ('constancy, fidelity') and its antonym, *unstæte(keit)* ('inconstancy, infidelity') are two of the most significant ideas prevalent not only in Thomasin's *Der Welsche Gast* but also throughout medieval German literature.[26] *Stæte* is a cardinal virtue, and is associated early on in verse 1013 with the virtuous woman (note also 1203).[27] In conjunction with his discussion of what is to be expected of good lords and princes in Book II (where *stæte* and its cognates are cited more often than anywhere else in *Der Welsche Gast*), Thomasin emphasizes in 1789 that absolute constancy is considered a necessity for the ideal ruler. This is reinforced in 1815–24, in particular, in 1819–20: "die andern tugende sint enwiht, / und ist dâ bî diu stæte niht" ('The other virtues are negligible if constancy is not present'). Thomasin immediately links constancy to inconstancy, claiming that the former can only be acquired if one rejects its antithesis:

> niemen mac die stæte hân,
> ern well di unstætekeit verlân.
> swer unstætekeit verlât,
> die stæte er begriffen hât.   (1821–24)

> ('No one can achieve constancy unless he chooses to turn his back on inconstancy, but anyone who has abandoned inconstancy has grasped the true meaning of constancy.')

Stæte is viewed as the sister of *mâze* ('moderation' [12339]), just as *unstætekeit* is the sister of *unmâze* ('immoderation' [12338]). Even more significantly, Thomasin ascribes to *stæte* "a sacred dimension," for "[s]ie konstituiert den *ordo*, Maß, Geordnetheit und Gesetzmäßigkeit der göttlichen Schöpfung":[28] "an der werlde stæte lît / daz ieglîch dinc hât sîne zît" ('It is in the nature of the world's constancy that every thing has its time' [2197–98]).

When the concept of *êre* is raised with respect to medieval German society, it is inevitably pointed out that the emphasis is first and foremost on

---

[26] See Winder McConnell and Otfrid Ehrismann, "*stæte*: Der feste Charakter," in Ehrismann, *Ehre und Mut*, pp. 209–11.

[27] This may also be claimed for the concept of *triuwe*, a term, however, that Thomasin uses fewer than twenty times, just slightly more frequently than its antonym, *untriuwe*.

[28] McConnell and Ehrismann, "*stæte*: Der feste Charakter," p. 211.

"outer" honor, i.e., the position of the individual within society, the respect that he enjoys among his peers, thanks to his holdings, his worldly possessions, land, affluence, and the like. This is not to suggest, of course, that "inner" honor was secondary, to say nothing of nonexistent. The term *êre* occurs with great frequency in *Der Welsche Gast* and, given the nature of the work, it is not surprising that it is used primarily with an emphasis on the "inner" characteristics of the individual or country that is under discussion. When Thomasin employs the word for the first time in 90 with reference to "Tiusche lant" ('German lands'), it is clear that he cannot mean simply "external honor":

> Tiusche lant, enphâhe wol,
> als ein guot hûsvrouwe sol,
> disen dînen welhschen gast
> der dîn êre minnet vast.   (87–90)

> ('German lands, welcome, as a good hostess should, this Italian
> guest of yours, who dearly loves your honor.')

Moreover, it is honor when a man does not treat others with disdain, as Thomasin declares in 126 ("niemen versmæher, daz ist êre" = 'Let him treat no one with disdain: that will bring him honor'). The same holds true of 607, where Thomasin admonishes noble children never to say anything that might go "wider zuht noch wider êre" ('against good behavior or honor'). *Êre* might well be understood in both senses, inner and outer, in 11747 where Thomasin asserts that "elliu guot und alle êre" ('all our possessions and all honor') are derived from God. It is also intimately linked to the idea of *mâze*, which is also seen as a prerequisite for *êre* ("diu mâze gît uns êre und guot" = 'moderation bestows upon us honor and goodness' [9947]).

"[M]an sol die mâze wol ersehen / an allen dingen, daz ist guot: / ân mâze ist niht wol behuot" ('One should observe moderation in all things: that makes sense. Without moderation, caution is thrown to the four winds' [722–24]). Paradoxically, Thomasin has virtually nothing to say about moderation for most of his work until Book VIII. Moreover, *mâze*'s antonym, *unmâze* ('immoderation'), together with its cognates, constitutes approximately 40 percent of the entries dealing with 'moderation/immoderation' in *Der Welsche Gast*. As inconstancy's sister, immoderation is viewed by Thomasin as "the messenger of Foolishness, the playmate of Drunkenness, and the cousin of Arrogance . . . the power of Anger . . . the mouth of the glutton, the keystone of avarice, the hound of Desire . . . the tongue of Lechery" (note 9895ff.), and is further associated with Envy, Cowardice, Sloth, and Wantonness. Thomasin asserts that 'the man who cannot exercise moderation is cursed and damned' (9929). As would be expected in a treatise of this nature, Thomasin is principally concerned with *mâze* in its qualitative, rather than quantitative aspect.[29]

The word *erge* can mean either 'animosity, hostility' or 'avarice' and the translator may initially feel ambivalent as to the best choice within a specific context of Thomasin's work. The author devotes Book X of *Der Welsche Gast* for the most part to a discussion of *milte* ('generosity') and *erge*, and here it is clear that *erge* consistently means 'avarice.' However, in most other instances, the context also would indicate that 'avarice, greed,' is what Thomasin has in mind, and this appears to be reinforced by the frequent occurrence of *girde* ('desire') or *girescheit* ('greed') in the immediate proximity of *erge* (note comments below), as well as the manner in which it is contrasted with *milte* ('generosity'), as in verses 4475ff. and 5947ff. Thomasin claims in 7353 that avarice stems from cowardice and that it is "armed" with "unêr" ('dishonor' [7462]). There are, however, some instances when Thomasin may well have intended *erge* in the sense of the more general 'malevolence' or 'wickedness.' When Thomasin points to the foolishness of a person's giving only to people who already have too much, he claims: "daz macht erge und nerrescheit" ('this only creates malice and foolishness' [1292]). Clearly, 'avarice' would not make much sense in this context. In 2460–61, Thomasin lists the vices that the world has chosen to propagate, including conflict, lying, scorn, hatred, envy, and anger. He includes "erge" in his list, citing it immediately following "strît" ('conflict'). We have translated "erge" here as 'malice,' believing that Thomasin intended a more widely embracing term than the more specific 'avarice' in this particular context. This is also our reasoning for rendering "erge" as 'wickedness' in 3911, when Thomasin cites the vices that have led a man to forfeit his nobility. We are unambivalent about his use of the capitalized "Erge" in 7462, portraying it as one of four leaders of armies of vices that are intent upon attacking the noble knight. The other leaders are "Hôhvart" ('overweening pride' [7459]), "Unkiusche" ('Impurity' [7461]), and "Trâkeit" ('Sloth' [7463]). "Erge" clearly means 'avarice, greed' in this context, for we note that when Thomasin alludes to the leaders of the four armies of vices in 7385ff., he substitutes "Übermuot" for "Hôhvart" (7386) and "Girescheit" ('greed' [7396]), that arms itself with the forces of 'Profit, Robbery, Theft,

---

[29] Note Waltraud Fritsch-Rößler and Otfrid Ehrismann, "*mâze. Die höfische Mitte,*" in Ehrismann, *Ehre und Mut,* pp. 128–36, in particular pp. 135–36: "Als habituelle Qualität war *unmâze* 'Nicht-Mehr-*mâze*,' ein Akt und Ausdruck des Widerstandes gegen das zivilisatorische Reglement. Besonders in der Liebe und in der Kunst zielte sie auf Exklusivität, Negierung gesellschaftlicher Normen und Kontrollen, Radikalismus (im Wortsinn), ja zuweilen auf Anarchie."

Deceit, Perjury, Lying, Envy, and Frivolity' (7399–7400) for "Erge."[30] When Thomasin includes "Erge" among his list of vices in 7519–20, we are also inclined to render this into English as 'avarice, greed,' given the association with "Unkiusche unde Trâkeit" (7519) that we have already encountered in his description of the armies led by vice. Much later, in 12695ff., Thomasin cites a series of four vices ("bôsheit," "erge," "zorn," "nît") responsible for the lack of unanimity between secular and ecclesiastical courts. In 12705, he claims: "zorn kumt dick von girescheit" ('Anger often comes from greed'), and it would appear that here, once again, "girescheit" is employed as a synonym for "erge" in 12695.

Nît on the part of one's fellow noblemen or noblewomen is one of the tribulations constantly experienced and lamented by the *Minnesänger* of the High Middle Ages. Middle High German *nît* may certainly be conveyed in English as 'jealousy' in conformity with the meaning of *Neid* in New High German. However, it may also be used more generally, namely, in the sense of 'hostility, wickedness, hatred.' Thomasin uses *nît* and its cognates (the adjective *nîdec* and the verb *nîden*) almost seventy times in *Der Welsche Gast* in both senses of the term. *Nît* is virtually synonymous with *übel* in verse 9: "wizzet das sîn übel und sîn nît" ('know for a fact that his wicked and nasty ways [will transform what is good into bad]'). The term clearly conveys the connotation of 'jealousy' when it is used as an adjective in 6882 ("nîdigen muot") to describe the motivation of those who sold Joseph into slavery, and then as a noun in the reference to Cain's murder of Abel: "Kâyn sluoc Âbeln durch nît" ('Cain killed Abel out of jealousy' [11989]). In 7605–7, Thomasin refers to the Bible, claiming that it does not lie, and that the first man was deceived by the devil (the enemy) who was motivated by envy: "wan in der vînt betwanc durch nît" ('for the enemy put pressure on him out of envy' [7607]). In 7728, Thomasin states that "der vâlant het ze gote nît" ('the devil was envious of God'), and here, again, it appears that Thomasin intends the word to be understood as 'envy' rather than 'hatred.'[31]

---

[30] The relationship between *girescheit* and *erge* can be more complicated, however, as when the terms are used together ("mit dem guote wehset girescheit, / erge, vorht, sorge, müe, leit" [8139–40]). We do not discount the possibility that Thomasin has offered here a deliberate tautology, but have nonetheless elected, in this instance, to convey "erge" as 'wickedness,' one sort of which is, of course, greed.

[31] We need to distinguish between what Thomasin meant by *nît* and what is provided in the way of evidence in biblical sources for Satan's relationship to God after his expulsion from heaven. Given the dialogue between Satan and God in the book of Job and the adversarial "testing" of Job by Lucifer, it would appear that the latter is more envious of the power of the Almighty than motivated by hatred towards Him. However, in the apocryphal "Life of Adam and Eve," Satan provides Adam with an account of his expulsion from heaven and claims that "all my enmity

While the word *List* tends to conjure up somewhat less than benevolent images in New High German, its Middle High German equivalent conveys positive connotations of cleverness, shrewdness, and even wisdom.[32] Thomasin employs the term with a variety of meanings, ranging from 'skill' in 113, in a reference to the construction of his own work, through 'cleverness' in 847 when he intimates that the courtesy of noble women *precludes* the latter from being 'too clever,' 'a better idea' in 4035, the simple 'way' in 'a thousand ways' in 4051, to 'cunning' as in the 'cunning manner' in which an oath may be taken or the cunning attributes of the world (13289). In Book VII, however, Thomasin uses "liste" as a euphemism for the 'arts,' specifically the seven liberal arts. When it is used in close proximity with "kunst," as in 9122 and 9126, we have adhered to the rendering 'skill,' as is also the case in 9144 where "an guotem list" is paired with "an tiefem sinne" ('profound meaning and fine skill') and both are preceded by a reference to "kunst" in 9141.

One of the "key words" used most prolifically by Thomasin is the collective concept of *tugent* ('virtue'), with its antonym, *untugent* ('vice'), and their various cognates. They appear more than 450 times throughout the book and are often directly juxtaposed with one another. Thomasin's intention is to explain to his audience "waz vrümkeit und waz zuht sî / und waz tugende" ('what constitutes goodness and courtesy / what virtue is' [25–26]). He establishes a direct link between courtesy and virtue, claiming that the person who takes note of the former will enhance his virtue. Virtue is essentially inner goodness complemented by external acts of kindness and a person may demonstrate his virtue by choosing a good (*vrumen*) man as his model and emulating him (627ff.). When Thomasin refers in 1044 to "Gaweins reiner tugent" ('the pure virtue of Gawein'), it appears to us that he means this in a way that goes far beyond some of the meanings that Lexer provides in his dictionary: "brauchbarkeit, tauglichkeit, männliche tüchtigkeit, kraft, macht."[33] Thomasin views *tugent* primarily from a theological point of view. The steps of the ladder leading to heaven are the

---

and envy and sorrow concern you, since because of you I am expelled and deprived of my glory which I had in the heavens in the midst of angels, and because of you I was cast out onto the earth" (James H. Charlesworth, ed., *The Old Testament Pseudepigrapha*, vol. 2 [New York: Doubleday, 1985], p. 262). Lucifer thus expresses both sentiments, enmity and envy, as well as sorrow, with respect to his reaction to his expulsion by God from heaven. It may well be that Thomasin has both hatred and envy in mind when he uses *nît* in this context.

[32] Lexer, *Mittelhochdeutsches Handwörterbuch*, vol. 1, col. 1936.

[33] Lexer, *Mittelhochdeutsches Handwörterbuch*, vol. 2, col. 1560.

various virtues, while those of the ladder leading to hell are their antitheses, the vices. *Tugent* is, to cite Thomasin's admonishment in 14667ff. to those who might wish to pass on his book to others, a prerequisite for any potential recipient. It is the person who complements "daz er gelesen hât" ('what he has read' [14680]) "mit guotem leben / und mit guoter getât" ('with a good life and with good deeds' [14678–79]).

The reader cannot fail to note how often the word *reht* appears in *Der Welsche Gast*. Adverbial constructions with *reht* are legion, whether as "von reht(e)" ('by right, rightly' [1772]), "nâch rehte" ([to speak] 'in the appropriate manner' [566]), and a number of forms that connote quite simply 'rightly, correctly,' including "reht" itself ("ob ein herre reht tuon wil" = 'if a lord wishes to behave correctly' [3662]), "ze rehte" ("swer sîn ze rehte war tuot" = 'Whoever observes him correctly' [3693]), "mit reht" ("Mit reht hân ich gezeiget wol" = 'I have rightly demonstrated' [6027]). Book IX contains Thomasin's views on the state of society with respect to the concepts of *reht* and *unreht* in the sense of 'justice' and 'injustice.' The term *reht* is used to convey something quite different from what we find in 10628, where Thomasin refers to the Greek emperor's becoming a slave and no longer enjoying "keisers reht" ('the privileges of an emperor'). In a similar vein, Thomasin refers to "herren reht" in 10775, which we interpret to be a reference to a person's retaining his 'proper position as a master.' References to *reht* and *unreht* in Book IX are, however, predominantly related to the judicial arena. *Reht* is regarded as the brother of constancy and moderation. *Reht* can also connote the idea of 'judgment,' as when Thomasin emphasizes how important it is to keep the spiritual and secular spheres separate when it is a matter of meting out justice:

> dehein werltîch man
> sol sich nimmer nemen an
> dehein geistlîch geriht
> noch dehein geistlîch reht niht,
> ode im geschiht lîht ungemach.   (12813–17)

> ('No layman should ever preside over an ecclesiastical court nor pass ecclesiastical judgment, or he will easily land in trouble.')

Thomasin demonstrates his facility (if not necessarily exceptional stylistic talent) with Middle High German when he juxtaposes *reht* with *unreht* and the verb *rihten*:

> sô mag ich doch vür wâr gejehen
> daz der tuot vil unreht
> der iemen ân reht gît sîn reht.
> daz reht muoz rehtes namen lân,

> dem reht enwerde reht getân:
> der machet daz reht zunreht wol
> der anders rihtet danner sol.   (13230–36)

> ('I can say for a fact that he who gives someone his just deserts
> without justice is perpetrating great injustice. Justice must aban-
> don the name of justice unless justice is done to justice. He who
> judges otherwise than he should is certainly turning justice into
> injustice.')

The 'happy' or 'blessed' man in Middle High German is "ein sælic man" (8870; note also the cognates *sælde, sælikeit,* 'happiness, blessedness, good fortune'), but there are relatively few allusions to such a state in *Der Welsche Gast.* Thomasin links the concept, as well as its antonym, *unsælic,* directly to *tugent/untugent,* claiming that the state of being 'happy/blessed' (or 'unhappy/unblessed') emanates from the latter:

> swer iht sælic werden sol,
> er muoz ez von der tugende hân.
> sô ist der ein unsælic man
> der dâ ist untugenthaft.   (4598–4601)

> ('Anyone who has any wish to be blessed with good fortune must
> derive it from his virtues. Thus anyone who is not virtuous is a
> wretched man.')

Within the context of his discussion on the perpetual dichotomy between happiness and unhappiness, why one man is blessed and the other cursed, Thomasin adopts the traditional stance, namely, that the ultimate dispenser of such happiness or state of being blessed, or the opposite is, of course, God: "jâ weiz got wol wem er sol geben / unsælic ode sælic leben" ('Certainly, God knows well enough to whom He should grant an unhappy or a happy life' [5077–78]). The consolation for the good man who is not blessed in this world is the certainty that he will find happiness in the next: "und ist er hie niht sælic gar, / daz er dâ sælic werden sol" ('and even if he is not completely blessed in this world, he will be in the next' [6850–51]). It is noteworthy that Thomasin refers to the 'wretched' man more often than he does to the man who is blessed. Misfortune (*unsælde*) is also the lot of the man who helps his friend transgress against God (3132). Thomasin views the bestowal of *sælikeit* ('fortune') and *unsælikeit* ('misfortune') as something of a test for the wise, virtuous man, who must make the effort not to allow the latter to lead to "das êwiclîche leit" ('eternal suffering' [4957]), but have the wisdom to recognize that "im sîn sælikeit beginne / die êwiclîchen sælikeit" ('his fortune is the start of eternal blessedness' [4969–70]).

The positive term *guote/güete* ('goodness') appears fewer than two dozen times in *Der Welsche Gast*. Despite its infrequency, *güete* is used early on in the work to underscore Thomasin's belief that one cannot simply identify the inner with the outer as was the custom of his time. In his description of the beautiful woman who is devoid of loyalty or beauty on the inside, Thomasin states categorically: "schœne ist ein niht wider güete" ('Beauty is nothing compared with inner goodness' [956]). *Güete* may be viewed as a synonym for 'virtue,' as in 1007, when Thomasin warns a man of the dangers of judging a woman entirely "durch ir schœn niht durch ir güete" ('on her beauty and not on her virtue'). A noble man is only noble if he has directed his heart toward "rehte güete" ('true goodness' [3862]), and the virtuous man is one "der stæte an güete wesen kan" ('who can possess constancy in goodness' [4352]). *Güete* manifests itself in good deeds towards others and these, in turn, help to accord a man *sælikeit*:

> sîn güete und sîn gedultikeit
> erwirbt im zwivalt sælikeit:
> sîn guot getât gît im ein lôn,
> sîn gedultikeit ein ander krôn.   (4593–95)

> ('His goodness and his patience earn two kinds of blessedness for him: his good deed brings him a reward, his patience another crown.')

The highest *güete* of all is God's 'goodness,' through which we enjoy His grace (7658–59), and most of Thomasin's subsequent allusions to *güete* are in association with the Almighty. However, it is also through "die rehten güete" ('true goodness' [7698]) that one comes to God. God's *güete*, along with humility, bestows love upon the receptive man (8297–98), and Thomasin exhorts his audience to be happy to hear what they can about it (9397). God's *güete* is the antithesis and the opponent of "übermüete" ('arrogance' [10723]) and the source of the "triuwe" (11468) that He demonstrates towards man.

Thomasin's book is as much a condemnation of vices as it is an exhortation to his readers to strive to live a virtuous life. Just as striking as the emphasis on *tugent* ('virtue'), *stæte/stætekeit* ('constancy'), *êre* ('respect, honor'), *mâze* ('moderation'), *triuwe* ('loyalty'), and *zuht* ('courtly courtesy'), for example, are the allusions to their antonyms *untugent* ('vice'), *unstæte(keit)* ('inconstancy'), *unêre* ('disdain, lack of honor') *unmâze* ('immoderation'), *untriuwe* ('disloyalty, treachery'), and *unzuht* (or *ân zuht*, 'without courtly courtesy'), as well as the particularly grievous sins of *hôhvart* ('pride') and *übermuot* ('arrogance'). Underscoring contrasts through antonyms is an effective didactic technique, particularly when Thomasin complements his

words with graphic illustrations, as in the case of the two ladders whose steps
are formed from either virtues or vices and which lead to either heaven or
hell, respectively. *Hôhvart* and *übermuot* appear to be used interchangeably
throughout *Der Welsche Gast*. When Thomasin recommends that a woman
should guard against "hôhvart" in 992, he has 'pride,' 'haughtiness,' or
'arrogance' in mind and this is echoed in 1364. *Hôhvart* and *übermuot* are
frequently associated with authority (*hêrschaft*), as in the case of 4403–6,
when he cites the reasons why a man in a position of authority may thrive
if he avoids *übermuot* but may encounter difficulty should he give in to *hôh-*
vart:

> sô ist im sîn hêrschaft guot,
> gwinnet er dervon niht übermuot.
> gewinnet er dervon dehein hôhvart,
> sô würre im sîn hêrschaft ze hart.

> ('That way his authority is good, if he does not become arrogant
> because of it. If he were to become at all overbearing, then his
> authority would cause him a great deal of trouble.')

While we have frequently elected to render *hôhvart* into English as 'arro-
gance,' there are several instances when it would seem that a better term
would be 'pride,' given the particular context. In 11370, Thomasin refers to
man's "unmâze" ('excesses, immoderation') and "hôhvart" ('pride') being
raised against God, and the latter term evokes the sense of the major capital
sin. Thomasin may well have been alluding to Proverbs 16:18 ("Pride goes
before disaster / and a haughty spirit before a fall"), or, perhaps, the Greek
tale of Icarus, when he employs the image of man setting his aims too high
and subsequently experiencing a fall in 11849ff., specifically, 11852–56:

> ze hôhe niemen varn sol:
> der vetich hât ein man niht
> die im ze vliegen helfen iht,
> dâ von muoz er vallen hart
> nider von sîner hôhvart.

> ('No one should aim too high. A man does not have wings that
> would help him to fly, and so he must fall down hard from his
> pride.')

Finally, it is the *biderbe* or *vrume* man (or woman) that Thomasin sets up
as a model for others and to whom he addresses his work. The *biderbe* man
or woman is the epitome of moral goodness, one who leads an upright life,
an individual who cannot be discouraged or led astray by the vicissitudes of
life because of his or her strong sense of faith and constancy. The two terms,

biderbe and *vrum*, appear over a hundred times in *Der Welsche Gast*, occasionally in close proximity to one another. They might both be translated simply as 'good,' although *vrum* may also be appropriately rendered into English within specific contexts as 'brave' or 'honorable.' It is no coincidence that Thomasin concludes his work with a reference to "der vrum man" (14747), who will not only learn from his book but whose deeds will be superior even to the instruction he has received from *Der Welsche Gast*.

Thomasin's work is not without a touch of pathos, as when he repeatedly points to the ills of his time and, in particular, in his reference to an earlier "golden age," a time when every child could read, when noble children were well educated (9197ff.), a time when the world was without rancor and hate (9201–2). His treatise on etiquette and, above all, on ethics was composed with the primary intent to edify, as Thomasin had become aware of just how badly his contemporaries were behaving. On the surface, *Der Welsche Gast* might appear to betray a somewhat cynical view of the world. In 2822, Thomasin declares that "von grôzer liebe kumt grôzez leit" ('great suffering derives from great joy'), echoing a popular topos of his age. The context makes it quite clear that by "lieb" Thomasin is referring specifically to one's cherished possessions and by "leit" to the inevitable loss of the latter (through enemies, fire, gambling, death, thieves), thus underscoring the transitory state of this world and what it has to offer. The joy-sorrow dichotomy is also emphasized by Thomasin within the context of male-female relationships: "Wan daz geschiht zaller vrist, / an swiu grôziu vreude lît, / da lît grôz leit zaller zît" ('For it happens all the time that, however great the joy, it is always accompanied by great sorrow' [3988–90]). Yet, he does not always confine himself to specific contexts when alluding to this dichotomy. He recognizes how, in every aspect of life, "wie leit bî liebe gât" ('how sorrow goes hand in hand with joy' [4108]).[34] At first glance, Thomasin's sentiments on the nature of joy and sorrow in the world could appear to have much in common with those expressed by the anonymous poet of the *Nibelungenlied*. The latter's ominous "message" at the conclusion of his epic of how it is *always* the case that 'joy gives rise to sorrow in the end' ("als ie diu liebe leide z'aller jungeste gît" [B: 2378,4]), betrays a remarkably nihilistic view of the world that may be unique in its time. In contrast to that poet, however, who may well have been his contemporary, Thomasin allows his primer on ethics to end on a relatively positive note

---

[34] The same might be maintained about 3947–48 following Thomasin's comments on the wretchedness that may befall the man who follows his desires with abandon and acquires "zehant derbî ein leit sô grôz / daz wol der vreude ist genôz" ('he immediately brings upon himself such great suffering which is, after all, the companion of joy').

(despite his apocalyptic prediction at the conclusion of Book II), assuming, as he does, that his book will fall into the receptive hands of a man who will complement the good teachings found therein with even greater deeds.

We were encouraged to produce this first complete translation into English of *Der Welsche Gast* by a number of factors.[35] It is not a work of great literary merit, nor does it set out to be. Yet it was written at a time of significant literary flowering in the German Middle Ages, and it cannot properly be separated from that. Given the time and probable place of its composition, the work must reflect the influence of some of the dominant poets of the early thirteenth century, although it is rarely possible to point to precise imitation. Echoes of Hartmann von Aue, Gottfried von Strassburg, Wolfram von Eschenbach, and the *Nibelungenlied* are present, as well as of the lyric poetry in Middle High German, but sometimes these are very faint and may reflect no more than a generalized acquaintance with the literary language of the day. When it comes to Walther von der Vogelweide, with whom Thomasin may indeed have crossed paths at the court of Wolfger von Erla, some verbal echoes are easier to detect, but the greater impact is in terms of content.

Our translation is in prose and thus sacrifices the rhythm and meter of the original in favor of providing our readers with a relatively smooth, flowing narrative. A major consideration that informed our own approach to translating the work was the rendering of the original into readable English prose, without, however, "improving on" Thomasin's style to a point where our translation might lose completely much of the repetitiveness and formulaic quality of the original text. We have, therefore, attempted to keep any stylistic embellishment of the original as much as possible to a minimum. Occasionally, we have used a variation for the same word (note the comments on *muot*, for example, above); Thomasin's German, while quite competent, is somewhat limited with respect to vocabulary. Throughout

---

[35] Excerpts of Thomasin's *Der Welsche Gast* were first translated into English by Eugene Oswald in *Early German Courtesy-Books. An Account of The Italian Guest by Thomasin von Zirclaria . . .* in *A Booke of Precedence. The ordering of a Funerall, &c., Varying Versions of The Good wife, The Wise Man, &c., Maxims, Lydgate's Order of Fools, A Poem on Heraldry, Occleve on Lords' Men, &c.,* ed. F. J. Furnivall, *With Essays on Early Italian and German Books of Courtesy,* by W. M. Rossetti and E. Oswald (London: N. Trübner & Co., 1869), pp. 79–140. See Eva Willms's partial translation of the work into modern German (*Thomasin von Zerklaere*), to which we frequently make reference. Willms provides a useful introduction and notes, and it is to be hoped that she will eventually provide us with a complete NHG translation of this work.

Der Welsche Gast, he is given to repeating the formulaic "wizzet das" ('know this'). It is not a medieval equivalent of the current and colloquially ubiquitous "you know" but is rather much more of an exhortation to his audience in the sense of 'take note of this.' Here, too, we have sought to provide some variation for a modern audience without, however, altering the basic tenor of the original formulation. On occasion, we have felt it prudent to augment the text modestly. Any additions to the original are enclosed in square brackets, as are insertions of words or numbers clearly missing in Rückert's edition. In this regard, a part of Thomasin's prose foreword (Book III, section IX) was reconstructed from the von Kries edition. In a number of instances, we have elected to change the punctuation found in the latter to produce a rendering that seems to reflect the sense of the original. Thomasin uses the subjunctive mood frequently throughout his prose foreword because he is, as it were, quoting himself. We have normally retained the indicative mood in our translation of that section.

Thomasin is no master of style, and no one knows this better than he. Nor is this weakness due, as he implies, entirely to his uncertainty in the command of a language not his own. His German is actually extraordinarily good, and it is likely that some of the problems the modern reader encounters with it may even stem from the fact that he was most closely acquainted with the language of the region where he had spent much of his life and possibly uses idioms and linguistic features current there but not part of the language associated with his linguistically more sophisticated predecessors and close contemporaries. Yet, before this discrepancy becomes a negative aspect of his work, it must also be noted that his intention is very different from theirs and that he fulfills it to a remarkable degree. Whereas the courtly literature of the day frequently sets out to teach *and* to entertain, the latter ingredient seems not to have been part of his purpose. Indeed, he admits that writing this huge work has not given him a great deal of pleasure. What prompts him—and this exudes from the work—is his awareness of the imperfections of the society in which he lived and his commitment to lead his audience to a more proper way of living, notably more in accordance with the overall purpose of God.

Moreover, he is conscious of an audience comprising a wide range of people, young and old, in many different walks of life, and coming from estates high and low. He often shows himself fully aware of the need to address this diversity in differing ways, repeating himself, reformulating his point, and employing sometimes quite surprising examples in his effort to make himself clear. He is, for example, relentless in his employment of the phrase "beidiu in alter und in jugent" ('both in old age and youth') to underscore the validity of his teachings for young and old alike, the need on the part of an individual throughout his entire life to adhere to virtue and

defend himself against vice and wickedness: "wirn müezen alle mit untu-
gent / vehten an alter und an jugent" ('we must all fight against wicked-
ness throughout our lives' [7703–4]). It is his commitment to his purpose
which accounts for some of his sudden jumps in thought and his abrupt
leaps from quite homely comparisons to complex and obscure analogies.
That he is capable of this speaks for a man of considerable intelligence and
an understanding beyond his years, but there are times, too—and Books
IV and V are an example of this—when one senses a man grappling with
his own thoughts and his sincere wish to present them coherently to a less
obviously informed audience. His erudition is apparent but may simply be
attributable to a sound education in a church school and a career in some
ecclesiastical capacity which has left him a ready access to biblical and classi-
cal references. He is informed about political events of his day, as one might
expect an intelligent observer to be in a time of immense social upheaval.

Combined with these intellectual qualities are his personal awareness
of the behavior of his fellowmen and an insight into what motivates them
and, overriding all these aspects of the picture that emerges of the person
of Thomasin von Zirclaria, is his sincere and zealously pursued wish to rec-
tify such situations as are in his power to rectify. This combination of ingre-
dients makes for a work which, admittedly rambling and unwieldy at times,
has considerable intrinsic value and serves as a significant adjunct to the
literature of medieval German, much of which expresses, in fictional terms,
the values and aspirations of the court.

If he appears to begin with the relatively modest aim of guiding his
audience, particularly its younger members, in proper courtly behavior,
and supplies some very detailed and sometimes seemingly trivial hints on
correct social demeanor, one has the impression that he widens his concept
of his task as the work proceeds, emphasizing much deeper ideals and con-
cerns. From rules of etiquette he moves increasingly to abstract virtues, to
what makes a human being virtuous, and to man's relationship with God
and the nature of God Himself. As the lengthy work proceeds and seems
to gather momentum, he appears to gain in confidence about his objec-
tive, so that by the time he reaches his conclusion, he is able to commend
his beloved book, which in the meantime has itself become the "Italian
guest," only to those who deserve to read it because they are already virtu-
ous. Scoundrels will not wish to read it, nor should they have the opportu-
nity to do so.

As he sends it out into the world, he expresses a more lofty sense of
the purpose of his work, but the progress towards this climax has not been
smooth or consistent. The flaws which Thomasin's sternest critics have seen
are for the most part undeniable, and one must avoid the temptation to
redress such criticism by elevating the work above its rightful place and

ignore the frequently expressed intentions of its author. There are, as we have noted, repetitions and digressions, and Thomasin seems at times in danger of losing his way. One could justifiably point to a lack of proportion in the time he expends on some topics, although he himself rarely seems to doubt the relevance of what he is saying to what he intends to say. However, the work remains a remarkable product of an important period in German literature and indeed in medieval European culture; it may be argued with considerable justification that *Der Welsche Gast* is the most significant didactic work of the German High Middle Ages. Unique in its own time, yet apparently valued by Thomasin's contemporaries and immediately succeeding generations, it belongs very much to its own age, yet, like so much of the literature of the German Middle Ages, it touches chords in the modern reader which cannot and should not be ignored.

SELECTED BIBLIOGRAPHY

EDITIONS, TRANSLATIONS

Disanto, Raffaele, ed. *Di Heinrich Rückert e le varianti del Memb. I 120, Gotha.* Quaderni di *Der Welsche Gast—secondo il Cod. Pal. Germ. 389, Heidelberg con le integrazioni* Hesperides. Serie testi 3. Trieste: Edizioni Parnaso, 2002.

Kries, F. W. von, ed. *Thomasin von Zerclaere. Der Welsche Gast.* 4 vols. Göppingen: Kümmerle, 1984–85.

Neumann, Friedrich, and Ewald Vetter, eds. *Der welsche Gast des Thomasin von Zerclaere: Codex Palatinus Germanicus 389 der Universitätsbibliothek Heidelberg.* 2 vols. Facsimilia Heidelbergensia 4. Wiesbaden: Ludwig Reichert, 1974–80.

Rückert, Heinrich, ed. *Der Wälsche Gast des Thomasin von Zirclaria.* Mit einer Einleitung und einem Register von Friedrich Neumann. Deutsche Neudrucke, Reihe: Texte des Mittelalters. 1852. Reprint, Berlin: Walter de Gruyter & Co, 1965.

Wenzel, Horst, ed. *Thomasin von Zerklaere: Der Welsche Gast. Farbmikrofiche-Edition der Handschrift Ms. Hamilt. 675 der Staatsbibliothek zu Berlin.* Codices illuminati medii aevi 51. Munich: Edition Lengenfelder, 1998.

Willms, Eva, ed. and trans. *Thomasin von Zerklaere. Der Welsche Gast. Text (Auswahl), Übersetzung. Stellenkommentar.* Berlin: Walter de Gruyter, 2004.

REFERENCE WORKS

Auty, Robert, et al., eds. *Lexikon des Mittelalters.* 7 vols. Munich: Artemis-Verlag, 1977–95.

Bumke, Joachim. *Höfische Kultur. Literatur und Kultur im hohen Mittelalter.* 2 vols. Munich: dtv, 1986. [Translation: *Courtly Culture: Literature and Society in the High Middle Ages.* Translated by Thomas Dunlap. Woodstock: Overlook Press, 2000.]

Charlesworth, James H., ed. *The Old Testament Pseudepigrapha.* Vol. 2. New York: Doubleday, 1985.
Gärtner, Kurt, et al. *Findebuch zum mittelhochdeutschen Wortschatz.* Stuttgart: S. Hirzel, 1992.
Harvey, Sir Paul. *The Oxford Companion to Classical Literature.* 2nd ed., edited by M. C. Howatson. Oxford: Oxford University Press, 1989.
Lexer, Matthias. *Mittelhochdeutsches Handwörterbuch.* 3 vols. 1872–78. Reprint, Stuttgart: S. Hirzel Verlag, 1974. See also the online version prepared at the University of Trier <http://germazope.uni-trier.de/Projects/WBB/woerterbuecher> and note in addition Gärtner et al., *Findebuch* (provides access to glossaries since issued for individual texts).
Porter, J. R. *The New Illustrated Companion to the Bible.* London: Duncan Baird Publishers, 1995.
Strayer, Joseph R., ed. *Dictionary of the Middle Ages.* 13 vols. New York: Scribner, 1982–89.
Wander, F. K. W. *Sprichwörter-Lexikon: Ein Hausschatz für das deutsche Volk.* Vols. 1–5. 1867–80. Reprint, Darmstadt: Wissenschaftliche Buchgesellschaft, 1964.

SECONDARY WORKS

Blaschitz, Gertrud. "Die Frauenkleidung in den Bildinszenierungen des 'Welschen Gastes.'" In Wenzel and Lechtermann, *Beweglichkeit der Bilder,* pp. 216–37. Cologne: Böhlau Verlag, 2002.
Boesch, Bruno. *Lehrhafte Literatur: Lehre in der Dichtung und Lehrdichtung im deutschen Mittelalter.* Berlin: Schmidt, 1977.
Borst, Arno. "Bild und Wort und Zahl bei Thomasin Zerklaere." In *Barbaren, Ketzer und Artisten. Welten des Mittelalters.* 2nd ed., edited by Arno Borst, pp. 429–47. Munich: Piper, 1990.
Brinker-Von der Heyde, Claudia. "Der 'Welsche Gast' des Thomasin von Zerclaere: eine (Vor-)Bildgeschichte." In Wenzel and Lechtermann, *Beweglichkeit der Bilder,* pp. 9–32.
———. "Durch Bildung zur Tugend. Zur Wissenschaftslehre des Thomasin von Zerclaere." In Schaefer, *Artes im Mittelalter,* pp. 34–52.
Burdach, Konrad. "Die illustrierten Handschriften des Welschen Gastes." In *Vorspiel. Gesammelte Schriften zur Geschichte des deutschen Geistes,* vol. 1, part 2, pp. 108–21. Halle: Niemeyer, 1925.
Carroll, William Francis. "'Der Welsche Gast' Thomasins von Zerclaere und 'Der Renner' Hugos von Trimberg. Perspektiven des Fremden in der didaktischen Literatur des 13. Jahrhunderts." In *Fremdes wahrnehmen— fremdes Wahrnehmen. Studien zur Geschichte der Wahrnehmung und zur Begegnung von Kulturen in Mittelalter und früher Neuzeit,* edited by Wolfgang Harms and Stephen C. Jaeger, pp. 137–52. Stuttgart: Hirzel, 1997.

Cormeau, Christoph. "Thomasin von Zerklaere." In *Die deutsche Literatur des Mittelalters. Verfasserlexikon.* 2nd ed., edited by Kurt Ruh et al. Vol. 9, cols. 896–902. Berlin: Walter de Gruyter, 1995.

———. "Tradierte Verhaltensnormen und Realitätserfahrung. Überlegungen zu Thomasins 'Welschem Gast.'" In *Deutsche Literatur im Mittelalter. Kontakte und Perspektiven. Hugo Kuhn zum Gedenken,* edited by Christoph Cormeau, pp. 276–95. Stuttgart: Metzler, 1979.

Curschmann, Michael. "Der 'aventiure bilde nemen': The Intellectual and Social Environment of the Iwein Murals at Rodenegg Castle." In *Chrétien de Troyes and the German Middle Ages,* edited by Martin H. Jones and Roy Wisbey, pp. 219–27. Cambridge: Brewer, 1993. Reprinted in Curschmann, *Wort—Bild—Text,* vol. 1, pp. 447–55.

———. "Interdisziplinäre Beweglichkeit—Wie weit reicht sie?" *Zeitschrift für Deutsche Philologie* 123, no. 1 (2004): 109–17. Reprinted in Curschmann, *Wort—Bild—Text,* vol. 2, pp. 851–59.

———. *Wort —Bild—Text. Studien zur Medialität des Literarischen in Hochmittelalter und früher Neuzeit.* 2 vols. Saecula spiritalia 44. Baden-Baden: Valentin Koerner, 2007.

Dallapiazza, Michael. "Artusromane als Jugendlektüre? Thomasin von Zirclaria und Hugo von Trimberg." In Schulze-Belli, *Thomasin von Zirklaere und die didaktische Literatur des Mittelalters,* pp. 29–38. Trieste: Associazione di Cultura Medioevale, 1996.

Davidson, Judith A. "The Two Examples of Manuscript D of *Der welsche Gast* (Dresden, Sächsische Landesbibliothek. M. 67)." *Neuphilologische Mitteilungen* 82, no. 2 (1982): 132–49.

Disanto, Raffaele. *La parola e l'immagine nel ciclo illustrativo del Welscher Gast di Thomasin von Zerklaere.* Trieste: Parnaso, 2003.

Düwel, Klaus. "Lesestoff für junge Adlige: Lektüreempfehlungen in einer Tugendlehre des 13. Jahrhunderts." *Fabula* 32.1, 2, 3 (1991): 67–93.

Ehrismann, Otfrid, et al. *Ehre und Mut, Aventiure und Minne. Höfische Wortgeschichten aus dem Mittelalter.* Munich: Verlag C. H. Beck, 1995.

Engelen, Bernhard. "Eine Studie zur Geschichte der Jugendlektüre um 1200: zu Thomasin von Zirklaere, Vers 761–1166." In *Aufsätze zur Kinderliteratur: Geschichte—Rezeption—Sprache,* pp. 13–42. Frankfurt am Main: Lang, 2005.

Göttert, Karl-Heinz. "Thomasin von Zerclaere und die Tradition der Moralistik." In *Architectura poetica. Festschrift für Johannes Rathofer zum 65. Geburtstag,* edited by Ulrich Ernst and Bernhard Sowinski, pp. 179–88. Kölner Germanistische Studien 30. Cologne: Böhlau, 1990.

Grubmüller, Klaus. "Eine weitere Handschrift von Thomasins 'Welschem Gast.'" *ZfdA* 97 (1968): 206–15.

Harris, Nigel. "Didactic Poetry." In *German Literature of the High Middle Ages*, edited by Will Hasty, pp. 123–40. The Camden House History of German Literature 3. Rochester, NY: Camden House, 2006.

Haug, Walter. *Literaturtheorie im deutschen Mittelalter. Von den Anfängen bis zum Ende des 13. Jahrhunderts.* 2nd ed. Darmstadt: Wissenschaftliche Buchgesellschaft, 1992.

Helm, Karl. "Zu den Watzendorfer Thomasin-Fragmenten." *PBB* 70 (1948; Halle a.d. Saale): 303–4.

Höfer, Susanne. "Zur gesellschaftlichen Verortung und Funktion des Gelehrten und des gelehrten Wissens im 'Welschen Gast' des Thomasin von Zerklaere." In *Literatur—Geschichte—Literaturgeschichte: Beiträge zur mediävistischen Literaturwissenschaft. Festschrift für Volker Honemann zum 50. Geburtstag*, edited by Nine Miedema and Rudolf Suntrup, pp. 865–77. Berlin: Lang, 2003.

Huber, Christoph. "Der werlde ring und *was man tuon und lassen schol.* Gattungskontinuität und Innovation in moraldidaktischen Summen: Thomasin von Zerklaere—Hugo von Trimberg—Heinrich Wittenwiler und andere." In *Mittelalter und frühe Neuzeit. Übergänge, Umbrüche und Neuansätze*, edited by Walter Haug, pp. 187–212. Fortuna Vitrea 16. Tübingen: Niemeyer, 1999.

———. *Die Aufnahme und Verarbeitung des Alanus ab Insulis in mittelhochdeutschen Dichtungen: Untersuchungen zu Thomasin von Zerklaere, Gottfried von Straßburg, Frauenlob, Heinrich von Neustadt, Heinrich von St. Gallen, Heinrich von Mügeln und Johannes von Tepl.* Münchener Texte und Untersuchungen zur deutschen Literatur des Mittelalters 89. Munich: Artemis, 1988.

———. "Höfischer Roman als Integumentum? Das Votum Thomasins von Zerklaere." *ZfdA* 115 (1986): 79–100.

———. "Thomasin von Zerklaere." In *Deutsches Literatur-Lexikon*, edited by Walter Killy. Vol. 11, pp. 345–46. Gütersloh: Bertelsmann, 1991.

———. "Zur mittelalterlichen Roman-Hermeneutik: Noch einmal Thomasin von Zerklaere und das Integumentum." In *German Narrative Literature of the Twelfth and Thirteenth Centuries. Studies Presented to Roy Wisbey on His Sixty-Fifth Birthday*, edited by Volker Honemann, Martin H. Jones, Adrian Stevens, and David Wells, pp. 27–38. Tübingen: Niemeyer, 1994.

Kästner, Hannes. "'Seit mir, chan si daz?' Reflexionen über Deutsch als Fremd- und Literatursprache bei Thomasin von Zerklaere." In *Das Buch der Bücher: seine Wirkungsgeschichte in der Literatur*, edited by Tom Kleffmann, pp. 45–59. Göttingen: Univ.-Verl. Göttingen, 2004.

Klare, Andreas. "Thomasins *unstete*-Begriff in Wort und Bild." In Wenzel and Lechtermann, *Beweglichkeit der Bilder*, pp. 174–99.

Klein, Karl Kurt. "Zum dichterischen Spätwerk Walthers von der Vogelweide. Der Streit mit Thomasin von Zerclaere." *Innsbrücker Beiträge zur Kulturwissenschaft* 6 (Germanistiche Abhandlungen) (1959): 63–91. Reprinted in *Walther von der Vogelweide*, edited by Siegfried Beyschlag, pp. 539–83. Wege der Forschung 112. Darmstadt: Wissenschaftliche Buchgesellschaft, 1971.

Knapp, Fritz P. "Integumentum und âventiure: Nochmals zur Literaturtheorie bei Bernardus (Silvestris?) und Thomasin von Zerklaere." *Literaturwissenschaftliches Jahrbuch* 28 (1987): 299–307.

Kries, F. W. von. *Textkritische Studien zum Welschen Gast Thomasins von Zerclaere.* Quellen und Forschungen zur Sprach- und Kulturgeschichte der germanischen Völker. Neue Folge 23 [147]. Berlin: Walter de Gruyter, 1967.

————. "Zur Überlieferung des 'Welschen Gasts' Thomasins von Zerclaere." *ZfdA* 113 (1984): 111–31.

Kühn, Claudia. "*Swer niht enmerchet, daz er siht, er enbezzert sich davon niht.* Die illustrierten Fabeln und Tierbilder im 'Welschen Gast' des Thomasin von Zerclaere." In Wenzel and Lechtermann, *Beweglichkeit der Bilder*, pp. 200–215.

Kuhn, Hugo. "Thomasin von Zerklaere." In *Die deutsche Literatur des Mittelalters. Verfasserlexikon*, edited by Karl Langosch, vol. 4, cols. 466–72. Berlin: Walter de Gruyter, 1953.

Lechtermann, Christina. "Affekterregung und höfische Literatur im 'Welschen Gast.'" In Wenzel and Lechtermann, *Beweglichkeit der Bilder*, pp. 143–55.

Leitzmann, Albert. "Zum Wälschen Gast." *PBB* 63 (1939): 298–300.

Lerchner, Karin. "Narration im Bild. Szenische Elemente im Bildprogramm des 'Welschen Gastes.'" In Wenzel and Lechtermann, *Beweglichkeit der Bilder*, pp. 65–81.

Müller, Jürgen. *Studien zur Ethik und Metaphysik des Thomasin von Circlaria.* Königsberger Deutsche Forschngen 12. Königsberg: Gräfe und Unzer, 1935.

Neumann, Friedrich. "Einleitung." In *Der Wälsche Gast des Thomasin von Zirclaria*, edited by Heinrich Rückert, pp. v–li. Deutsche Neudrucke. 1852. Reprint, Berlin: Walter de Gruyter, 1965.

Neumann, Friedrich, and Ewald Vetter. *Zucht und schoene Sitte. Eine Tugendlehre der Stauferzeit mit 36 Bildern (16 davon farbig) aus der Heidelberger Handschrift Cold. Pal. Germ. 389 'Der Welsche Gast' von Thomasin von Zerclaere.* Wiesbaden: Reichert, 1977.

Oechelhaeuser, Adolf von. *Der Bilderkreis zum Wälschen Gaste des Thomasin von Zerclaere. Nach den vorhandenen Handschriften untersucht und beschrieben (mit 8 Tafeln).* Heidelberg: G. Koester, 1890.

Ono, Shoji. "Konflikte und Verhaltenslehren im 'Wälschen Gast' Thomasins von Zerklaere." *Neue Beiträge zur Germanistik* 1, no. 1 (2002): 166–79.

Ott, Norbert H. "Mise en page. Zur ikonischen Struktur der Illustrationen von Thomasins 'Welschem Gast.'" In Wenzel and Lechtermann, *Beweglichkeit der Bilder*, pp. 33–64.

Ranke, Friedrich. *Sprache und Stil im Wälschen Gast des Thomasin von Circlaria.* 1908. Reprint, New York: Johnson, 1970.

Rapp, Catherine Teresa. *Burgher and Peasant in the Works of Thomasin von Zirclaria, Freidank and Hugo von Trimberg.* Studies in German 7. 1936. Reprint, New York: AMS Press, 1970.

Resler, Michael. "Thomasîn von Zerclære." In *German Writers and Works of the High Middle Ages: 1170–1280*, edited by James Hardin and Will Hasty, pp. 133–40. *Dictionary of Literary Biography*, vol. 138. Detroit: Gale Research Inc., 1994.

Richter, Dieter. "Zur Überlieferung von Thomasins 'Welschem Gast.'" *ZfdA* 96 (1967): 149–53.

Rocher, Daniel. "Die *ars oratoria* des Thomasin von Zirklaere in seinem 'Wälschen Gast.'" In Schulze-Belli, *Thomasin von Zirklaere und die didaktische Literatur des Mittelalters*, pp. 63–77.

————. "Thomasin von Zerclaere: ein Dichter . . . oder ein Propagandist im Auftrag?" In *Wolfger von Erla. Bischof von Passau (1191–1204) und Patriarch von Aquileja (1204–1218) als Kirchenfürst und Literaturmäzen*, edited by Egon Boshof and Fritz Peter Knapp, pp. 325–43. Germanistische Bibliothek, Reihe 3, Untersuchungen, n.s. 20. Heidelberg: Winter, 1994.

————. "La Leçon des Elements à l'Homme dans le 'Wälscher Gast.'" In *Les Quatre Elements dans la culture médiévale*, edited by Danielle Buschinger and André Crepin, pp. 149–52. Actes du Colloque des 25, 26 et 27 Mars 1982. Université de Picardie, Centre d'Études Médiévales. Göppinger Arbeiten zur Germanistik 386. Göppingen: Kümmerle, 1983.

————. "Pour la Connaissance et l'Étude du 'Wälscher Gast.'" *Études Germaniques* 21 (1966): 46–51.

————. *Thomasin von Zerklaere "Der Wälsche Gast" (1215–1216).* Paris: Diffusion H. Champion, 1977.

————. "Thomasin von Zerclaere, Innocent III et Latran IV ou la véritable influence de l'actualité sur le 'Wälscher Gast.'" *Le Moyen Âge: Revue d'Histoire et de Philologie* 79 (1973): 35–55.

Rockar, Hans-Joachim. "Von Ziffern und Proportionen. Eine wissenschaftsgeschichtliche Betrachtung zu Codex Gothanus Memb. I 120. Thomasin von Zerclaere: Der Welsche Gast." In *Das Buch als Quelle historischer Forschung. Dr. Fritz Juntke anlässlich seines 90. Geburtstages gewidmet*, edited by Joachim v. Dietze, Jutta Fliege, Karl Klaus Walther, pp. 71–78. Leipzig: Bibliographisches Institut, 1977.

Röcke, Werner. *Feudale Anarchie und Landesherrschaft: Wirkungsmöglichkeiten didaktischer Literatur: Thomasin von Zerklaere "Der Wälsche Gast."* Bern: Lang, 1978.

Romeyke, Sarah. *"Swaz ein herre spricht ia oder niht, daz sol gar sin schephes schrift.* Das Aufzeichnungsgebot in Bild einundvierzig und seine Abschriften im 'Welschen Gast' des Thomasin von Zerclaere." In Wenzel and Lechtermann, *Beweglichkeit der Bilder,* pp. 156–73.

Ruff, Ernst Johann Friedrich. *Der Wälsche Gast des Thomasin von Zerklaere. Untersuchungen zu Gehalt und Bedeutung einer mittelhochdeutschen Morallehre.* Erlangen: Verlag Palm & Enke, 1982.

Schaefer, Ursula, ed. *Artes im Mittelalter. Wissenschaft—Kunst—Kommunikation.* Berlin: Akademie Verlag, 1999.

Schiewer, Hans-Jürgen. "Thomasin von Zerklaere." In *Lexikon des Mittelalters,* edited by Robert Auty, vol. 8, cols. 727–28. Zurich: Artemis, 1996.

Scholz, Manfred G. "Die 'Hûsvrouwe' und ihr Gast. Zu Thomasin von Zerclaere und seinem Publikum." In *Festschrift für Kurt H. Halbach zum 70. Geburtstag am 25. Juni 1972,* edited by Rose B. Maulbetsch-Schäfer, Manfred G. Scholz, Günther Schweikle, pp. 247–69. Göppinger Arbeiten zur Germanistik 70. Göppingen: Kümmerle, 1972.

Schulze-Belli, Paola, ed. *Thomasin von Zirklaere und die didaktische Literatur des Mittelalters. Beiträge der Triester Tagung 1993.* Trieste: Associazione di Cultura Medioevale, 1996.

Schüppert, Helga. "Bildschichten und ihre Funktion im 'Wälschen Gast.'" In Schulze-Belli, *Thomasin von Zirklaere und die didaktische Literatur des Mittelalters,* pp. 7–28.

Schumacher, Meinolf. "Gefangensein—*waz wirret daz?* Ein Theodizee-Argument des 'Welschen Gastes' im Horizont europäischer Gefängnis-Literatur von Boethius bis Vladimir Nabokov." In Wenzel and Lechtermann, *Beweglichkeit der Bilder,* pp. 238–55.

———. "Über die Notwendigkeit der *kunst* für das Menschsein bei Thomasin von Zerklaere und Heinrich dem Teichner." In Schaefer, *Artes im Mittelalter,* pp. 376–90.

Siegert, Ernst Peter. "Der Wälsche Gast des Thomasin von Zerklaere. Didaktischer Gehalt und künstlerischer Aufbau." Diss., University of Frankfurt, 1953.

Spartz, Charlotte. "Der Wälsche Gast des Thomasin von Circlaria." Diss., University of Cologne, 1960.

Starkey, Kathryn. "Das unfeste Geschlecht. Überlegungen zur Entwicklung einer volkssprachigen Ikonographie am Beispiel des *Welschen Gast.*" In *Visualisierungsstrategien in mittelalterlichen Bildern und Texten,* edited by Horst Wenzel and C. Stephen Jaeger, pp. 99–138. Philologische Studien und Quellen 195. Berlin: Erich Schmidt, 2006.

———. "From Symbol to Scene: Changing Strategies of Representation in the Manuscripts of the 'Welsche Gast.'" In Wenzel and Lechtermann, *Beweglichkeit der Bilder*, pp. 121–42.

Stolz, Michael. "Text und Bild im Widerspruch? Der Artes-Zyklus in Thomasins 'Welschem Gast' als Zeugnis mittelalterlicher Memorialkultur." *Wolfram-Studien* 15 (1998): 344–72.

Teske, Hans. *Thomasin von Zerklaere. Der Mann und sein Werk*. Heidelberg: C. Winter, 1933.

Wandhoff, Haiko. "*[B]ilde* und *schrift, volgen* und *versten*. Medienorientiertes Lernen im 'Welschen Gast' am Beispiel des 'Lektürekatalogs.'" In Wenzel and Lechtermann, *Beweglichkeit der Bilder*, pp. 104–20.

Weichselbaumer, Ruth. "Normierte Männlichkeit: Verhaltenslehren aus dem 'Welschen Gast' Thomasins von Zerclaere." In *Genderdiskurse und Körperbilder im Mittelalter: eine Bilanzierung nach Butler und Laqueur*, edited by Ingrid Bennewitz and Ingrid Kasten, pp. 157–77. Bamberger Studien zum Mittelalter 1. Münster: Lit, 2002.

Wenzel, Horst. "Der Dichter und der Bote. Zu den Illustrationen der Vorrede in den Bilderhandschriften des 'Welschen Gastes' von Thomasin von Zerclaere." In Wenzel and Lechtermann, *Beweglichkeit der Bilder*, pp. 82–103.

———. "Die Beweglichkeit der Bilder. Zur Relation von Text und Bild in den illuminierten Handschriften des 'Welschen Gastes.'" *ZfdPh* 116 (1997): 224–52.

———."Sagen und Zeigen. Zur Poetik der Visualität im 'Welschen Gast' des Thomasin von Zerclaere." *ZfdPh* 125, no. 1 (2006): 1–28.

———. "'wan die vrumen liute sint, unde suln sin spigel dem chint': zum Verhältnis von Zeigen und Wahrnehmen im 'Welschen Gast' des Thomasin von Zerclaere." In *Kunst der Bewegung: kinästhetische Wahrnehmung und Probehandeln in virtuellen Welten*, edited by Christina Lechtermann, pp. 181–215. Bern: Lang, 2004.

———. "*zuht* und *êre*: höfische Erziehung im 'Welschen Gast' des Thomasin von Zerklaere (1215)." In *Über die deutsche Höflichkeit. Entwicklung der Kommunikationsvorstellungen in den Schriften über Umgangsformen in den deutschsprachigen Ländern*, edited by Alain Montandon, pp. 21–42. Bern: Lang, 1991.

Wenzel, Horst, and Christina Lechtermann, eds. *Beweglichkeit der Bilder. Text und Imagination in den illustrierten Handschriften des "Welschen Gastes" von Thomasin von Zerclaere*. Cologne: Böhlau Verlag, 2002.

Winter, Ursula, and Heinz Stanescu. "Ein neuentdecktes Fragment aus dem Welschen Gast des Thomasin von Zerclaere." *PBB* 97 (1976; Halle a.d. Saale): 291–98.

Zips, Manfred. *"Reht tuon daz ist hüfscheit:* der Gedanke vom Seelenadel im 'Welschen Gast' des Thomasin von Zerclaere." In *Nouveaux mondes et mondes noveaux au moyen age,* edited by Danielle Buschinger and Wolfgang Spiewok, pp. 171–86. Actes du Colloque du Centre D'Etudes Médiévales de L'Université de Picardie Jules Verne. Greifswald: Reineke-Verlag, 1994.

Figure 2. Thomasin von Zirclaria, "The Italian Guest." Heidelberg, Universitätsbibliothek, Cpg. 389, fol. 2r (bottom). In accordance with the text above, a messenger (*der bot*) presents the book (*der welsch gast*) to the personified 'German Tongue' (*teuscheu zunge*) who inquires after the poet's own ability to write in that language ("sait mir chan si daz"). (Right margin) Again in accordance with the text, the poet/narrator mediates between two contrasting attitudes: An evildoer (*bosvaht*) obeys the dictates of evil (*bosheit*), while a good man (*der frum man*) stomps on another personification of evil and declares victory ("du bist unter minen vuoz"). Photo: Universitätsbibliothek Heidelberg.

THE ITALIAN GUEST

THOMASIN VON ZIRCLARIA'S PROSE FOREWORD

Whoever wishes to know what substance this book relates will find the [separate] subjects dealt with one after the other.[1] This book is divided into ten parts and each part has its chapters. Some parts have ten chapters, some more, some fewer, and each chapter has its sections, some many, some few. Before I begin the book, I shall state in my Foreword that every man should make the effort to complement with actions the good things he has read about, and how the wicked man can twist good words, and then I will say what I want to about the virtues, and what goodness and breeding are, and excuse myself for not being able to speak the language well, and request of the German language that it receive my Italian book well and not allow any inconstant man to see it, and then I shall begin my book as follows.[2]

Book I

I. I'll speak first of all about leisure, and what one should do at all times, and why one ought not to be lazy, and how laziness brings shame upon a man, and how one cannot get out of the habit, and which teaching one ought to be ashamed of, and how bad that fellow is who brags, lies, and mocks, and how one ought not to boast, and how boasting is less fitting in women than in men. II. I shall also speak of how the young lords shout when they come from the court to the inn, and how inappropriate that is, and how they ought to take to heart what they have seen at court, and how they should treat their companions well, and I will tell how and why one ought to honor strangers. III. I'll tell why one ought not to laugh too much, and that a man should not learn his companion's secrets, and that one should beware of the man who would like to learn them, and that a man should loyally keep silent about what his companion tells him, and why one does that, and that one should be careful of whom one speaks and

43

to whom, and how and when one should speak, and why young folk should be wary of the lords. IV. Why one ought to talk little and listen a lot, and why one ought to instruct the young folk with fear. And how the young folk themselves should be fearful, and how they might practice self-control, and that every young person [should] admit a good man into his heart, and turn his thoughts to him, and that it should seem to him that, whatever he does, this man might be watching him, and whom one should follow, and that one should be accustomed at home and at court to conduct oneself appropriately, and that one should take care when joking, and that one should not give in to anger and wickedness. V. That one should avoid gaming, and that one should consider the man who talks too much to be a fool, and also the person who is too taciturn, and that no one should speak of, or act on, everything that comes into his mind, and that one should speak and act sensibly, and how foolish that person is who, in his youth, believes he knows [something] without having been taught, and why one should be happy to listen to good stories, and let bad ones go. VI. And how one cannot take Helen [of Troy] as a good model, and that a woman should not be pleased if another woman behaves badly, and that women should improve themselves by comparison with Helen, and that beauty is nothing without good sense, and what type of sense a woman should have, and what sense is sufficient for a woman, and how beauty, birthright, wealth, love are nothing without it, and how beauty [does harm to] honor where good sense is not present, and how beauty and nonsense are bound together. VII. And that one should not sacrifice honor for the sake of beauty, and that beauty is nothing without breeding. Every cloth has its [own] quality. One's eyes can deceive one. A malevolent woman is not entirely without beauty. Some virtues are more appropriate in women than in knights, and some are more appropriate in knights, and certain vices are worse in women, and certain others are worse in knights. VIII. Concerning the fools' nets, and who is a good woman, and what young ladies and gentlemen should be happy to learn, and whom they should follow, and what those who have emerged from childhood should listen to and read, and that a well-spoken man should not deviate from the truth. IX. [I have said] that I have exceeded my goal, and what is the nature of love, and how one should watch over a woman, that one should not bewitch, force, nor buy [her], that love bought is not love. That love would be a vassal if one could buy it, and that it is free, and what one should give for the sake of love, and that a gift does not make evil good. That a man gives [presents] to a woman who considers him a fool. That a man gives [presents] to a woman who herself has sufficient [goods], and does not give [anything] to the woman who has nothing. A fool takes note of the adornments that a woman has externally, on her body; the wise man sees how she is adorned on the inside. That a man should not rob a woman of her possessions. A woman should also behave in like manner. X. What a woman may accept from her gentleman friend. That women remain faithful to their men, and why chivalry is useless.[3] What I like best in a woman. That no decent woman takes pleasure in being molested. That a man should not be too quick to request a favor of a decent woman, and that she should consider it bad if anyone does that. That some women think more highly of themselves if someone keeps asking them for something, that faithless women have experienced more than good women. That a false man [hurries off] to where he knows there is a false woman. XI. How one recognizes what an old woman was like in her youth. How one behaves toward a woman that one cannot court. What I have stated and where one can find out more about it. That a woman should know to whom she may offer her body. That one should honor love before possessions, and that one not love loose people. Why one should love goodness and good advice. That a woman not be given to maliciousness in her speech, so that one does not ignore or disbelieve [what she says]. That one should not court someone while chastising them, or praising oneself. After that I will turn to my subject matter.

Book II

I. Here I begin to speak about the lords, and that one ought to better oneself in old age, and how the country is led astray under a bad lord, and I liken us to the ladies and the lords to a mirror, and the malevolent lord to a light that has been extinguished, and advise one to take constancy as the starting point for virtue. II. What inconstancy is and regarding its nature, and how one carries it everywhere, and that one should remain constant to one thing, and how inconstancy is divided into four parts. III. How inconstancy is ill-suited to lords and why they should abstain from lying, and how nasty lying is, and how anger and lying are the progeny of inconstancy, and how a lie deceives, and that a lord should see whether he wants to give and can give what he promises [to give]. IV. How our inconstancy comes from the heart, and how the inconstancy of the world has emanated from us, and how the world still retains a part of its constancy, and we do not, and which things come and go according to their time, and how the heavens and stars follow their course. V. And then, what is below the moon is made up of four elements, and that it is a miracle since four contradictory natures are united in us, and that we are not united, and that among these four elements the one does not deprive the other of its nature, and how one separates us from our nature, and how the fifth nature is placed above all the four elements, and the nature of the seven stars, and why everything that is above the moon is well united and constant, and why what is below the moon is not united and not at all constant. VI. Here I provide examples of how those constancies grow that unite well together, and how their honor is constancy, and how that which does not unite is not constancy, and how the world is at present completely disunited and that one might comprehend the inconstancy of the world through this and other things, and know that the end of the world is at hand.

Book III

   I. Why nothing is so inconstant as man, and why God does not force us to be constant. II. That all things maintain their nature and order but man does not, and that every man would prefer to give up his role in life to assume that of another. III. How everything is evenly distributed, and how the poor man is no worse off than the rich man, and what both of them need, and what a man might truly need [on the one hand] and according to his foolish notions [on the other], and who is rich or poor on account of foolishness, and how some do not believe in living with this and what God has given them, and how we expend more energy on things we do not need than on those things that we do need, and how the fool thinks that he can have for free what he buys with his body, and how one has to abandon completely one's possessions at death, and how, then as always, where there is great joy there is also great sorrow. IV. That possessions do not make a man good, and that white makes white and black makes black, but whoever is bad is also bad if he is rich. How wealth more often brings us sorrow than joy. How a man thinks of possessions if he is rich, and what he ought to be thinking about. That worldly riches are [actually] poverty. That the person is secure who wishes to make use of his wealth, and that wealth [in itself] is not good. V. How wealth plagues the thoughts of a poor man, and the edifice he then builds, and what he then buys, and how he quarrels with his rivals, and whom he brings in to watch over his pennies, and thus he has anxiety with wealth even before he acquires it and afterwards. VI. That the [common] people are better off than the lords, and that it is foolishness for every man to want to be a lord, and how they speak about what they then would like to do, and that authority is not good, and that one should not set one's sights too high. VII. How a man is burdened with arrogant thoughts when he does not have it (i.e., authority), and what grand thoughts he then has, and how he takes one office away from one person and bestows it on another, and how he is then praised, and yet has nothing at all to show for it. VIII. That the powerful and the powerless are equal, and that the powerful are worse off than the powerless, and that the powerful are constantly concerned as to how they can subject others and never arrive at any conclusion. How a man takes on great worry when he believes he has escaped it, and how power abandons the powerful when he least expects it, and how we are deceived by power, and that the powerful man derives his power from the powerless, and that wealth, authority, and power do not follow their [true] nature. IX. How thinking about power causes us anxiety, and how quickly we put together a large army and slay our enemies, and that [a man shows God something that] he does not dare show another man. X. What good does it do that a man spreads his reputation? That a lord should be angry when someone praises him unjustly, and that he should take note of the person who is praising him, and how we ought to know if we are not worthy of praise, and that an evil man does not want to recognize his vices, and that a lord ought to consider whether the person who is praising him is telling the truth, and that miserable fellows praise [someone] to his face but malign him behind his back, and that one maligns the man whom one praises with lies, and that that man is a fool who is more inclined to believe a miserable fellow than himself, and that the lords create these miserable fellows and liars. That one ought not to do anything for the sake of fame. That whatever one does for the sake of fame cannot be virtuous, and that it is a vice, and how fame does not last a long time, and how it is foolishness for a man to seek a thing where it is not to be found. XI. Concerning the man who is not courageous, how he worries about it, and what gifts he conjures up, and what valor and what tournaments, and how people will tell marvelous tales about him, and that this is all a dream. XII. I also state that a dream with a foolish notion makes us noble, and how a noble man defiles his nobility through wickedness, and that one ought to make oneself noble so that one does not act in an ignoble fashion, for every man is noble, and that no one is noble, except the one who acts justly, and that the courtly man acts justly and is noble. XIII. How every man has his desires, and how everyone suffers on account of this. I'll tell about this in six sections. After that I'll talk about how one does not recognize wickedness in one's wife, and that every man should be on his guard against debauchery, and about the person who is more inclined to watch over his wife than over himself. Here I talk about those men who cannot follow their desires, however much they may suffer as a result.

Book IV

I. Here I will talk briefly about how inconstancy troubles us with respect to six things, and how I am amazed that we love what so thoroughly confounds us, and how the six things I have in mind—wealth, authority and power, fame, nobility, and desire—are seldom without vices, and that one ought not to concern oneself with them at all, if one does not wish to serve vice. [II. I will speak throughout the chapter about the characteristics of the lords, (and) how fettered those men are who follow some of those six things.][4] III. Here I say that I would like to speak about constancy, and tell what constancy is, and that one virtue does not make [a person] virtuous, and that the virtues are useful, and how everything that is good for the good man is bad for the wicked man. I will tell in six sections how these six things herald the virtue of a bad man and how the good man turns to good everything that happens to him and the bad man to bad, and I will then tell in three sections how the good man is always blessed, and the bad man always cursed. IV. How that man is cursed who does another man an injustice, or the one to whom he does it, why God permits an evil man to do so much injustice to a good man, and how everything that happens is right, and that it is right that God allows us to sin so much, and to what purpose the court exists, if everything that takes place is just, and whether it is right that the devil at times has power over a man, and whether it is right that the devil is powerful, and that evil people are also powerful. V. Why the good man suffers and the evil one fares well, and the good fare well and the evil suffer. VI. That no one can know why all sorts of things occur, and that no one should assume that he knows that, and that God treats everyone according to his due, and that no one should say that God acts any differently from the way He ought to, and that, whatever He does, one should consider it good. VII. By what right a good man should fear nothing, neither poverty nor illness, nor that one might banish him, nor that one might take him captive, nor that one might slay him, nor that one might bury him, and that he should pay no attention to how long he might live, other than to how he might live, and that he not pay any attention to where he might die, all of this is covered throughout the chapter. VIII. How a person should console himself over his dead friend, and that one lament him in moderation, and not let him remain without lament, and how long a man should be without a woman, if his wife dies, and a woman without a man, and that they should take care that they are not secretly doing evil, and that every man be a witness to his misdeeds. IX. Whether one shall recognize one's friends in the next world.

Book V

I. Here I will say first of all that virtues bring us to heaven, and before I show how, I will tell how two ways are good and two are bad. The fifth is both evil and good. The first thing is the highest good, the second is completely good, the third is the lowest form of evil, the fourth is completely evil, the fifth is both evil and good. II. Here I will state what can be considered the highest good, that [it] has to be completely good, and how one ought to build the ladder that will lead to it, and what constitutes the rungs, and what the person who wishes to fashion them should be wary of, and what constitutes those [rungs] that lead to the lowest form of evil, and how it is easier for one to arrive at the lowest form of evil than at the highest good. III. This chapter relates of the hooks that pull us [down] from the highest good, and how the devil likes nothing better than what enables him to attract people and how he really enjoys doing that. IV. Here I tell that I have quite rightly shown that vice will not bring us to God, and then I demonstrate that no man will ever arrive there except through virtues, and will also demonstrate that no one can have all the virtues in their entirety, other than God alone, and I will also provide examples of those who have gone to hell because of their vices, and how they deceive themselves who believe they can ascend to God on account of their wealth, and how foolish that man is who sins in the belief that he can eliminate his sin through goodness, and how the poor man can give just as much as the rich man in God's name. [V.]⁵ Why a lord who is not subject to God unjustly has authority, and how a man who wishes to separate us from God does us great violence, and why there are not so many virtuous people in our day as there were earlier, and how the lords are responsible for this situation, and how good knights are hidden, wherever they are, and how the lords should find them. VI. I say the same thing about the priests and tell why they are incapable of doing anything, and how good they were in former times, and how one treated the good [men] well back then, and how one mistreats them nowadays, and why that happens, and how all sorts of things get stood on their head, and why one should love wise people, and that the lords should help those who want to learn, and how, in particular, the bishops should do that, and why they do not do it, and how in this way they transgress against the law, and how they bribe one person with possessions, and allow great skill to go to waste in another through poverty. VII. Why knowledge is unpleasant, and that one does not send those off to study who have a good mind, and that that man is arrogant who does not seek to acquire virtues, and that the person who does evil is completely indolent, and that through evil and laziness one accumulates many sins, and that one is therefore evil, and how we commit a wrong by following the lords so that we all end up being captured, and that the lords come off worse than we do, and how we are all nonetheless "bathed," and how one is scrubbed in the bath and washed and whipped with the chains of vice, and how one is tied there, and what these chains are made of, and how one ought to stay clear of the bath and the chains, and how one ought to bathe on this earth, and turn away from vice; that will serve him well.

Book VI

I. Here I admonish all types of people not to neglect their virtues, and show them that, if they do not always practice them, they will nevertheless emerge with them in the end, and provide an example of many a man whom God has also brought to great honor in this world through his virtue. II. How it is right for a man who is himself not praised to praise a good man, and that the rich man mocks the poor man, and how happy the usurer is when one complains of lacking something, and how foolish the usurer is and how other people are better off with what he has than he is, and in what way one ought to take pity on one's children. III. Here I tell how the usurers are happy to hear these stories, and that one has great trouble as a result of vices, and that the virtuous man has a serene life, and what serenity modesty gives, and what trouble arrogance creates. And what serenity that man has who is not envious, and what trouble the wicked man has, and what serenity that man has who is not given to anger, and what trouble anger brings, and what serenity chastity gives, and what trouble licentiousness creates, and what comfort that person has who does no one an injustice, and what trouble the robbers and thieves have, and the serenity those [men] have who live with their goodness, and the [trouble] those people have who lie, and how easily one can tell the truth. IV. That one rarely takes from the generous man, and always takes from the parsimonious one, and how the miserly man follows the fool, how avarice emanates from cowardice, and how both cowardice and avarice defeat a man, and that a good knight should fight against vice, and how the vices amass against him, and how the virtues should arm him, and how one should persevere over the vices, and how he should take care, whenever he has defeated them, that they do not assemble forces against him, and how one should protect oneself from the devil, and the world, and desire, for these three help the vices against us. V. Why the vices have the power to fight against us, and why we should be happy to fight [against them], and for what there can be no help, I shall relate in four sections, and I will state that possessions interfere with our fight, and admonish the knights to think of their Order, and tell them then what they ought to do, and also what the priests ought to do, and that the lords live well with their people, and that vassals are happy and willing to serve, and that one should not be a tyrant, and that one should allow one's squire to live according to the rights of a vassal, and that no man may be completely enslaved, and how God offers us nothing but justice, and how we order our squire to do evil and injustice, and how we do not let our people live a Christian life, and how one should force one's squire to lead a good life, and how one must answer to God for one's people, and how both the lord and the squire have sins, and that the squire should not transgress against God for the sake of his lord, and that no lord should issue a command that is against God, and how one should adhere to the same thing in a friendship, and how we incite our friends to do bad things. VI. I have this to say about bad advisers, and how they[6] incite their lords to avarice, and how possessions are the devil's grindstone and his net, and how the [money] collector is a foolish money-changer, and how one can become rich quickly, and how the value one has from possessions is worthless, and how a man who has nothing and is not a craftsman should acquire possessions, and that one should not despair on account of poverty, and how I advise the lords to lead us well, and be a beacon of light for us, and that we should believe God's laws, and how the priests and the laymen are rushing off to hell, and that every man must go to the place that he has deserved, and how that man is lost who does not believe this.

Book VII

I. Here I begin to tell about the soul and the body and the power of both, and how the power of the soul is better than the power of the body, and how one can do with one's mind what one cannot do with strength [alone], and that a man's reputation does not lie in his strength or in his agility, and how God has honored us with a mind, and how one should apply it to acquiring virtues, and how we turn our mind to bad things, and how the mind contains God's image within us. II. I say that our mind turns to bad things and to good things, and how both priests and knights deal in both cunning and violence, and how the parsimonious rural judges hold forth at court, and how they turn their minds to nonsense, and that that man is wise who relies on God, and how foolish that person is who relies on profit, and how he has lost the best two of the four qualities: Imagination, Memory, Reason, and Intellect, and how no one in this world can be fully informed. III. I will relate that there is no knowledge so small that one can know it in its entirety, and then I shall talk about the seven Arts, and what purpose each of the seven serves, and who were the greatest masters with respect to these seven, and how not one of them was a complete master of his art, and how an uneducated man believes that he is wise about something [even] Solomon did not know about, and how I compare this same fool to a person who has never emerged from a dungeon. And then who might recognize the mind's heights, depths, and breadth, and [how] one can recognize them in this world, and then I will show who knows the seven Arts best of all, and thus demonstrate that a peasant could master them, if he wishes to do so. IV. And then I will speak of the two Arts, of Theology and Physic, and of their respective functions, and how the one heals the soul, and the other the body, and how one might know the nature of all things that are below the moon, and what is between the moon and the heavens, and what is in heaven, and I will tell you why people do not pay attention to Theology, and why one has more love for the decrees and the laws. V. Here I indicate that I would be happy to say how one Art relates to the other, but that one would not understand them, for there are now fewer educated laymen than was formerly the case, and how one hitherto taught children to read books, and I enumerate several lords of whose skill people still speak, and state how I would like the lords to teach their children, and that they should retain good masters at their courts, and that all noble people should have their children educated, and that no better legacy can be left to a child than virtue and common sense, and how some demonstrate that they are not capable of anything, and how the priests act worse than the laymen. On this point I will respond to them. I will also answer to them that they demonstrate to God in this way that they do not know what a sin is, and I respond to the retort spoken by many fools, namely, that, since that person does evil who reads about it in books, then I have no sin if I am to do it, and I say that if it enters the eyes of the priest, then it goes into the ears of the laymen. VI. Then I say that every man has five doors in his body, and those are the five senses: touch, hearing, sight, smell, and taste, and I show how the five senses are the servants of the four powers that I have mentioned previously, and I tell you how one lives well by the four senses and cannot live without the fifth, and how the senses are awakened when it becomes light, for they do not serve the four powers well when they are asleep, and how Reason shall educate the senses, and how the soul is the queen of the body, and how the four powers are the advisers of the soul, and [that] the senses can deceive. VII. How it stands with the soul in the body as with a king in his land, and why the soul does greater penance for what the body does than the body itself, and how and by what right it does penance in the final analysis for both, and that no man need endure the fire of hell, and how one ought to gain wisdom in the appropriate fashion, and how one can easily do that. VIII. Here I state briefly what I have said, and how one should sensibly arrange five things in one's body and five outside the body, and how each of the ten things will create confusion if one does not do this, and how one thing is constituted that is both inside and outside the body, that one should order with the power of the soul.

Book VIII

I. Here I state what I have said regarding inconstancy and its clan since I began my book and how I would now like to say something about its sister, and how immoderation is its sister, and what immoderation is, and about its power and its customs and its activity, and what moderation is and what immoderation and moderation do, and by what means one can learn moderation. II. Here I tell how one can turn virtues into vices through immoderation, [for example] modesty, and generosity, and other virtues. III. How one can transform vices into virtues through moderation, [for example,] both anger and arrogance, and other vices. IV. Here I relate that nothing is good that is immoderate, and what moderation a man should observe while praying, and about those who make fine requests and do evil, and about those who make malevolent requests, and what moderation one should practice when fasting. V. And how one should practice moderation in one's speaking, laughing, sleeping, and waking, and how moderation should be observed in one's weapons and attire, and I begin to speak about some immoderate people. VI. In this chapter I give nothing other than examples of people who, in our time, have come to nothing through their arrogance and immoderation, and some who have ascended through their modesty. VII. Here I show how the same thing happened in olden times, namely, that many were brought down through their arrogance and their immoderation, and I demonstrate how that person is worse off who does not want to take heed of the example that evil happens to evil men, and that that man is better off who does not follow the evil man. VIII. Here I tell how I have often observed that all those who are troubled with arrogance fall; how one should not take any notice of frivolous people, and I will relate that that person is arrogant who does not wish to serve his lord, just as the one is who rules in a way other than he ought to, and that we should be happy to be subject to those men whom God has given to us as lords, and that we should take as an example the Greeks, who did not want to follow that [advice], and also provide the same example in Aaron's sister and others in the Old Testament, and how it comes about that one sometimes has a malevolent lord as a result of one's sins, and how we do not want to follow him, even if he is decent, and also provide an example of what happened here before as a result, and then I relate that God has given us a master whom we always defame: I am referring to the pope, and how the person who has never seen him acts this way, and I state how bad that is, and why one ought not to do it, and how the pope sent his emissaries and his letters in the service of the Holy Grave, and [how he] did that out of goodness and how we turn it into something bad, and I will tell you as well about the good squire, who sang about the man, and how one can easily confuse a good thing, but not so easily a bad one, and how one can go astray so that one is happy to do it, and I talk a little bit about the heretics, that there are so many of them that the one does not give the other any advice other than to be happy to do it, and how it is unnecessary that one advise against perhaps traveling across the sea in the service of God, for one is not happy to do it anyway. IX. Here I admonish the German knights to cross [the sea] in God's name, and show them in many ways how it is right that they should do that, and answer those who speak against it. X. I admonish here the princes from German lands to do the same thing, namely, that they cross the sea, and I also say what King Frederick might acquire there, if God wishes it. XI. Here I tell how I have deviated a bit from my subject matter and wish to return to it, and why arrogance is so named, and how one must out of arrogance land up in five chasms, and how one thus falls into all [sorts of] vices, and then show through what skills one should flee from vices, namely, arrogance, and avarice, and wickedness, and injustice, and perjury.

Book IX

I. Here I provide a little introduction and tell how my pen is complaining that it writes too much, and how I answer it, and then I begin my Book. II. And I say that a lord ought to follow the eagle and the lion and carry both of them in his heart, neither less nor more, and what lies between high spirits and arrogance, and then I relate what is right and how good it is, and how a lord ought to better himself through a poor man's misfortune, and whom one ought to take as a lord, if one has a choice, and that a lord should treat the poor man and the rich man evenhandedly at court, and what breaks the wings of justice, and in what way one ought to show mercy to the thief, and how one ought to refrain from anger while in court, and how one ought to bring peace to the lands. III. How one ought to refrain from things that break the wings of justice, and how justice has two wings. IIII. Here I say why worldly and ecclesiastical courts do not complement one another, and how priests and laymen live in a state of adversity, and of their chiding, and how maliciously they chide [one another]. And how one can refrain from doing so, and how a layman should not subject himself to a religious court, and how the religious man should act who deals with secular courts, and how a lord should act, whose vassals do not want to be subject to him, and how he dishonors God who neglects his court out of fear, and how no man was ever conquered who fought for the sake of justice and with modesty. V. Here I demonstrate that a lord should not be in too much of a hurry, and that he should act on advice, and why he ought to take advice, and how a lord ought to pay attention to three points when it comes to advice, and what they are, and how one should take note with advice what the poor man and the rich man advise, and what the old man and the young man might want to say, and why one ought to do that, and how one ought to let the man whom one has asked for advice take time to reflect. VI. Here I state that one ought not to pass judgment for the sake of fame, or affection, or for the sake of profit, and I also advise that a lord should not trust too much, and I provide an example of those who trust and do not dare to act, and compare them in the final analysis to the malevolent oppressors, to the wolf and the malevolent driver who dares not do anything when someone does something to his donkey. VII. Here I advise that one not believe too quickly what anyone says, and demonstrate that there are three types of injustice and from where injustices emanate.

Book X

I. In this final book I will tell how justice admonishes me to speak about generosity, and that justice applies generosity, and what they give by rights as well as according to the law, and what justice might give, and what generosity might give, and [how] justice brings it about that the one is with the other, and how generosity brings it about that they love one another. II. Here I tell why I have left it to the last to speak about generosity, and how virtues are as nothing where there is no generosity, and how generosity that one acquires for the sake of fame and fortune is worthless, and that that person is generous in old age and in his youth who is not generous for the sake of fame or fortune, and how there is no virtue more constant than generosity, whenever it emanates from the heart, and how virtue and vice, as they grow, justly retain their names, and how avarice is increasing, and how avarice emanates from a cold nature, and how the parsimonious fellow cannot free himself from avarice, and how one ought to understand the value of generosity, given the malevolence of avarice, and how every man would like one to say of him that he is generous. III. Here I tell what generosity is, and whether that person who has nothing can be generous, and I demonstrate that that person is just as generous who is willing to give as the person who actually gives something. IIII. Here I show how we have lost the designation of generosity, and how we deceive ourselves when we think that that person is generous who gives us something that he has acquired illicitly, and how that man is more malevolent who gives in such a fashion than the person who gives nothing, and how we have stood the substance of generosity on its head, and how justice and injustice cannot coexist, and how many a man believes he is generous who is not capable of understanding what generosity is, and here I introduce a rule of generosity: the first rule is that one take note where the gift is most appropriate, the second rule is that one neither give too little nor too much. V. The third rule states that one ought not to be tardy with one's gift, the fourth, that one be joyful in one's giving, and throughout the chapter I will speak about this subject matter. VI. Here I relate why a man becomes ungrateful, and afterwards that a person should forget the gift that he himself gives, and think about the gift that he receives, and how one should adhere to giving and receiving. I talk about all of that in the same chapter. VII. Afterwards I tell that one should give some gifts publicly and some secretly. and that one give no one something that will shame or injure him, and that one not give [superfluous][7] gifts, and that one should enjoy giving gifts that last a long time. [VIII.][8] Here I state how I wish to give my book to virtuous folk and how it will mean nothing to malevolent people and what it is called, and that it should not remain with any scoundrel, and how no good teaching can remain within a bad man, and how afterwards I conclude my book.

PREFACE TO BOOK I

Whoever enjoys reading good books and is himself good will find that his reading will have been put to good use. Every man should strive to realize through good deeds whatever he has found to be good in his reading. If someone hears or reads good tales, but is himself bad, know for a fact that his wicked and nasty ways will transform what is good [into bad]. Any man who likes to proclaim the virtue of another man should do all he can to emulate him, for everyone should try to have others speak well of him too. One should read about honest and respected people and should try to be a decent person oneself. This is a piece of advice that all would do well to heed. (20)

For a long time I have been hearing that a great deal is achieved in this world by virtuous people, and now the time has come for me to say what constitutes goodness and courtesy, what virtue is, and how men and women alike can come to do good things, even if they cannot manage it by themselves. If someone takes note of courtesy's lesson, this will enhance his virtue both in youth and in old age. (32)

First I want to let you know that, however well I know Italian, I do not intend to intersperse my poem with Italian words. The mantel that adorns courtesy's lesson should, by its nature, be the same color all over. I am not saying this because it displeases me if someone intertwines his German with Italian if he can do this effectively, for then a German who knows no Italian will learn many a fine turn of phrase if he chooses to do so. I am afraid that I should be wasting my efforts if I set out to teach you how to speak Italian. I have something else in mind to which I am keen to apply my efforts and I propose to turn all my thoughts to making people understand me. That is my constant aim, and for this reason you should not take me to task if I happen to miss out on some rhyme or other and not render it quite correctly. It naturally bothers me greatly that I am not proficient in the language.[1] Because of this I ask all young people, as wise people have already been asked by virtue of their experience and their good sense and their kindness, that they should not take it amiss if there are any failings in my language. It should not surprise anyone if I make mistakes in speaking German, for I am an Italian through and through, as one can plainly see from my German. I was born in Friuli and shall not take offense if anyone in all sincerity corrects my poem and my German. My name is Thomasin von Zerclaere, and I am indifferent to the mockery of malevolent people. If I enjoy the favor of Gawain, Sir Kay may mock me if he wishes.[2] Anyone who pleases all the good folk invariably displeases the bad. If someone receives the praise of good people he can certainly forget about the bad ones. If a virtuous person behaves well, that does not seem good to bad people, for whatever good a virtuous person does must be a blow to the malicious. (86)

German lands, welcome, as a good hostess should, this Italian guest of yours, who dearly loves your honor. If you will listen to him he will tell you many tales of courtesy. You have often enjoyed hearing things that have been taken from the French and that German people have translated, and so you shall today hear whether an Italian can perhaps say things in German that may be pleasing to you. He is prepared to put all of his heart and soul into this. May God grant that it may seem good to you, for he has not taken what he is saying from any Italian source.[3] However, it is a good carpenter who knows how to position stone and wood in his work where they belong. Nor is it a vice if I can perhaps with skill insert within the wall of my poem a piece that another hand has fashioned, so that it fits just like the others. A wise man once said: "Anyone who can skilfully insert into his poem a passage that he did not write himself has done as much—do not be in any doubt about this—as he who made it up in the first place. It immediately becomes his own creation." It is my intention that one should underpin one's writing with the teaching of other good folk. Let him treat no one with disdain: that will bring him honor. (126)

My hostess, bear in mind that if my book falls into your hands, and if there is anything that you do not like about it, let that be made good by a man who is beyond reproach. You should not let it be seen by anyone who is not free of inconstancy. A malevolent man is more inclined to look at a good piece of writing closely so that he can reject it than on account of its message. (136)

This is where my preface ends. Now I propose to start another section and ask God for the wit to do it. This is how I begin my book. (140)

BOOK I

I have heard and read that people should avoid becoming idle. Every respectable man should all the time speak, act, and think in a proper manner, and he should not deviate from that path. Idleness is a vice among young people; laziness ill befits youth. If one has nothing to do one should have the good sense and the wisdom either to speak well or to consider that one should do so. Anyone who wishes to be courtly and adroit will always find enough material from these three things, and he will achieve much success through them. A man who lives idly in his youth will rest shamefully in his old age, because he did not wish to do what he should have done when he was able to do it. Anyone who devotes his youth to bad behavior will have brought absolute dishonor on his old age. Anyone who wishes to live honorably in his old age should strive for honor while he is young. (164)

One never throws off a vice if one has practiced it constantly in one's youth. Whenever there is no fruit to be had, a child will spend his time walking up and down in the orchard, and his craving is greatly increased. Take note of this: the gambler is even more drawn to gambling when he has nothing. The glutton agonizes for food; the drinker is dying for a drink, and even when he has nothing to drink he does not want to do without it. And so it is with an old man: he cannot free himself from the bad things and the vices he practiced in his youth. That is why I offer my advice that one should build one's youth firmly on courtesy and virtuous things. We cannot go wrong with them. (184)

I am directing this advice at young people and if they then want more of it they can gain it afterwards if they put their minds to it: they should practice modesty in proper measure, for anyone who practices modesty must abandon boastfulness, mendacity, mockery and villainy, and all manner of inconstancy. If anyone desires to practice modesty properly, he should preserve it in three respects: firstly, one should not speak dishonorably; secondly, one should hold fast to the instruction that one should behave well and correctly; thirdly one should do what one ought to do. Even if a woman behaves correctly, if her demeanor is not good and if she does not speak nicely either, her good deeds are uncrowned, for fine behavior and good speech crown the deeds of a woman. I tell you that her good deeds can never amount to anything if she cannot deport herself well and speak as she should speak. Unsightly behavior reflects inconstancy and wrongful deeds follow on the heels of bad speech. Sometimes a woman thinks she is conducting herself in a womanly fashion if she behaves in a haughty manner, but a woman who wishes to behave in a ladylike way should guard against haughtiness. Young ladies and young gentlemen should both practice modesty. (216)

Boasting, mendacity, mockery: anyone who engages in these three things cannot be called "free," for he is a slave to villainy. May my service be denied to him! Good breeding commands that no one should endure mockery from another person, and that neither man nor woman should lie to one another. Boastfulness is the worst villainy, and mockery can never be separated from boastfulness. The boastful one is devoid of all shame, and lies are second nature to him. If he boasts that he is telling the truth then he can very easily break his oath. For this reason any man who can discern courtly matters should strictly beware of boastfulness. He should bear in mind: "Either I do not speak the truth or I am guilty of perjury, for if it is true I vowed that I should not go on talking about it." If a man behaves in a reprehensible manner, he is not immune to boasting. By behaving in a reprehensible way, a man is certainly showing off foolishly. Anyone who goes riding about at night for the sake of boasting, or lies down under a hedge[1] will stand to profit from everything that I would like to pass on to him for free. (246)

I shall demonstrate precisely that one should not boast, for one knows that a worthy man should have the skill to do what a worthy man should do. His boasting is absolutely meaningless, for everyone says that he can attract real love if he turns his mind to it. If, on the other hand, he is a scoundrel, he need not boast so that people will treat him better. All he achieves through boasting is that people will say that she has done what she has done for the sake of a scoundrel and that she is a bad woman who has defiled her body. If a man brags [about his conquests],[2] he heaps shame upon the ladies and brings precious little honor to himself. It goes completely against the dictates of propriety. No one knows how to praise himself for his goodness and decency better than the worthless fellow. No one becomes a boaster unless he has no respect for women. A man who is nothing in the eyes of women is given to boasting. To be sure, nothing so ill becomes a man as boasting. However, boasting becomes a woman even less, if you want to know. She would do better to keep quiet than to tell her husband who is wooing her. Her boasting and her frivolous behavior cause her husband great distress, and bring suspicion on herself, for her husband will trust her less, and she will incur great hostility from her husband towards her friends, you can be sure. In the end she will also lose the man who would like to serve her at some point. A woman can certainly do what she ought to do without boasting. Her good deeds are absolutely nothing if she does not guard against boasting. You should know for a fact that the woman who does not guard against boasting is behaving as badly as the one who is actually behaving improperly. (296)

I find it hard to put up with yelling and shouting and boisterous antics. They say that barflies behave like this, but, unfortunately, so do young people at fine courts. They yell and bluster more than gentle courtesy ever teaches them. Shouting and boisterousness are very much the game of ill-bred youngsters. Whenever they come over from the court to the inn, a base young person will yell: "Bring that wine and mead over here! Look, I'll give this much, and he can give that, and my mate will give the same," and then in his blustering way he overestimates what his companion can afford and so always upsets him. Then all the young fellows shout out: "That's just the way it should be." Once the rounds have been given out, if one of them has nothing left, he has to leave his coat at the inn, whether he likes it or not. Anyone who upsets his companion like this is behaving very badly. Then these coarse young people shout out: "Now let's wager for wine. We really don't want to be greedy." They think they are avoiding stinginess but end up falling into wanton behavior. Anyone who has any finer feeling is condemned by them, and anyone who has nothing to gamble away has to be a villain, and they all make a noise about this ignoble man from time to time. Anyone who wished to take it upon himself to be generous when he could be would not need to boast the way that scoundrel demanded. I want noble young people to follow these instructions about correct behavior. Let noisy talk and bragging be completely unacceptable. One should leave that to the coarse barflies, since it is their job to be yelling all the time. (342)

So when noble young people leave the court they should be thinking quietly to themselves: "That was how that good knight behaved at court today: I must try very hard to emulate him." Anyone who does not take note of what he sees will not improve himself. He might just as well be in the woods as at the court. Because a youngster does not notice how a respectable man behaves at court, the court has often produced some foolish young people. I don't mind telling you that a bear is never going to be a good singer, and it's the same with these uncouth young people. The more they are at court, the less they become anything: they only take note of the bad things, not the good. (362)

I want my young people, who are of noble stock, to treat their companions well. Any noble youngster should help his friend with his intentions and his deeds. If that friend owes a debt somewhere, he should immediately pay it for him. Whatever he has to do on his behalf, he should not begrudge him that. I want one person to respect another, if they obey the lessons about good behavior. No one should push through the door in front of everyone else. (376)

Both ladies and gentlemen should respect strangers, and even if a stranger does not deserve it, they will have brought honor on themselves. On the other hand, if he does deserve it, then both of them gain honor. Since one does not know who the stranger is, one always ought to respect him. Whenever an unknown guest arrives at court, the young squires should serve him well, as though he were their master. That is desired by the lesson of courtesy. They should speak wholesome words, for that is the very essence of good breeding.[3] (390)

A lady should allow herself to be seen, if a stranger comes to visit her. If she does not allow herself to be seen, she should never be known outside her chamber. Let her pay the price for that, let her remain unknown. A lady should not speak recklessly if she is to behave in a ladylike manner. Moreover, I wish to emphasize that propriety demands that a lady should not stare at a stranger. It should please a noble young gentleman to look courteously at knights and ladies alike. (404)

A noble young lady should certainly speak softly, not loudly. A young gentleman should also be astute enough to take to heart what people say to him, so that it is unnecessary for them to repeat it. Good behavior forbids all ladies from sitting with their legs crossed. A young gentleman should under no circumstances stand on a bench, whether it be long or short, if he sees a knight sitting on it. A lady should never walk with firm or long steps, and you should know that it is wrong for a knight to ride while a lady is walking. Believe me, a lady should face the horse's head when she is riding, and be assured that she should not sit sidesaddle. A knight should not ride up to ladies in an impetuous manner, for, to be sure, a startled lady has often taken a leap that she might better not have taken. I cannot imagine that any knight who allows his horse to run free so that it spatters a lady will be the master of his wife either. Good manners dictate that knights should not keep looking at their legs when they are riding.[4] Indeed I believe that people should look straight ahead. A lady should not stretch her hand out over her dress when she is riding, and, believe me, she should keep her head and her eyes still. A gentleman and a knight should also pay heed to this and not fidget with his hands when he wants to say something. He should not swing his arms about in the direction of a good man's teeth.[5] Anyone who believes in proper courtesy should not place his hand on the head of anyone of higher station than himself, nor on his shoulder: that is proper respect. (450)

Any lady who wishes to adhere to decorum should not travel without a cloak, and she should hold her cloak together at the front if she is not wearing a long tunic. If she allows any part of her body to be seen uncovered, that is completely contrary to proper behavior. If I have any understanding of the matter, a knight should not appear barelegged in the presence of the ladies. It seems to me that a lady should not keep looking behind her. She should walk straight ahead and not often look back. If she hears a noise she should be mindful of propriety. A young lady should rarely speak unless someone asks her a question, and if a lady believes me, she will not speak much at all, and note that when she is eating she should certainly not speak. (470)

Anyone who wishes to behave correctly should take care at table, where very good manners are called for. Any host worth the name should see to it that everyone has enough, and his guest should be so correct that he behaves as though he did not notice anything. When a man begins to eat he should bear in mind that he should only touch his own food: that's good behavior. One should not eat the bread until the first courses have been served. A man should take great care not to put food into both sides of his mouth, and at the same time he should be careful not to drink or talk while he has anything in his mouth. Anyone who turns to his companion with the cup, as though he were wanting to give him something to drink, before he has taken it away from his own mouth, must be prompted to this action by the wine. Nor is it courteous to peer over one's cup while one is drinking. A man should not be too quick to take something he likes from his companion for one should stick to one's own food. One should always eat with the hand furthest from one's neighbor. If your companion is sitting on your right, always eat with your left hand. One should also take pains never to eat with both hands. One should also not be too quick to put one's hand into the dish at the same time as one's companion, for he will remove his at once. A host should also avoid any dish which his guests do not like or which is unfamiliar to them. The wolf prefers to eat alone; the camel does not eat alone if he sees another wild animal around him. Mark my words: the host will derive more honor by taking the camel as his example rather than the wolf. It is fitting that the host should provide water after the meal, but it is also appropriate that no squire should wash at that point. If a young nobleman wishes to wash himself, he should go to one side, far away from the knights and wash himself in private: that is polite and pleasing to the eyes. (526)

Here is another lesson that noble children should observe: they should not laugh too much, for laughing is the practice of fools. When two people are laughing together, their conversation does not have much meaning. Any man who has his wits about him need not regret if he does not hear what a man says while he is laughing. No man should be inclined to pester his comrade to reveal his secrets to him: that is my advice. One should be very wary of anyone who wishes to discover one's secrets, for people are inclined to blabber about those things they have been pressing someone to divulge. (544)

Let every fine young gentleman be so aware of his good manners that whatever his friend tells him he loyally keeps quiet about it. If he betrays his confidence and his friend comes to hear of it he will never trust him so much again. Things told in confidence are often spread abroad. Let me tell you that if a man cannot use good judgment with regard to whom he talks about, with whom, about what, how and when, this will sooner or later cause him harm. One should consider whom one is talking about. The decent man is quite distinct from the malevolent one. No man should tell secrets to a big mouth. Anyone who has a virtuous disposition should speak nothing but good. If anyone wishes to speak well, then good things should be spoken in a good way. Anyone who knows when it is appropriate to speak will also speak in the appropriate manner. Children should stop their whispering, since whispering gives rise to mistrust. Things which one is reluctant to make known are never correct and honorable, for that which one says openly should be embellished with courtesy. It very often happens as a result of whispering that someone takes offense at another, for he quite rightly believes he does not esteem him as he should. When pages go before their superiors or stand in front of them, they should refrain from whisper-ing, laughing, or [idly] looking around. (580)

I will not withhold my third piece of advice: listen a lot and say little. Lis-tening does us no harm: talking can often get us into trouble. One ought to learn in silence so that one can afterwards be eloquent. Anyone who does not wish to learn in silence tends to say a lot of foolish things. One should refine in private what one proposes to say in public. A child should learn with discipline anything he wants to recite well at a later date. Discipline is a positive thing inasmuch as it sharpens the mind of a child for listening and understanding. A child will not soon forget something it has been taught through discipline, for his mind will seek it out at all times. If a child grows up without discipline he has lost the true measure of instruction. Thus noble children who lack a firm hand should bear in mind and see to it that they acquire discipline for themselves. Their sense of honor should engender discipline in them so that they never speak other than well, and never say anything that might go against good behavior or honor. They should keep this advice in their minds and in their spirits: he who does this is truly noble. Where there is neither control nor discipline, good breeding and honor are also lacking. Every noble child can practice self-control daily. If a person wants to, he can learn a lot from observing and hearing and thinking. He should also be so inclined as to take note of how the best fellow behaves, for virtuous people are mirrors for children, and so they ought to be. The child should recognize in them what is good and what is bad. If he sees something he happens to like, let him not lose sight of it, but if he sees something that does not seem good to him, then let him strive to improve it. (626)

In his heart a man should silently select a virtuous person and should copy him in every way: that accords with virtue and good sense. If he can he should think about him day and night. He should not desist from this and, whatever he is called upon to do, he should take this worthy man as his example: then he cannot go wrong. Anyone who can cut along a straight line will cut exactly as he should. Anyone who can follow virtuous people is himself a good man. (640)

A child should be disposed to think that, whatever he does, a good man is watching him; that way he will be better able to protect himself from disgrace, for he would have to be ashamed in that man's presence if his foot were to slide towards misbehavior. One should gladly follow the man who is better to observe than to hear, for that is the man who so adheres to the lessons about courtesy that he follows up his good words with even better actions. (652)

Anyone who wishes to behave well at court should take care when he is at home that he does not behave in a discourteous way, for you should surely know that good manners and courtesy derive from habit. If a child is given to joking, let him joke in such a way that no one becomes unhappy because of it. Bad jokes have serious consequences. One should joke in an appropriate way. Joking around with the truth often causes heartache.

Just look how the peasant jokes and larks about in a very nasty way. Malevolent tricks lead to hostility, anger, suffering; anger to animosity, animosity to death. Bad joking creates more aggression among friends than among rivals. (670)

Anyone given to aggression or anger has turned his back on proper courtesy. Anyone who submits to his anger says and does things he regrets afterwards. For this reason one should be careful not to let one's anger get the better of one. One should fasten it with the bonds of good sense to the wall of correct behavior. If a person maintains his composure when he is angry, good behavior will accompany him. If someone envies another his good fortune, this stems from the stupidity of his heart. Envy and anger often make for a sad disposition and an unpleasant countenance, pointless chatter, lopsided gait, peculiar behavior, and lots of miserable thoughts. (686)

Anyone who wishes to watch what he says should be wary of gambling that leads to much bad talk about us and conflicts with fine behavior. Rarely does any man play and lose the game without saying plenty of things that a courteous and correct man would be very reluctant to say. How can a man more demean himself than by choosing to bring shame upon himself with his talking and because of some trivial loss? Even if he lost what he once had, he might nevertheless have refrained from blabbering about it. This is the result of great inconstancy. Gambling produces hatred and much anger. Avarice and hostility are gambling's companions. A man who hazards what is his for the sake of what is mine must be desperate for possessions. It is a very true saying that gambling does not make a man rich, for if that were the case everyone would decide to gamble and all virtues would be lost. (710)

Anyone who talks a lot is a child, and wise people think he's a fool. Because of this, a child should be careful that he is not so foolish as not to hold his tongue, for if a child fails to do that he has no time to think and his tongue can easily run away with him. On the other hand, one should not be too quiet, for often the same can happen from excessive silence as from a lot of chatter. One should observe moderation in all things: that makes sense. Without moderation, caution is thrown to the four winds. (724)

Anyone who talks and behaves only according to his own impulses is nothing but a beast. A man should possess senses, but a beast is devoid of sensibility. There is no difference between them other than virtue and common sense. Sense separates a man from a beast that knows nothing. The man who has the mind of a beast has brought disgrace on his humanity. Anyone without virtue and ability is an animal on the inside and a man on the outside. Anyone who does not regret being a man should always make the effort to have the mind of a man, just as he has the body of a man: that is how it should be. If he has the face of a man, it's useless for him to have the mind of an animal. A beast does not think much about what it should do, for it lacks the sense that might guide it properly. Let a man pursue his desire with good sense, so that he does not go astray, and let the intention of an action be clear to the man who is virtuous. (750)

Anyone who thinks he knows without [receiving] tuition is closely following the beasts, and anyone who does not learn while he can has wasted his day. A great many days are lost, and time does not come back to us. Anyone who thinks he is wise in his childhood will be full of stupidity in old age, for he did not wish to learn what he should when he was in a position to do so. Children should consider themselves foolish, and they should delight in reading and hearing good stories and reject the poor ones. Anyone who enjoys poor stories does not better himself by them. Therefore everyone, men and women alike, who have a proper understanding, should turn their attention to taking in what is good and what has been composed well and simply ignore the bad stories. (772)

Young ladies will do little to better themselves by emulating the beautiful queen who once upon a time lived in Greece.[6] The lady who first read the story did not do the right thing, for poor examples are inclined to ruin good breeding and good advice. After all, we can read bad stories that it would be better to leave alone. Anyone who does not know them does not really know what he should be wary of. If a woman has a pure heart it will not matter to her whether she hears good or evil. If she hears or sees something bad that will serve as a warning to her to be on her guard. On the other hand, goodness gives her models,[7] so that she may act rightly and well, and shows her the way she ought to follow. If someone is incapable of recognizing good examples so that he can see what one should do, let him think what one should do and really take his example from that. If men and women cannot pay heed to proper matters they tend to take bad examples of good and evil, for their minds are always inclined towards the worst things. (799)

Some women are happy when they hear something discreditable that has happened to another woman. They say: "Her husband may be better disposed towards her afterwards. But we are not going to come to grief if we do what she has done."[8] No decent woman—I venture to give this advice—should be pleased if another woman does not deport herself correctly, for I am telling you for a fact that men and women completely deceive themselves if they believe they can conceal their own misdeeds behind the fickleness of someone else. Therefore, a worthy woman should be sad if another woman behaves badly. A virtuous woman should take a firm line on misbehavior, for she should be very much afraid that the same thing might happen to her. (820)

Women should learn from the misfortune of the woman whose name was Helen. She was a powerful queen over all the lands in Greece. She had great beauty but little sense. Her beauty brought great shame upon her. Beauty without good sense is paltry surety. A lady should have the sense that if anyone speaks to her of love she should be inclined, whether people speak well or badly of it, to answer straightaway, whoever the man is and whatever he may have asked for: that way the lady and he are both satisfied. (836)

It suffices for a woman to know that she is both courteous and composed and can also deport herself well with fine speech and modest demeanor. If in addition she has good sense then let her have the courtesy and the wisdom not to show what good sense she has. No one is asking her to be a high official. A man should possess many skills. The training of the noble lady requires that a lady who is excellent and noble should not be too clever. Simplicity is a good thing in a lady.[9] However, it is right that a lady should have the knowledge and the good sense to avoid animosity. Often people call something "love" when it might better be called "hatred". (854)

To whoever does her no injustice let me say that I am not criticizing proper Love. Beauty, friendship, birth, wealth, love, are all turned upside down without good sense. Beauty is nothing if it is not accompanied by good sense and good breeding. If a man lacks good sense, then he will give bad advice to his friend. If a man is well-born but lacks sense, then his nobility is completely wasted. The wealth of a man is as nothing, if it is not complemented with good sense. Love often turns to animosity if it is not governed by good sense. (868)

A beautiful woman with neither good sense nor sound education has little honor in her person. Beauty very easily damages honor if it is not accompanied by good sense. If a beautiful woman lacks good sense, she has two chains attached to her body that drag her towards misconduct, and she will never prove successful. Beauty encourages a man to seek her favor, but lack of good sense prompts him to urge the lady to do what she should not do. (880)

A man who abandons honor for the sake of beauty goes to market for a bad buy. There have been many women—I'll tell you this for a fact—who forfeited their honor for the sake of beauty and later regretted it bitterly. A woman's beauty is completely dissipated if it is not crowned with virtue. If she adorns her body and not her soul, then she is adorning herself for disaster, for she is telling the bird catcher to be ready to catch her with his stick. If someone adorns himself a lot and does not have proper intentions, the disease inside him will soon creep out. The fastenings round the cask are often snapped by strong wine, or so we have often heard, and the same can be said of our bad thoughts, which are very quickly brought to the fore by bad deeds. Even if there is a lot of water in a barrel, in time it will run out.

If a person is sick in his mind his body will not take long to learn it. On the other hand, if someone is healthy inside, his body will easily feel that too. At no time, then, does anything come out that is not inside, whether it be bad or good. (911)

The body adjusts to the mind. Physical gestures often indicate to us whether a man is happy or sad. Thus every man who can discern the state of someone's body can understand all manner of things from it, if he is so inclined. Every inner movement has its particular trait, if anyone has the knowledge and the insight to recognize it. Love has its special characteristics, too, and I'll tell you in truth that fear, envy, hostility and covetousness, joy, sorrow, generosity, irritation and anger have none of them lost their particular qualities. Yet there are plenty of people who skillfully conceal their hostility and their anger, so that no one can notice them, for the company of wise people has nothing to do with the multitude of fools. One can understand the thoughts of fools to a great extent by means of their speech, if one wants to, but anyone who wants to recognize the wise man needs some measure of common sense and anyone wishing to find out what is in his mind needs a bit of good sense himself. (938)

Appearances often deceive a person. To be sure, not all bright lights are day and the white one sees is not always snow. Both men and women often reveal things that are nowhere in their bodies or in their hearts: their wicked cunning is responsible for this. (946)

A woman is not beautiful at all if she has no kind of goodness in her heart, for, however beautiful a woman may be, if she is given to disloyalty and wantonness, her outer beauty is nothing: she is not beautiful inwardly. I would rather have a virtuous woman who is not beautiful than a beautiful woman who misbehaves, for the former has beauty in her heart. Beauty is nothing compared with inner goodness. I would prefer to pay my debts with gilded copper than with silver. One should well consider a beautiful but false woman as gilded copper that has little gold to show for it. There may be falsity beneath a beautiful skin. Let it be known that dishonest people have nothing more beautiful than their skin.[10] (964)

Anyone who sets out to trick us with sweetness will offer poison mixed with honey. The tongue of a treacherous woman is like honey, but, God knows, her intentions are gall. Falsity is becoming to no one. A woman should guard against falsity more carefully than a man, for falsity is less fitting in women. Generosity, on the other hand, suits everyone. Every woman should practice generosity, yet you should know that generosity is even more fitting to knights than ladies. Modesty suits both of them well. A knight and a lady should practice modesty, yet humility is more fitting to the ladies, for their goodness should be adorned with virtue both in youth and in old age. Bravery befits a knight, loyalty and honesty the ladies. A timid knight is as nothing, as is a false woman. A stingy knight is completely lacking in honor, a foolish woman devoid of goodness. Roguish behavior is unbecoming in a knight, while it's a good thing if a lady guards against inconstancy and disloyalty and haughtiness. If she lacks these virtues, her beauty is absolutely nothing. (994)

If a woman is beautiful but lacks other fine qualities, then may the Lord preserve me from ever really trusting her. Whoever does so will come to regret it bitterly, for he will certainly get to know her falsity and her disloyalty, you can be sure of that. Just when she appears most sweet to him, she will be demonstrating her wicked cunning. The beauty of a woman is a snare for fools and anyone who falls into it will find himself the subject of mockery. A man who bases his judgment of a woman entirely on her beauty and not on her virtue lands in this trap, for if she turns out to have a false disposition, nothing but misfortune will be in store for him. Wretchedness and everything that goes with it will be his lot. If, however, a beautiful woman possesses loyalty, steadfastness, and a gentle disposition, then she is a good person, and she can catch me without a net: I will soften my heart on her account and wish that her simple heart be my fly hook without any pain, so that she can pull me whichever way she wants. Nothing that she commands will be too much for me, for the pure heart of a good woman outweighs every other commodity. (1022)

I have stated that bad tales should be repulsed by children, and I have indicated which they are. Now I'm going to say what children should hear and read and what can be of use to them. Young women should enjoy hearing about Andromache, from whom they can take their examples and good instruction. They will derive both virtue and honor from that. They should hear about Enite and readily follow in her footsteps, and emulate the lady Penelope and Oenone, Galiena and Blanscheflur, . . . and Sordamor. Even if they are not all actually queens, they would qualify as such as far as their fine minds are concerned.[11] (1040)

Young gentlemen should hear about Gawein, Cligès, Erec, and Iwein, and should lead their own young lives according to the pure virtue of Gawein. Follow the noble King Arthur, who sets a very good example before you, and you should keep the emperor Charlemagne, that fine hero, in your mind too. Do not allow your youth to go to waste: think of the virtue of Alexander and copy Tristan, Segramors, and Kalogreant in behaving correctly.[12] (1052) Look! Look! How they pushed forward, those knights of the Round Table, each one ahead of the other in bravery! Children, do not sit back idly, but follow the instructions of brave people, and this will bring you great honor. You should not copy Sir Kay, whose disgraceful behavior causes me much dishonor: he causes me to despair greatly.[13] To be sure, Sir Kay is still alive and in any case he has lots of offspring, so that I don't know which way to turn. His children have the same name as he does: once upon a time there was one Kay, now there are more of them. It seems that Parzival is not alive at all: only Sir Kay is striving for honor with lies and inconstancy, with mockery and mischief. You should believe me when I tell you that if I were Parzival I would deal a certain Kay a blow and break one of his ribs. Alas, where are you, Parzival? for if there were a Grail somewhere and if it could be procured for the surety of just a penny, Kay's hand would not redeem it. (1078)

Now you have heard all about what a child should hear and read, but those who have come to maturity should, in truth, be educated differently from a child, for they should turn their backs on false tales that plague young children. I do not criticize any man who can tell tales of adventure. Adventure stories are good, because they broaden a child's mind. Also, anyone incapable of learning in a better way should derive his examples from them. A person who can write should write and anyone who can paint should stick to painting. Everyone ought to do what he can do well. An uneducated person and a child often find enjoyment in a painted picture: if someone cannot understand what a smart fellow is meant to understand in a piece of writing,[14] let him make do with pictures. Let a priest look at the Bible while the uneducated man should look at the pictures, since he cannot understand what is written there.[15] A man who cannot understand deep meanings should do the same: he should read adventure stories and enjoy them, for in them he will find things that improve his mind. When his understanding increases, then he ought not to waste his time on adventure stories. He should follow teaching about good behavior and good sense and truth. Adventures are often clothed in very beautiful fabrications: fabrications are, in fact, their adorned crown. I am not criticizing adventure stories—even though the message of adventures leads us to distort the truth—because they depict courtesy and reality: truth is [simply] cloaked in fabrications. A wooden image is not a man, but anyone who is capable of comprehending anything understands well enough that it is supposed to represent a man. Even if the stories are not [strictly] true, they can nevertheless indicate what a man should do if he wishes to lead a good and virtuous life. Therefore, I wish to thank those who have rendered many stories into the German language for us. A good story enhances good behavior. However, I would have thanked them even more if they had composed tales completely devoid of lies: they would have derived even more honor from that. If anyone wants to he can tell us a great deal about truth: that would be a good thing. He will improve our mind much more with the truth than with lies, be sure of that. Anyone with a gift for writing poems will always find plenty of material in the truth: let him steer clear of lies. Therefore, a courtly man who decides to take up composing poetry should take extreme care not to get into the way of lying. If he is himself a liar, then his stories will be very unpleasant. Any man who is gifted in speaking should apply his words to good things; that way things will never go badly for him. (1162)

I have gone beyond my goal and have said a great deal that I would [otherwise] not have said. Would it not have become irksome to the young folk, I would have liked to have held forth on another topic, but I have omitted it for their sake.[16] And if there were time I would like to say more about how knights and ladies ought to live, if they wanted to strive for honor, just as I have already stated in my book on courtliness that I wrote in Italian.[17] I said that one should endure the power of love with dignity if one wanted to live without dishonor. (1178)

The nature of love is such that it makes a wise man wiser and makes a fool even more foolish. That is the way of love. The spurs guide the horse through the trees when it is galloping without the reins. It is just the same with a foolish man who believes he can play with the love of a lady. She will lead him through the trees if he does not guide her with the reins of his good sense. Fire is a useful and good thing if a man does not abuse it, but if the fire gains the upper hand, so that people let it take control, then in truth anything it touches is destroyed and laid to waste. It's just the same with love when it overwhelms the senses: it blinds the mind of a wise man and brings disgrace to the soul, body, honor, and possessions. Anyone who gets too close to a fire will often singe his beard. (1200)

I have taught that a man should compel his lady by gentle means to be constant to him. Anyone who keeps her captive would do better to protect her with his service. Now tell me, what use is it to confine her body if her inclination is not as it should be? No lock can imprison the spirit. A body without a heart is a paltry thing. Locks produce great animosity, good treatment closes more securely. Love that is bewitched and forced and bought is the opposite of love. Know that anyone who dabbles in magic has won by force whatever he gains by those means. He does not display the manners of a courtly gentleman: anyone who uses violence on women has a decidedly uncourtly disposition. (1220)

I taught that anyone who wished to possess good love should not try to gain it with gifts. Anyone who woos love with material things does not understand the heart of a woman: whether she is truly well disposed towards him or whether she prefers gold to his person. He does not know whether she will be happy because of his courtly ways. However, if he subsequently realizes that she is turning her thoughts in his direction and if she wants something that he has, let him take my advice and give it to her. I know only too well that what I am saying is not what malevolent people want to hear, because a villain cannot woo with courtliness. He likes to have a guarantee for everything. He gives and takes simultaneously. Anyone who cannot woo with courtliness might just as well be a merchant. Love that is bought has not the power of proper love. One cannot really possess it. (1242)

Everyone has the sense to know that if one were to try to buy love, that love would be a vassal. Otherwise love, in truth, is free. Anyone who thinks he can buy love in exchange for money knows neither love nor the heart, for our senses and our virtue, not our material possessions, should track down for us both love and the heart. One should give one's heart in exchange for another heart; one should desire fidelity by being faithful; one should bestow affection with affection; one should secure constancy and truth with constancy. Anyone who thinks he can make evil good through gift-giving is deceiving himself. (1258)

A man who never knew throughout his life how to give anything, whether little or much, either for the sake of honor or for the sake of God, often brings mockery and shame upon himself by giving a grand gift to a woman who turns her heart away from him. She also considers him to be a fool and a simpleton. She shows a lot of affection for him when she actually wants to do something else, for if someone else gives her more, he will be dearer to her. I am not speaking here of those women who have a virtuous heart, but there is another kind of man who knows nothing about courtliness and gives a woman whatever she wants, even though she has too much already, while another woman who has nothing is left high and dry. A man often denies himself to give to a woman who is worse off than he is. In truth, what one gains through dishonor one should also completely lose through dishonor. If, on the other hand, he were to give to a poor woman something he had denied himself, he would probably receive God's praise for that. Otherwise he is making a mockery of himself by choosing to give only to those who themselves have too much. Now know the truth that this only creates malice and foolishness. A man who gives when he ought not to does not have his wits about him, and a man is not without wickedness who does not give when by rights he should. He is leading a shameful life. (1303)

A foolish man takes note of how a woman adorns her person. He does not see what she has inside her by way of fine virtues and sensibility. In contrast, a worthy man observes her gestures and her comportment. If a horse has no saddle that does not make it worthless. A wealthy woman who leads a disgraceful life cannot be compared to a virtuous woman lacking affluence. If I were to buy a horse I would not want to examine the reins more than the horse: I would certainly rather see what shape it was, and what kind of legs and hooves it had. Anyone who wants to choose a good woman should do the same. He should not take too much notice of her possessions, but he'll do better to observe whether she is a good woman, for one can have great happiness with a poor but virtuous woman, and be unhappy with a wealthy, malevolent one. (1329)

I have taught that no worthy man should ever turn his thoughts to depriving a woman of her possessions, for while, if a woman were to do that, it would suit her very badly, it suits a man immeasurably worse, believe me. I'm telling you that I would rather commit robbery. (1337)

I have taught what it is seemly for a woman to accept from her gentleman friend: gloves, mirror, ring, brooch, chaplet, posy. A woman should be careful not to accept anything bigger, unless she has great need of it, in which case I would permit her to take more but not so much that it precludes her from showing that her gentleman friend is more important to her than the material things, otherwise she would be a false woman. If she happens to take anything else, but does not really need it, then her friend is not really dear to her. One should certainly take note of this. (1353)

No matter what I have said hitherto, I am now speaking about truth and reinforce it with my advice that ladies should be constant to their menfolk, for true love has little presence at this time in the world of courtesy. That comes from falsity, boasting, evil surveillance, inconstancy, and arrogance. If a lady is virtuous in her youth and complements it with the virtue of guarding against haughty behavior, and if she is affectionately disposed towards her man and loyally devoted to him, then she is a jewel above all jewels. I say the same thing with regard to the man: to be sure he should not turn towards another woman. Anyone who already has a woman should keep away from others. (1371)

I have always cherished the honor of the ladies. If there was anything I could do to be useful to them, I was happy to place it at their service. The thing I value most in a lady is that she guards against falsity. Falsity quickly turns love into animosity, and good into bad, and white into black. Falsity turns sweetness into bitter gall, and its lovely greeting into gracelessness. Its promise is a lie, its gentleness anger, its laughter tears, its softness a thorn. The talk of false people, their gestures, their desires, all three have a different intention. Mendacious people shield themselves behind fine gestures and sweet words, but their evil intention is a sword that seeks only to cause suffering. If a man is capable of discerning a false disposition, this can often protect him from harm. (1391)

I have taught that no decent woman should allow any man who has no right to do so to take hold of her. A woman's breeding instructs her in this way. I have also instructed that no man should do such a thing. Furthermore, I have taught that no man who knows about courtly matters should make any request of a decent woman without first determining in a courteous manner that he is pleasing to her. Good breeding demands that he should do this. Anyone who makes even a small request steps outside the bounds of proper conduct, if he asks immediately before he is known to the person of whom he is making the request, regardless of whether this is great or small. At the same time, any man with proper understanding should take note that he should serve a lady with courtesy for a long time before he asks that something of her on account of which she might completely transgress against her good breeding, her modesty, her excellent behavior, her loyalty and her steadfastness, her reputation and her courtesy, her good name and her nobility, and all her virtue, and thereby bring herself into disrepute. That is indeed a strange man who, on seeing a lady for the very first time, wishes her to abandon so much on his account, and it should not please the lady if it comes about out of arrogance that he advances so swiftly and approaches her with his suit. However, let me tell you this: there are some women who think themselves better and believe that they will derive much honor from it, if a man becomes more and more pressing with his requests. (1432)

When a woman is lying in her bed she will think to herself: "This man has done so much for me, but that man has courted me even more. On the other hand, a third man has made great demands of me. I know only too well that I am beautiful and noble, since these so honorable men come here desiring my love with all their hearts and all their senses." In this way she becomes so vain that she thinks no one has anything like her. (1447)

However wealthy a stingy man may be, people ask very little of him, for even if one does ask anything of him he does not give it anyway. However poor a generous man may be, people make requests of him, and they do it on account of his generosity. It's the same with a woman. However contented she may be and however beautiful, if she wears the crown of constancy, a villain and a bad man will not dare to ask anything of her. If she is lacking in virtues, people will always attach themselves to her. Even if she is not a beautiful woman and behaves in a frivolous manner, she will attract plenty of improper and false lovers who ask for her love to the detriment of her honor, for the false man will not ask too much of a woman unless he finds her ready to give it. He likes to avoid the effort. The king's treasury is protected against thieves, and they are very much afraid. Even though they love silver, precious stones, and gold, they do not wish to approach the chamber, for they will not be able to take anything from it. If they know a poor man who cannot protect himself, they will break down his fences and his walls and steal a flimsy garment from him. It is the same with a false man who acquires love: if he recognizes a woman who cannot refuse him he rushes up to her and tries with all his might to make her do what she is glad to do. Then he is satisfied. When he has gained little honor through his mendacity it seems to him that he will gain honor by talking everywhere about it. Therefore I'm telling you for a fact that a lady who believes that it is an honor if someone keeps asking something of her is deceiving herself completely. I've told you often enough that people behave like this

not because of her nobility but because her manner tells them that she is
enjoying it. A man who happens to have many women should not think too
highly of himself. Women do not do so much for anyone as for the one who
chooses to ask them. There is no honor to be had at court if one is a beggar.
(1512)

Whenever an old woman tells me what misery and what trouble she
caused people when she was young, she reveals to me all there is to know
about her lack of virtue. If one were of a mind to do so, one would gladly do
what one would like to recount in old age. Old people may have lost much
of their strength, but not their desire. Their strength may diminish but in
their hearts they are always ready to sin. An old woman says: "I was so beauti-
ful that on account of my beauty they were all eager to serve me. Nowadays
young women are nothing to look at, and no one courts them. In my youth,
people cultivated joy and great courtesy." She goes on saying this day and
night. Since her ability has faded she substitutes it with something else. She
never had much sense and still has not. (1534)

I have taught that a man who cannot serve a lady and also cannot bring
it about that she act with him in mind is best advised to turn away from
her in a kindly manner. He should bear in mind this advice, in order that
he does not through his own fault forfeit her greeting and even her favor.
A man who blames a woman for not wishing to do something with him
in mind brings disgrace upon himself. Indeed he brings too much shame
upon himself and if he persists in this, he will lose both her body and her
heart. (1548)

If you have noticed, I have had a few words to say about falsity. Anyone
who wishes to hear more about this can hear many a treatise against falsity
that I have delivered in the Italian tongue. I did it in honor of a lady who
asked me for that advice. I taught how a lady who wished to protect herself
should recognize false lovers who have turned their back on honor. I rec-
ommended many a handy trick by which one might better protect one's
honor against false, treacherous people. Anyone who does something for
their sake will regret it. (1564)

A woman should know a man well if she is to commit her heart to him.
Indeed a respectable woman should know to whom she intends to commit
herself, for she would also wish to know to whom she should entrust her
material possessions. (1570)

Anyone who cannot combine material possessions with honor should
give up thinking about them, for possessions without honor are nothing. I
would not want to have them that way. Robbers, thieves, faithless women,
all surrender honor and their very selves for the sake of material things.
They will even give up their salvation and their souls out of greed. Profli-
gate women and thieves are all the same to me. A worthy man should be

prepared to protect his estate from thieves and even more fiercely his very self from a badly behaved woman. Likewise, a respectable woman should protect her person very carefully, if some immoral fellow incapable of fidelity makes an approach to her. (1588)

A woman who wishes to enjoy true love should also have the good sense to turn to someone who is her equal: that is the counsel of proper love. If he is not her equal but if she has ascertained that he is a good and decent fellow, I would be prepared to accept her proceeding with the relationship. However noble and rich he is, if in addition he has bad intentions and tends to be a braggart, ladies should not want anything to do with him, for you can be sure that a villain is absolutely no good to a woman. One should always turn to where one finds virtue and good sense. One should seek good counsel from a person displaying virtue and good sense. (1606)

A woman may perhaps think: "I'll be better off with a fool than with a wise man who will be able to notice everything I say and do," but she is deluding herself with such thoughts. A wise man overlooks much that a fool cannot and will not overlook. Bear in mind that a foolish man wreaks all sorts of havoc, whereas a wise man has the self-control to bring about only the good. They have completely different temperaments. Therefore I'm telling you truthfully that a good woman has a better life with a wise man than with a fool: you should hear this and take note of it. (1624)

A lady should not think: "If I do something for the sake of a villain, he will have to keep it quite quiet, for he will not dare to talk about it. But if he does prattle, people will certainly say that no one should believe him." Don't count on this and know for a fact that a villain certainly does dare to boast: that's all part of the villainy. Whatever is said about a woman is believed about women far and wide, for what the one does brings all the rest into disrepute. However, one of them may say: "If people speak ill of me, no song was ever so long that it was not concluded. Whatever people are saying now will probably be kept silent in a year's time." That is small comfort, and it is of no help to anyone, for if someone does not speak about my wickedness because he is disinclined to do so, he is behaving exactly like the person who pulls someone to and fro in the mud and leaves him where it is deepest. However, if someone cannot say anything bad about me he should leave me with my honor intact: one should be grateful for the silence. (1656)

I have taught that any man who aspires to courtesy should be careful never to say anything less than favorable to a woman about her man, for if she is able to understand anything correctly he will not have honored her either by doing so. Anyone who badmouths the lover or the husband of a woman is badmouthing her in the process, too. The neighbors of a man who likes to praise himself do not praise him much. No decent man has

taught anyone to criticize, and anyone who seeks to acquire love in this way
has some weird ideas. If one could gain love by these means then the fool
and the wise man would be alike, for the fool is also given to badmouthing.
(1676)

I have taught what is befitting for virtuous women, and how a noble
knight should behave in order to be pleasant and pleasing to the eyes of
women, and how ladies should behave, how they should conduct them-
selves, and how they should speak to young and old alike. I said all this in
Italian, and if I am now to say it in German I cannot speak too quickly, or I
will deviate from my subject and distort my message. A man who often rides
out far beyond his own territory may get carried away. Now I'll return to my
subject: I propose to tell you about how gentlemen should cultivate their
virtues. Anyone who abandons any of this along the way has completely lost
his virtue. Gentlemen should not be angry: some of them think they are vir-
tuous who do not recognize the power of virtue. What I taught them may be
too much. Nevertheless I'm telling you that, if you all think it a good idea, I
intend to demonstrate my own inclination, if I am capable of doing so. My
good intentions should herald my deeds. (1704)

I have concluded the first part and may God speed us for the second!

BOOK II

I have intimated in the first part that a person must cultivate virtue
and courtesy in his youth. Anyone who fails to do this should make amends
by leading a virtuous life in his old age, for anyone who does not do so
has truly forfeited his life: it would be better if he had never been born. I
intend to say much more about this general teaching of mine in respect of
princes and noble gentlemen. Their good example shines far and wide. If
I do something wrong, I am on my own, whereas the sins of princes affect
everyone. If the leader has an angry countenance, he will lead us all into
peril. If a man's head bothers him constantly, it causes a lot of trouble to
the other parts of his body. After all, the branches of a tree wither if there
is something wrong with the roots. If some impurity flows into a river, the
brooks are polluted also. Similarly I say: if a land is in the hands of a mas-
ter who cannot accomplish anything, fears everyone, and does not dare to
take control, that land is being led astray by a scoundrel. It will bring great
injury upon anyone who elects to remain in that country, for the lethargy
of the masters often harms the poor people. A master who does not dare
to govern really makes fools of his people. A cowardly lord can make a
humble man appear bold in comparison with himself. If he does not dare
to give orders, then he surely offends his authority. The sea is nothing with-
out water. A bad person tends to do bad things. The forest, too, is nothing

without wild things. A bad master without a bad image is hardly conceivable. Throughout each day you lords must provide us with an example of how we are to behave. If you act well, then we shall gladly follow your good example, but if you behave improperly, then we have no idea whom we should follow, and we shall wander around lost at night until the morning. If you behave badly then you are like the night that takes the power of light away from us. We should be able to see ourselves reflected in you: you are the mirror, we the ladies. If the mirror is distorted, one sees a strange image of oneself: one seems too short or too long, too broad or too skinny. A lord should avoid the narrow way, the broad, the short, and the long: the narrow in order that he may keep to the right path, where the way is broad and straight. He must not neglect the honors that he has acquired by right. A lord must shun the broad path, in order that he may exercise his power in such a way that his foot does not slip and he ignore the right of someone else; the short, for he must not be in too much of a hurry to realize his desires. A lord must do no less than he is by rights called upon to do. A lord must shun the long path and not delay in behaving well. A lord should only ever do what justice desires him to do. If a mirror is bright, as it should be, and whole and round, then one can see oneself clearly. A lord should also be very bright, so that he projects a clear image. He should be the epitome of constancy, so that neither joy nor sorrow produces any change in him. Let him never step outside the compass of virtue, no matter what is going on in the world. One must be steadfast in virtue: that has always been my advice. If a virtuous lord is weighed down with wickedness, I compare him in my mind to a light that has been hung up high: if it goes out now and then, it would be better to take it down. If a man has placed an extinguished candle on a candlestick, he should be ashamed of himself, if he were so inclined and if he were to do what he should do. He really ought to throw it away and replace it with a burning candle. If someone were to do the same with wicked lords, I would perhaps have some advice for him. One must abandon vice before one can attempt to achieve virtue. One must clear the fields properly if one wishes to sow good seed: if there are stones and thorns in them, then the wheat can easily get choked. I want people to apply their efforts first and foremost to constancy: that way, believe me, they can more easily acquire the other virtues. The other virtues are negligible if constancy is not present. No one can achieve constancy unless he chooses to turn his back on inconstancy, but anyone who has abandoned inconstancy has grasped the true meaning of constancy. For this reason I should first discuss the concept of inconstancy. I have very often heard it said that anyone who wishes to build a bridge should tear down the old one and put a good one in its place. We must leave the bridge of inconstancy right behind us and above all demonstrate constancy by focusing on performing good deeds.

There is a great deal of inconstancy about, some examples of which I will now impart to you. (1836)

What *is* inconstancy? The shame of noble gentlemen, an aberration throughout the land. Inconstancy means constancy in respect of evil things. No one can force it to confine itself to good acts. Inconstancy is not free. Rather, inconstancy is at all times a slave to vice. Inconstancy follows on the heels of vice in youth and in old age. Every vice enjoys both its service and its advice. Inconstancy never rests for anything at any time. Whatever inconstancy may undertake today will not appear good to it tomorrow. It is constructing something that its fickle counsel will soon have destroyed. Inconstancy quickly turns a square into a circle, but then it will not leave the circle alone if it is better with four corners. It always prefers to desire what it does not want. It was never dismayed by change. It makes the little big, and then the big little. One moment it is running, the next walking along slowly. Now it's climbing, now it's falling down. Today it goes away; tomorrow it comes back again. Off to the mountains, then towards the sea! Today it's alone; tomorrow it will have an army around it. At one time away into the forest, then into the town. Now and then it checkmates itself, for it knows deep down that it is chasing around all over the place. It can travel from town to town, but not for a single day can it leave its heart. (1874)

If someone fastens a little bell to the tail of a pup, he will run about and twist and turn this way and that and not know that what he is trying to get away from is tied to him. It is the same with the inconstant man who does not know what is the matter with him. Note that he is wearing something that chases him from place to place. Inconstancy tries out many different kinds of food that do not suit it at all, since its stomach is upset by various bad dishes. Inconstancy has its own stomach: this is its desire which quickly vanishes, for what it craves in the morning never lasts throughout the day. Its desire grows cold from the many dishes. Anyone who strives for many things does not keep faith with any one of them. Anyone who wishes to be constant should stay with one thing only. We have often seen that if a person is not inclined to be constant to one thing he will prefer three things to one: look what he has achieved! Anyone who wants to gallivant around in the world has many lodging places and not a friendship anywhere. This is what happens to anyone who wishes to be equally involved with everything: he will miss out on a great deal along the way. (1904)

Let the priest who has many books stick to one of them, that's my advice, for if one day he wants to become familiar with all of them, he will not be able to take in the meaning of every one. If anyone wishes to derive wisdom from books, let him hang on tightly once he has taken hold of the branch of meaning. One cannot see well through a door if one wants to run ahead too fast. There is no deed so good that it is of any use if left on its own. If a man hears a good word he should not hang about in front of the gate but go in with great steadfastness, until he discovers its very essence. Water does not make a hole in a stone by force, but when it drips frequently. A man who does not take notice of what is said does not have a high opinion of a good speech, but anyone who takes good note derives great pleasure from it. (1926)

Someone who does not take in what he is reading often wastes a lot of time, but someone who can understand a good word has not wasted his day at all. Anyone who wants to understand should think deeply about fine words. I often dismiss today what will please me more tomorrow. When it comes to good things, one must establish a solid foothold in constancy. If in the process the foot is injured, walking will not heal it. A man must lie still for a while if he wants to walk on that foot in the future. Eating is no use to the body which is going to die. A sick man who wishes to get better should not keep changing his diet. If he wishes to recover quickly, this will come about as a result of the advice of the doctors. It does not do a sick man good to try out medicine on him. Consistency should reign in all things. Anyone who is seeking to be cured through one remedy would in truth be a complete fool to try out any more. A man who likes to try what he should not try often discovers something he does not want. Anyone who undertakes one thing should first of all finish that before he takes on something else: that's right and sensible, for a person who starts lots of things never completes what he wants to complete. Anyone who thinks too much damages his mind. Things become less if they are divided up; a person who is everywhere is nowhere: I have known all this for a long time. (1964)

Anything that is whole must be unique: inconstancy is universal, for it wishes to be everywhere [at once]. It is not whole and has no goal. It is divided into at least four parts: one part is joy, the other sorrow, the third is "yes," the fourth is "no." It both destroys and is itself destroyed, for anyone who follows it at some time or another criticizes the person he will have to praise, for while he may heartily dislike someone today, he'll probably be according him respect tomorrow. One should not abuse anyone so much since afterwards one may well be praising him to the skies, for someone who is a villain now can easily become a saint at a later date. (1980)

Inconstancy is universal, but nowhere does it appear more wretched than in noblemen, whose every deed should be steadfast. A nobleman should maintain constancy in everything he says or does. To be sure, a common man brings shame upon himself if he cannot resist telling a lie, but look how a nobleman is protected if he falls into the habit of lying. He who ought to be advising us about propriety and about truth, were he so inclined, presents us merely with examples of lying, for he never tells the truth himself. There is no one who so likes to tell lies or to deceive people that it does not upset him if someone calls him a liar. Let a nobleman take this example to heart, unless he wishes to be accused of the same vices as his knight. In that case lying is a strange garment if it manages to bring honor on the master and much disgrace upon the knight. However, I'll tell you for a fact: a master is not honored by something that brings disgrace on a knight, because something that is not worthy of a knight does not well befit a master, and anything that is supposed to adorn a lord must also be adornment for a knight. Thus you should take note of the following: since lying ill befits a knight, it also detracts from the honor of a noble lord. (2014)

To be sure, it is dishonorable if the speech and heart of someone are at variance with one another, for the worst evil of all is a smooth tongue accompanied by a wicked intention. Simple speech and an ambivalent heart make evil look good. Just look: if someone's hair were cut unevenly, he would be upset, but we do not find it shameful if someone's heart and someone's speech are at variance with one another: [yet] we are inclined to consider such a[n uneven] haircut shameful.[1] It is great inconstancy when we have joy in our hearts but outwardly display sorrow. (2028)

Inconstancy is the mother of lies. Inconstancy can never be true: anger and lying are the children of inconstancy. They have many other siblings, and I'm going to name all of them to you before I come to the end of my talk. However, if it is not quickly told, you must put up with this for the sake of courtesy, for I cannot cover many things in haste. If I think of the family of inconstancy, I swear on oath that I cannot find among all the relatives anything to which I take more offence in noblemen than lying, believe me. Lying is completely abhorrent to me. In one hand it carries joy, in the other sorrow and suffering. One embraces, the other slays; one loves, the other hates; one caresses, the other tears out hair; one gives, the other sells; one beats, the other moans. When one praises, the other says that it is all a pack of lies, and that's how they often get into one another's hair. If it does not bore you, I will briefly tell you: lying promises good things but it has its roots in a false heart. The liar has fine words and nice promises, but brings poor reward. The master should with a host of courteous ways level out his will and completely hack down useless talk, so that both his heart and his talk are good. (2064)

Anyone whose tunic hangs down below his coat by a yard appears a fool. If a man wears his coat long in front and then at the back it goes up to his knees, a wise man will consider this man an idiot, too. In this respect I offer a piece of advice which will stand fine noblemen in good stead: that their tunics should be in line with their coats. That is to say, that their gifts should be as generous as their promises, for I have known for a long time that if someone promises more than he gives, he will spread his lying far and wide. Let a gentleman be cautious: indeed he should look very far in front of him and behind him. In fact you should be thoroughly ashamed of yourself if you promise something and then have nothing to give when the time comes. If a man's coat reaches down to his feet, let him see what it looks like from behind. If someone regrets his promise afterwards, he is regretting it too late, unless he intends to prove his intention false. Even so, it is preferable if damage is done to material things, for in the mind and in the heart, damage is a shameful agony. Now a nobleman may perhaps say: "I often have to promise more than I give, for I do not wish to keep refusing." But I say that it is more honorable to refuse and one attracts less animosity, than when one becomes obligated through one's promises, for afterwards one does not refuse so easily. If a lord reneges on a promise, he is not being loyal and brings great harm on the person to whom he has made his promise, because that person has been relying on him completely. A nobleman who chooses to promise something, whether it be great or small, should give careful thought to whether he has pledged it in full [already]. Whatever the usurer lends or the master promises must be paid back in full. One must redeem a loan, but a master must also maintain his loyalty, for there is no question of regret once a promise has been given. I redeem my deposit before it is due, and it should be the intention of a gentleman swiftly to make good his word: that is the noble thing to do. I redeem my letter of credit, so that the usurer does not put pressure on me with it. The nobleman should redeem his promise, since lying is the gateway to hell. Whether a gentleman says "yes" or "no" he should confirm it in writing. (2124)

I shall incur the wrath of noble gentlemen. It is on their account and through their fault that constancy has been lost, but I do not mean to say anything to incur their disfavor: I truly mean well. If my lord is fickle, then I must be ready to partake of this inconstancy. If my lord declares that he does not wish to go away tomorrow, and tonight changes his mind and thinks it a good idea after all that he should go somewhere else tomorrow, then I have to go away with him. Now I have once learnt that whichever way one sets the rudder, the ship must go in that direction: if a master changes his mind, then his people must be capricious. Indeed, we have often seen that the whims of inconstant masters give rise to much inconstancy in the world. Thus the world has become very unstable because of us, disloyal and inconstant. That comes about as a result of our misdeeds. The world was created absolutely stable, but now it has no stability left, as anyone can see if he wants to. There are many examples of inconstancy in the world: in the summer we complain of showers, in the winter of ice and snow. There's rain today and wind tomorrow, and both of them often cause us injury. A thunderclap after a lightning strike often brings the blackness of death. I see that it often snows when summer is approaching, and it is also often very hot, and then soon afterwards the frost comes along. We often get rewarded with clouds just when we thought the weather was fine. The world has fickle ways, and our own inconstancy matches it. (2168)

I venture to declare that if we were not inconstant it would not come about that there was inconstancy in the world. Now why would there be rain and wind? If Adam and his children had been constant, why would there be snow? We would never suffer from the cold. (2176)

And so I have said: When the world was first created, it was made completely constant. We can see that in the fact that night always comes before day. Summer only brings heat after winter, that's true. The world would still be constant, exactly as it was created, if it were not for the power of our own inconstancy. This gives it a great deal of instability that it exploits to cause us suffering, for its inconstancy does not harm it: all the damage falls on us. It brings us disease in place of good health, by changing all the time. (2192)

However, the world retains part of its constancy and that serves us well, for we retain nothing at all, that's the remarkable thing. It is in the nature of the world's constancy that every thing has its time. Flowers and foliage, fruit and grass, everything has its time. One fruit comes before the other: one ripens early, the other late. Leaves and grass drop according to their time, and that which was green withers away. In summer the day is long, which it cannot be in winter. The heat is great in summer, and the frost never became too tedious for the winter. But we do not hold back what we have in mind. Whether it be good or bad, we want to follow our inclinations. Anyone who gives full rein to his desires pays no attention to any holy day. (2214)

It is an aspect of the constancy of the world that the sun shines above the earth by day, and under it by night.[2] You should not be surprised at this, for it is its nature and its custom to travel all the time towards the heavens and back again. It is written in the book: "For that was always the constant in the world that the heavens moved around the earth."[3] The course of the seven stars occasions the earth to become weak in comparison with the strength of the heavens, so that it has not turned it round.[4] Each one has its own course in which it goes around: it does not travel outside its own orbit, as often happens to us, for we travel to and fro and try more ways than one, and yet because of our wrongful actions we are inconstant in all of them. A person is always trying new paths and does not want to pursue the best one. We think that the bad and wrong way is good and noble, and we follow it to the point where we are completely shamed by it or perhaps dead, or we come back with great difficulty, for anyone who wishes to travel afar will face many a burden on the way home. I'm talking about the penance one has to do for sinning. (2248)

The world itself is always constant. When the sun is close to the moon, the moon becomes small, and afterwards it gets bigger and bigger, and thus

the further the distance, the larger it becomes. Likewise when we lose that
which we have gained by our sins we do not better ourselves in the slightest.
On this matter, the German says: "When the sick man recovered he was just
as he had been before."[5] (2260)

It must always be a constant fact that the sun shines by day. By day its
light completely hides the host of heavenly stars, for its light ensures that we
can see the stars better by night than day: it is a fact that the greatest tends
to dominate the least. However, we do not have the light that conceals our
misfortune from us: that's reason for regret. I can tell you in all truth that it
has come about that people do not feel the least bit ashamed of committing
unjust and wrongful actions openly in front of people. (2276)

Whatever lives has remained constant, whether it crawls, walks, flies, or
swims, and whatever is to be found beneath the moon must consist of four
elements. I am referring to the four elements of nature from which we have
all been created and formed. I will describe to you the nature of these four.[6]
(2284)

Fire, air, water, earth: these four elements are at variance with one
another. Earth is dry and cold; water holds sway over coldness and wetness,
and air cannot desist from being hot and wet too, but then fire is hotter and
dry as well. Now anyone who is not a fool should take note that, since these
four are united in our bodies, the fact that nevertheless we are not united in
our desires is due to our great resentment. Between water and earth there
is nothing; air desires nothing between itself and water. Fire is to be found
above in the air. It always rises higher but does not come lower down. Take
note that this is caused by its lightness. Look how, when one is joined with
the other, they are always at variance with one another. I think these four
elements must have something that binds them together. They do not part
from one another by night or day. However, no matter how dry the earth
may be, it does not want to make the water dry. Water does not have the
power to make the air cold. Air dampens, fire does not, for it will in no way
come about that the nature of the elements can be changed. One can make
water very hot, or put out a fire, if one wants to, but fire does not abandon
its heat and dryness, and one cannot take them away from it by any cunning
as long as it is not extinguished. Nor does boiling water change its nature,
whatever coldness and wetness it encounters. Observe the following: how-
ever hot a man may be, he can cool himself with hot water. I'll tell you too,
since I know it full well, that neither air nor earth can depart for a single
day from their true nature. So how is it that a man keeps deviating so much
from his true nature? We are always deviating greatly from it when we eat or
drink in excess: this goes against our nature. Anyone who wishes to follow
his true nature should not do anything in excess. A cow has no inclination
to eat when it has filled its empty belly, nor does it drink unless it is thirsty,

for if we do something to excess that is completely against our nature: know that for a fact. (2348)

I have stated the following: beneath the moon there are the four elements, and the moon represents their limit. The fourth "nature" ends there, and the fifth begins right away. Heaven and the seven planets have constituted the fifth "nature." The other stars all cling to the firmament, but these seven do not: they are designed to hang suspended from it. Their beginnings are high above and their end is down here with the fourth element. The first is called Saturn, known for its coldness and dryness. The second is Jupiter, and it is hot and wet. The third is Mars, which is always hot and dry. Then the fourth is the Sun, which revels in heat and dryness. The fifth is called Venus, and it appears cold and wet. Mercury is the sixth planet, hot and wet in its effect. The seventh is called the Moon, which is often cold and wet. One can perceive in all things that the Moon makes them completely wet. At the time of the full Moon, the veins are full.[7] (2380)

A star is described as cold because it has the power to produce coldness: no star is actually cold. It is designated "hot," "dry," "wet" because it often causes the air to be very dry, hot, or wet, after it has passed that way, for as I have said, that which is above the moon has a separate, fifth, "nature." For that reason you should not be surprised that whatever exists between the moon and the sky is always constant. Here there is only one nature, and they are obliged to share this trait. It is just like someone who goes along with another who completely shares his nature. Whatever the one is inclined towards, the other desires also. There is no conflict up there. However, down here there is no constancy with anything that is to be found beneath the moon, for the four elements are at variance with one another. Believe me, because of that nothing down here is constant. Even if not one of the four denies its nature, as long as it exists, it always denies itself, for every day air turns to fire, water likewise to air; and earth behaves in a similar manner: this comes from its opposing nature. Heat does not remain still opposite cold, and if it comes about that the wet fights against the dry, one of them is fortunate, for whichever is stronger, the other one submits and must surrender to it. This battle is waged every day. Above the moon is constancy and there no conflict is to be found. (2422)

Anything that forms a proper unit should by rights be called constancy. We never agree when there are three or four of us gathered together. While Rome was united in its purpose, it gained much honor, but once it was no longer united its honor fell away completely. Remember that when it was united it conquered much of the world, but once it was not united its power did not extend very far at all. It inspired fear everywhere, this side of the ocean and also abroad. Now its honor is as nothing and not even the people of Viterbo fear it.[8] (2438)

Why am I talking about things that happened in the world a long time ago? For in our own time many towns have been destroyed by discord and hostility, war and misfortune. I am not yet thirty years old, but even so I can remember, truly, when Verona was crowned with honor and its towers and houses were intact: now they are flattened. Brescia has been brought to shame by war and hatred, and that has happened in our time. One can say the same of Vicenza and Ferrara. (2454)

What I'm talking about is just a small sample. Disloyalty has spread so far abroad that now no one can discover loyalty and constancy for even half a day. Where is constancy in our time? The world has chosen conflict, malice, lying, scorn, hatred, envy, anger: virtues have fallen completely by the wayside. The world is full of inconstancy: where are loyalty and truth now? Wherever one may choose to look, they are of no consequence. They have been driven out of England and are not to be found among the French,[9] for those two kings, that warring pair, have devastated their lands.[10] Loyalty and truth have been chased out of Provence as well where they suffered under the heretics.[11] Are they in Spain? No, they are not, because much tribulation came to them there at the hands of heathens and apostate Christians who abused them there.[12] They are no longer in Apulia,[13] for they were long ago driven out of there. Now, what if they are in Rome? It does not take long for anyone who has business there to discover the falsity of the Romans. One should not seek them in Tuscany: the pilgrims know very well, when they are plundered at Monte Fiascone,[14] if loyalty resides in Tuscany. It is not in Lombardy either, for there the people of Milan frightened it off with their heathenism, fire, war, and pillage.[15] As to whether it is in German lands, people know that near and far.[16] It is not present in Hungary either, for it has not been there for a long time. You can easily see the disloyalty and senselessness of the Hungarians in the treatment of their queen.[17] (2496)

I could name more lands. I can find loyalty and truth nowhere, and inconstancy has brought this about. You can clearly see the power of inconstancy: its power gives us so many clear signs that the world is soon coming to an end. Indeed we can tell that the end of the world is at hand by the fact that we are all possessed of hatred. We have it written indeed that before the end of the world there will be hunger and bad years, storms and earthquakes: now we are seeing it come about. Before that time there will be war, hatred, anger, and jealousy. Empire against empire; land against land. After that the end of the world will not come straightaway, however. These are harbingers that forge a way for it: disloyalty, mendacity, perjury, inconstancy, and all kinds of wrongdoing. Messengers have come to us with a message: now turn your hearts firmly towards God in order that you do not pursue the inconstancy of the world, for this quickly vanishes, but come instead into His kingdom. There you will always be steadfastly filled with joy without sorrow: the constancy of joy is there. (2526)

Here ends the second part: my pen will now proceed to the third.

BOOK III

I have now told you what I can about inconstancy, according to what I believe, and have still not said everything about it. It has an extensive family. Even if a vice is not its kinsman it is nevertheless related to it by marriage. Because of this I must say more about it, if this is not irksome to you. (2536)

A man spoke to me and asked me a question: "Now tell me, my dear friend, how has it come about that we are all so inconstant? For God gave us the power of authority over all things. We are the best things created by God, with the exception of the angels. Therefore you must listen to me and say why there is nothing so close to inconstancy with more constancy than ourselves. Tell me what you think." Then I answered him as follows: God gave constancy to the first man when He gave him a mind, but then he lost the gift of constancy of his own volition and through his own fault, because he squandered the favor of God and thus succumbed to inconstancy. Ever since Adam passed from joy into sorrow, we must be inconstant beings, for the anguish of his inconstancy is given to us by him at our birth. In that way he brought the anger of God upon himself. Nothing else squandered its constancy, and so whatever inconstancy we might ourselves exhibit has emanated from that man, as I have just told you. Moreover, He gave us the capacity to distinguish between good and evil. Were He to force our hearts to wear the crown of constancy, to what purpose would He give us anything as a reward? He wants our steadfast inclinations to motivate us to proper constancy, for Adam, the first man, departed thence because of his inconstancy. He has given us a free choice: we can live as we wish. (2578)

One thing puzzles me greatly. I have often heard it said: people say that if God wished it to be so, they would not transgress against His commandment. I'll tell you for a fact that what people do against Him is completely contrary to His will. Some man might take it into his head to think that He cannot compel us in any other way than by His command. Anyone who fears God will be compelled by that. To be sure, a master also is accustomed to inflict suffering on a servant if he does not do what he tells him to and to force him to do it simply by saying "Do it." It's the same with our Lord God: if we break His commandment, He very firmly makes it clear to us that people should be in no doubt that evil deeds are committed against Him. Let anyone who cares to have common sense take note of that. (2602)

As I have stated before: from the sky and as far as the moon, the seven planets have remained constant in their orbit. From the moon down towards the earth four elements have remained in conflict with one another according to their respective properties. Heat is higher than coldness. Each thing has its own place: that corresponds to the law of nature, with the single exception of man who cannot retain his position. Anything in the world that is very insubstantial always rises up, whereas that which is heavy has no choice but to drop down towards the earth. Everything heavy is drawn towards the center, otherwise the earth would have fallen to pieces. Iron has the property of being drawn towards the magnet. The salamander does not try to leave the fire where it lives.[1] The rivers hasten towards the sea. There is nothing in the world so grand that it wishes to exist outside its rightful place, with the single exception of foolish man. The birds fly in the air; wild animals are in caves in the mountains and in the forest; the fish swim in the water where they live. It is different with us, for we do not wish to preserve our rightful place or our way of living. Everyone would like to exchange his lifestyle for someone else's drudgery: that is great inconstancy.[2] (2638)

The peasant would like to be a squire, because he thinks his life is easy. The squire would like to be a peasant, whenever he becomes disaffected with his own life. The priest would like to be a knight, when he gets bored with reading his books. The knight would like to be a priest when the thrust from a lance causes him to vacate his saddle. Whenever the merchant falls on hard times he says: "Oh dear, I wish I were dead. I have a hard lot. The craftsman has a good life: he spends his time at home. But because I have no craft I have to travel all over the place and am hard-pressed." Then the craftsman says: "The merchant is lucky, for I have to stay awake all night working. The merchant can sleep when he wants to." What this one likes, the other hates: that is great inconstancy. If the hound were to want to pull a cart and the ox chase after the hare, we would think both of them very strange, and it is just as funny that a man is not ashamed that out of envy he wants someone else's job. The squire a peasant, the peasant a squire: neither of these is right. The priest is a knight, the knight is a priest. Both of them are behaving like monkeys, for the monkey is not ashamed to want all the jobs. Thus we are all completely deluded, for I'll tell you in truth that no one would want to give up his own way of life if he really knew what the other man's was like. (2676)

The poor man has his troubles, so has the rich man. Everything has been given in equal measure. A reasonable person can see that the poor man does not have a worse time of it. The poor man suffers because of his poverty, the rich man because of his wealth. If someone owes me something it grieves me if the payment is not available. On the other hand, if I owe something, it distresses me if I have not got the wherewithal to pay.[3] Anyone who can work it out properly will see that the two things have the same effect. If someone has nothing, no one takes anything from him; the rich man loses a lot. Because of his own wealth the rich man must often experience low spirits, conflict, anger, and great hostility: he would certainly be better off without these things. On account of his wealth the rich man must put up with much humiliation such as I would not wish to endure. However, even if he does not wish to endure it, he will experience suffering on account of his wealth. (2698)

The poor man needs money, but the rich man needs protection. While the poor man asks for money, the rich man is so concerned about it that he must ask for assistance. They are going in exactly the same direction. The poor man suffers in pursuit of money, but the rich man is even worse off trying to find ways to become richer. Wealth does not make anyone free of cares. If someone has sufficient and wants more, then his wealth helps him as much as smoke helps the eyes: he can never deny this to me. The man who has much is very poor if his heart desires more, and the man who has little and wishes for no more has much. The man who is rich in spirit is not poor, even though he owns little, but the man who is not satisfied with what he has cannot get rid of his poverty, for no amount of wealth is sufficient for the bitter spirit of a wicked man. The wicked man would find much in little, if his desires could be fulfilled. If a man cannot make do with little he must surrender himself to slavery. The virtuous man knows how to get along with both little things and big ones. (2728)

The man who lives according to his needs does not need much. A man who knows how to live according to his needs cannot be a poor man. Do not hunger, thirst, or long after riches that will never come your way. If a man has an abundance of riches, he gets the foolish notion that he needs more: this is something that plagues the wealthy man. What one needs is soon fulfilled, but a foolish wish is boundless. A fool cannot become rich and is not to be compared with the needy man, for he does not need anything. It is different with the wise man, for he always has needs and even so he has a vast inheritance [to draw upon]. (2746)

One man is rich because of his foolishness, another poor because of his stupidity. The person who, in his arrogance, thinks he is affluent, is rich through foolishness. Similarly, if someone out of weak-mindedness believes he lacks wealth even though he has enough possessions, then he is poor through foolishness. It is my wish and also my advice that a person should diligently recognize himself and his possessions and his friends too. Anyone who does that will often be protected from harm, for if he has good sense he will not get into harm without deliberately seeking out security. (2764)

If a man does not trust that he can live with what God has given him, I would like him to realize that lots and lots of elephants survive perfectly well in the forest. At the same time, a worthy man should know that he will get what he needs much better than the elephant does. He is small and has big thoughts. No matter how big the elephant is, he nevertheless always gets quite enough in the forest. How can a man be so inept that he does not trust himself to acquire enough with all the powers at his disposal? After all, does he not have fire, water, air, and earth in his hands? He has all these and still has nothing, and that comes about through great avarice. (2784)

We apply more effort and cunning to what we do not need than to what we need very much. That is an amazing course. One leaves one's wife and children at home and goes off to slave away, very often in return for little gain. So it would make better sense if one were to apply a little effort to acquiring virtue. In that case both wealth and possessions would be on hand for us: I mean in terms of a pure heart. Very often one barters one's whole life, one's freedom, one's soul, one's wife and children, for nothing—note how this comes about—and if we were to buy it for a pound we would leave it by the wayside. Very often the foolish man puts his life up for sale and does not know for what except for sorrow, tribulation, and regret. (2804)

If the fool purchases something with his own person, he thinks he is the one who benefits and does not realize at all that he is the one who has given up the most. He would be angry, if it were not for his wealth. Thus he has sacrificed his heart and his mind to wealth and must live in servitude. The man who sells his free spirit does not receive something of equal value in return. Whoever places a priority on his affluence trails behind it like a fool. Anyone who does an injustice to his wealth undermines his own spirit. Anyone who cannot master his own wealth is a slave to pennies. (2820)

Now listen to [this example of] great inconstancy! Great suffering comes about from great joy. That which one struggles to achieve one must nevertheless leave behind when one dies. Wealth does not make anyone well if he becomes ill at any point. Anyone who loves it is very much grieved to leave it behind, and yet it is inevitable: he does have to leave it in the end. (2830)

Sorrow can come to him from joy, even before the day of his death arrives: enemies, fire, gambling, death, and thieves, these can all turn joy into sorrow. For that reason I wish that the rich man might give up his wealth for an incomparably greater possession. What might that be? The grace of God: that would suit him better, for it would give to him forever more eternal riches and honor. A pure heart purchases that for the poor man too, and thus they have equal wealth. (2842)

The poor man will reach his goal sooner, if he will do this, while the rich man will fall by the wayside. The poor man always travels light and also travels without fear, whereas the rich man is burdened with fear and bad thoughts, and if he hears a noise it startles him. If a mouse stirs somewhere he thinks thieves have broken into his house and shouts: "Robbers!" This is what the love of pennies does. Meanwhile the poor man pushes ahead of the rich man towards the gates of heaven. Anyone who wishes to retain his wealth should give it as quickly as possible to the poor, for they will soon take it to the place where it will be kept safely for him. Anyone who thinks he can set up his treasure chamber here on earth, no matter how much he may watch over it, will eventually lose it here, and there in heaven too, be sure of that. Hell and the wicked man are never satisfied. Consequently, I believe it is right that the two should go hand in hand. If a man resembles hell, then he cannot attain the kingdom of God. (2870)

If material goods were not displeasing to us for the sake of God, they would be heavy enough in themselves for us to bear, for their power makes no one virtuous. (2874)

Now look: white makes white, and black makes as black as it can, but what we call possessions gives no one a virtuous heart. In the end Fortune and good come to the bad man to end poverty, but not badness. If poverty gives a bad heart to someone, no amount of material goods will improve him. Because poverty is so wearisome to us, that makes us sinful as far as material things are concerned. A lack of virtue is not to be found in the goods themselves, but in the heart and in the spirit. Similarly, virtue is never to be found in goods, for it is in the spirit of the man who is noble and good. I have said again and again that virtues represent courtesy. Why do we call something "good" that does not make our spirit pure?[4] That which is "good" makes for virtue, and the power of virtue must do that. Virtues improve a man: riches cannot do that. If a man who is bad but poor becomes rich, he does not cease to be a bad man. I know well enough no wealth can make a poor spirit rich. (2902)

You can lay a sick man anywhere you like, first on his bed, then on the straw, and his sickness will follow him. And it is the same with the wicked man: whether he be poor or rich, his wickedness goes along with him just the same. (2908)

What we all call "goods" more often brings sorrow than joy to us. Why is wealth called "good" when it often brings great shame upon us? Anyone who has it is carrying two heavy burdens. The one is that he would like to be richer: that's called greed. Then the suffering from the other burden is the fear that he must always endure because he is afraid of losing his possessions. All those possessions that Alexander had—silver, gold, castles, lands, people—will make you avaricious, so that you will crave even more after goods. (2922)

Whenever a man has sufficient, he thinks: "I'm still not well off: my neighbor is even richer," and he brings upon himself a bitter life through someone's wealth until through toil he becomes as rich as his neighbor. Then he says: "I still want more. That man is richer than I am, and so I have reason to be ashamed, for I am of more noble stock than he." If he then acquires more he is given to say: "I am not rich. I can hardly be compared with him in terms of wealth," and he goes on despairing like this until the day he dies. (2938)

Someone who can judge astutely should, whenever a rich man is walking in front of him, look behind and say: "For every man who is richer than I am, there are easily three who are poorer." And he should leave it at that. People don't do that: they just look ahead and see who is going out of the door in front of them, and they don't wish to see that if one is walking ahead, at least ten are walking behind. Worldly wealth is poverty: it makes a poor spirit poorer and does not make the rich man richer. Its name is false and worthless. The richness of heaven is good. It makes body and spirit rich, and so its name is good and true, since it truly enriches a man. (2956)

No goods that a man has will help him if he does not follow this advice: that he should not be concerned about losing his possessions. If a man wishes to enjoy his worldly goods, his spirit must be very secure, for worldly goods without security are small joy alongside great sorrow. For sure, there would be nothing evil about worldly goods if one did not turn one's heart to them. Anyone who wishes to pursue worldly goods has taken a lot upon himself, something he must always carry along with him, whether on horseback or on foot. That cannot be good. We have often seen this with malevolent folk. At no time is that virtue. Good cannot be found in evil, and evil cannot survive in good. If wealth were "goods," as it is called, it would have to flee a malevolent spirit. All virtues quickly take their leave when a wicked visitor comes to pay them a visit. (2980)

By now you have heard enough said about how useless wealth is. Now you are going to hear what wealth does to the poor man who has not a great many worldly goods. It troubles the poor man terribly when he comes to think about it. If at the time he can recall a little trick for winning, it will immediately appear to him that he possesses what his heart desires. When he has that in his thoughts he immediately searches in his mind for advice and tricks about how he might improve that wealth and gain even more. He applies all his thoughts to that. Once he has acquired great riches in his deluded mind, he sets about constructing tall castles and broad cities,[5] and turns all his thoughts to how he might build his palace in them. Once he has completed that, he seeks further advice as to how he might secure it firmly, so that it may be protected from attack, and he will not be the least bit afraid, even if the city is taken. So he very carefully makes a moat around his palace, with a wide stretch of water full of big fish swimming in it. Over the top of the moat he quickly builds very high round towers. These provide good protection against battering rams, for if it perhaps comes about that the stones are hurled down upon them, they do not do much damage to the towers. When, on the basis of his foolish counsel, he has done all this while lying on his bed and has gained plenty of worldly goods in his mind, he remembers above all that he must guard his goods securely and thinks of what he wants to buy straightaway, which cities and which lands. Thus he quarrels with his rivals who wish to do him harm because of his wealth and envy him on account of it. His heart is in conflict and he is wondering what he should do to prevent thieves getting hold of such wealth as he has. So then he looks for many a piece of advice. (3036)

When he has been tormenting himself with such thoughts for a long time, this man still only has what he had when he started, and yet he has tortured his mind with all this thinking. Thus there are a great many people who wage war at night without an enemy, for they fight the whole night through with their greedy thoughts. They cannot find any rest from the moment their bodies are lying very comfortably. It is only right that greed should cause suffering ahead of possessions, for it also causes suffering along with wealth, if you observe it correctly, and also creates sorrow once wealth has been achieved. I have already told you all this. (3054)

Now you have heard exactly how the poor man should preserve his place in life, and the rich man, too, for they are very similar. In truth, both of them suffer very much on account of their respective positions. The rich man endures fear and greed; the poor man only endures greed, that's the common factor: only the rich man has the fear. The poor man would not want to give up what he has if he really knew what the life of the rich man was like. (3066)

I want to speak of the same thing: the lord and the common folk have a single goal: and anyone who can understand it properly recognizes that the common folk have a better life than the man who is burdened with authority, for he is in despair all the time. The people need someone to rule over them. The lord never rests in his mind, for he has to work out how best to rule. The foolish mind of the people tells them that no one has wealth except the lord. Whenever he is borne in state, the people say that the lord has everything he wants.[6] [But along with that] he has distress and much worry. When the people are able to sleep, the lord is riding all day long in the interest of them all. He alone must bear the trials and tribulations of what might cause consternation to the people. He must always be prepared to pay compensation for anything less than good that befalls his people, whether inflicted by enemies or thieves. His people must be as dear to him as his own life. Our Lord protects the nobleman to whom He has granted the capacity to behave so virtuously. (3096)

Foolish people, just tell me, by what right do you wish to become lords? I have heard and read that anyone who wishes to transgress against his true nature will very often come to grief. Now why should a peasant wish to be a lord and lead a bitter life because he is not one, thinking about it all the time? To be sure, that peasant who wishes to deny his true nature should bear in mind, when he's lying comfortably, that his lord is having a wretched time. While the peasant is playing with his friends and laughing with his child, the lord is burdened with all kinds of trouble and with pressure and worries. I cannot tell you in detail about the misery that he has then. One man there says: "My lord ought to do this." Another man has a different opinion and says nothing. Their opinions differ on many things, and each man expresses his opinion, so that people may think him a wise man. He does not care if he gives worse advice and very often speaks against his better judgment, because of his friends or for the sake of gain. It is a wretched man who does that, someone who makes unjust pronouncements for the sake of material goods. One should not help one's friend transgress against God, that is His commandment, but if anyone does that, misfortune will befall them both, for they will be completely defeated. Know that for a fact. (3134)

A simple man who is not capable of much or anything at all often says: "If I were a lord I would behave well, like this, and act just as one should." He does not know what he is saying, for with his way of thinking the three little scraps of land that he owns are very badly organized and managed. (3142)

Foolish people: just think. A man who cannot steer a ship and puts himself forward as a ferryman is not sensible, for if he does not know his proper place, everyone who comes on board is lost. The master also gains something. I'll say this: if a man would like to achieve great honor and is not capable of doing so, his honor will turn into dishonor. It must dismay the people, too, if they have a wicked master. Honor is the harbinger of great dishonor if a man exercises authority without wisdom. A lesser man often goes unnoticed: if he becomes a master, however, his shameful ways become clear enough, and everyone ought to know this. So how does it come about that a man is so keen to acquire a great deal of authority? If authority were good in itself it would endow us with a good heart too, but authority does not do that, for very often it falls to a wicked man to possess it, who cannot do anything with it and will never be able to learn, even if he lives until the Day of Judgment. (3172)

If authority were good by its very nature, it would do what every living creature does by its very nature. Whatever is good here in the world ought to be good elsewhere, too. Fire is hot here as well as elsewhere: wherever it is, it always produces heat. Authority does not do that, for if a master has to travel to another land where he is probably not known, I tell you that people will pay as little attention to him as to someone who is virtually unknown in that country. Thus, to be sure, authority does not possess so much power in itself that it can demonstrate to us who is the master, whether he is close to us or far away. People must say to us: "Look who is there!" for authority does not have the wit to tell us who he is, however near we may be to him. Therefore it does not seem that good to me, so why does anyone torment himself so much because he wishes to have great honor? Tall towers collapse completely if the foundation is not very firm, and the same thing happens to a man whose arrogance is greater than his virtue: he can easily come to grief. Great boulders on the mountains crash down to the ground: the rocks which are on the plain lie very comfortably. Know that the wind that shakes the tall trees vigorously breaks their branches off completely, but it does not do so much harm to the little tree that bends with the wind. Thus I say that one should be happy to live beneath the lords, for the lord has to work hard if he wishes to live honorably. The mind of a lord is often troubled by conflict and by worries, and, as I have told you, he must contend with all sorts of trials and tribulations. (3220)

I have talked at length of the misery that authority produces. Now hear how it troubles the man who never even had it. (3224)

When a man greedy for honor thinks very hard about it he comes up with a clever solution. Once he has formulated it, he is immediately as happy as if he had acquired a whole land. He thinks he has what he wants: he has both honor and a great deal of authority. He rules his land as if he should have it by rights. He lacks nothing in terms of honor. He bestows the office of cupbearer,[7] and he determines in his head who is suitable to be the steward. Thus someone who was once good at his office loses it, because the fellow gives it away to whomever he wishes, for now he has much power. Thus the chamberlains surround him with great courtesy and consideration and keep the crowds away, and so he is very content in his fantasy. (3246)

If, for example, he desires to go hunting, in a very short time the dogs are made ready, and all the huntsmen appear with their hounds. Then they catch so many hares that there are too many for them to carry. A boar causes problems for the dogs as soon as it appears. In fact it causes them great suffering, but in the end it will also be dead. Then he fantasizes about catching a stag with its long horns, and finally that same lord stabs a bear to death with his spear. My! How bold he is as long as his fantasy lasts! Then they promptly blow their horns, for they have done enough hunting for now, and they ride home, along with their dogs, in a very happy mood. Then along come the falconers and provide reports on their falcons, so the lord has an enormous crowd around him. However, this authority does not last long, for when he gets up next morning and proceeds through the streets on his own, no one says: "Be seated, my lord." His chair is a long way away from him; his chamberlains have vanished; he does not have a single page with him. He has no idea where the game is that he has sought for so long. The boar with its long tusks is safe from his fantasy. Let him fantasize as much as he wishes: the steward and the cupbearer will not lose their positions because of that. Indeed they both still hold them. (3284)

Now you have heard enough about how the man who strives too hard for authority can make a fool of himself and lead a wretched life. Moreover, anyone who strives for power does not realize that power and lack of power have one consequence: they plague us day and night, but the one without power is better off, and that is very easily understood. (3294)

The man without power often rests while the powerful man is running around in fetters that he cannot break, for if he is a powerful man he wishes out of arrogance to catch everyone in his trap and very often finds himself shamefully ensnared. A peasant, if he's capable of anything, chooses to consider other people worthless and applies all his might to bringing others under his control. He wants to have his own way with them. If anyone opposes him, whether in small or large measure, he takes him to task and sees to it that some time or other his master directs his anger at him. In this way the poor man has lost a great deal. The same holds true for knights, and I do not exclude the priests either. The powerful man wants to draw all the other people under his control, but if anyone resists him he lures him in with false counsel, with deeds and by all kinds of means, for he wants to force him to do whatever he wants. Then he has his men inflict considerable suffering upon him. If the man comes to him and complains, he says: "I don't know anything about it. It happened without my knowledge," and he sees to it that people deal with him until—by fair means or foul—he "persuades" him to submit to him. (3330)

By the time he believes he has sorted out what was opposing his heart's desires he will find that another person pops up against him, and he turns his mind once more to devising a way to subject him. Then he has to lie awake worrying until he has subordinated this man. Then a third man summons up his strength and stands up against him, until he brings him down in the same way. After that a fourth man rises up against him, and you can be sure that he will have no peace as long as he is alive, for no one can subject everybody else to his will. One cannot find it anywhere in the Scriptures that any man ever had the strength to bring the whole world under his control. I can certainly say in all honesty that there have been many who have wanted this, but, as we can read, their wishes were never fulfilled. Our Lord God brought about much misery by His command: if people look for trials and tribulations, they will find any number of them. (3356)

A man often believes he has released himself and then he lands in worse straits. He says: "If I kill this one man, I shall be safe from my enemies forever more." He kills him and as a consequence he gains three enemies instead of just the one. Thus his bright idea has come to nought. And anyone who thinks he can lessen his misery through homicide will find his worries increased. Likewise I tell you for a fact that anyone who thinks he can make us subordinate to himself always has a great deal of trouble and will not be able to achieve what he would like to. Alexander had problems with this right up until his death.[8] If anyone fights fiercely to acquire power, that power does not last for long. Alexander enjoyed it for twelve years but then had to relinquish it completely. (3376)

I will tell you the same about Julius,[9] who had control of much of the world, but his power did not help him, for when he returned home having gained much honor by his conquests he only lived for two more years and then lost all his power. When he believed he was safe, his power did him no good and he was nevertheless slain. Hector, too, was dragged round his city like a cart: that was a miserable end.[10] (3390)

Why am I talking about those who relinquished their authority through the power of death, for there were many who had to give up their authority completely in their lifetime? At Troy, people who had power and honor were brought to their knees. Once Troy had been conquered they were terribly denigrated, for the aged queen of Troy was brutally dragged through the dust like a slave.[11] That was not appropriate for members of the court. And old Anchises was forcibly driven into exile. He suffered terribly in the fire, only to die in the water.[12] (3406)

When Hannibal gained the victory, many a man in Rome fell from a position of power into great weakness: indeed they lost all their strength and influence.[13] (3410)

Why am I talking about what happened long ago in the world? For it comes about in our own time that people cannot hold on to their power. Now hear about how great weakness and power go hand in hand. I know of an earl who lost his earldom. I know of many similar cases. I know of a march and a bishopric and even a dukedom, which have been lost in my lifetime: their very strength gave rise to weakness. I can also think of a king who in his time certainly possessed the power of a wealthy emperor and now does not even have the strength of a king.[14] (3426)

Power: we are deceived in you; we have been told many lies about you. Now tell me, power, what are you good for? For you have not even the strength to protect yourself. How do you wish to protect me? No matter how powerful Alexander was, he always sent his chamberlain ahead when he wished to visit his wife, to investigate whether there was a knife [in the room]: he wouldn't go in until this was done. His power did not help him not to fear a woman.[15] (3440)

The powerful man must seize his power from the weak, then if the weak move away, the powerful ones are like children in respect of their power. (3444)

As I have said, there are three things a man possesses that do not conform to their nature. No other creature emulates him in this respect. Good often leads to bad. And authority often tends to produce dishonor. Power, too, also teaches that it produces enormous weakness, if anyone relies on its strength. (3454)

Now I have told you enough about the misery and trouble that befall a powerful man on account of power. However, it also does not spare the man anxiety who has no power at all: it lures that man, too, with its cunning. For if he lies thinking as he does all night long, he lands on the idea that perhaps by marriage or perhaps by some other means he can bring it about and ensure that he can be powerful: he is very pleased about this. Then straightaway he thinks what harm or what shame he wants to inflict on his enemies. He imagines assembling a huge army, and then his enemy is completely defenseless. Thus he avenges himself very well, as a respectable man should. He gives the order that one man's house should be torn down, and no one dares to contradict him. He commands that another man be hanged forthwith. One man is slain here, another there; people are killed the whole night through with his impure and evil thoughts. (3482)

Then the master is furious and the enemies are vanquished. No matter how quickly he may have slain them, when he gets up next morning, he sees the power of the enemy that he slew during the night. So he has achieved nothing at this point but sin, and if anyone were to know the thoughts that he had been having during the night he would be mortified. What account has he given of himself before God, against Whom no doors can be closed? Because of this a man should purify his mind with virtue and goodness, for I can truly say that He can see into the heart of everyone, whether evil or good dwells in it. (3503)

Is this not foolishness? What a man would regret if someone were to hear it from his own mouth, he is revealing to God all the time through the thoughts in his mind. Look how careful the foolish man is: whenever he has spent the whole night killing people in his thoughts, in the morning he will go to church and dare to stand before God, whereas if a lord had been so defiled by him and were to come to know it, that man would never dare to look at him. (3516)

I have spoken about three things which have occupied my mind: about power and wealth and authority. Now I have a mind to tell about the power of a man who would like to be famous. In truth he seems to me to be a complete fool, for, when with much effort we have spread our name abroad, our name is of no help to us, once it is time for us to go to where others have gone before. The children follow their father, all according to their actions, whether these deeds be just or wrong. Wherever they end up, their name is not the slightest help to them. Look, Arthur was well known and is often mentioned today, but tell me: how does that help him? An "Our Father" would be of more use to him. If Arthur is to attain the grace of God, he can certainly do without our praise, but if he is in the depths of hell, our praise will only add to his sin, for he supplies us constantly with all sorts of lies.[16] For that reason I wonder how it comes about that people desperately want other people to say that they are good and courtly and virtuous, and that they should become famous. They do not care if the man who praises them like this is lying. His lie does not bother them the least bit. Yet a master who is capable of doing so should consider, when another man praises him, whether he is speaking the truth. If he does not recognize in himself those traits for which the other man is praising him, then he will not escape disgrace. (3560)

If someone speaks well of a lord without good reason, the lord should justly be angry that the man is lying about him so publicly. (3564)

A respectable man should be inclined to observe what the man who praises him is doing, for a scoundrel cannot praise another man. I do not consider myself valued if a man wishes to praise me whom I cannot praise back unless I am proposing to lie to him. If a man who is himself highly praised wishes to praise me I consider myself happy to be praised by him, but the other forms of praise cause me distress. (3576)

It came about once that Alexander was wounded. He said: "People are always lying and saying that I am a god. I am a man, and the wound from a little arrow has truly revealed this to me."[17] Thus greed, wickedness, and inconstancy provide us with proof that we are not so perfect as we have often heard. (3586)

We do not relate our dreams while we are [actually] dreaming. When I relate my dream it's obvious that I am awake. And so it is with a man who will not and cannot understand how burdened he is as long as his wickedness lasts. I tell you the same thing: the man who has recognized his lack of virtue has improved himself a great deal, nor does he immediately believe what the flatterer says about him. He does not find that at all pleasurable. (3600)

A respectable man should consider when someone says something nice about him: "Is it true what that fellow is saying?" But if the man is lying, he is distressed that the flatterer seeks to deceive him with such a charade. For later on, when he has left him, he demonstrates well enough that people should not mistake a puppet for a child, and he shows this by hiding the puppets away and then saying in truth that the man is a villain. Then he does not think any longer about his earlier praise. (3616)

There is never any more effective criticism than when one praises highly something that is not praiseworthy, for that way one immediately causes people to say: "My dear fellow, your praise is not sincere" and everyone criticizes that person even more. Thus the master is not highly honored when praise is mixed with lies. (3626)

Now note this: when children look into a mirror, it is not particularly sensible of them to imagine that there is actually a child there who will play with them. Much more foolish is the person who believes someone [who maintains] that there is nothing bothering his head when he has, in fact, a headache. I'm talking about the tendency of a nobleman to believe the flatterer and the wicked people more than he does himself. How can another person know his mind better? Hence it amazes me that he lets himself be deceived like this. When the flatterer tells him that he is doing very well, he believes that everything is just fine at that point, when actually there is much that is wrong. Likewise I say that when the heralds[18] call out at the tops of their voices before the knights: "Hurrah, knights, good chevaliers, noble and high-spirited," even the man who is actually a shameless lout among decent folk thinks he is a lion. (3652)

What a brave lord should consider to be bad, if he were so inclined, many people consider good. That arises from their feeble minds. They should consider all deception, mendacity and loose behavior evil: then there would not be so many liars and flatterers. (3660)

I still have a fair amount to say about how, if a lord wishes to behave correctly and if he is not lacking in virtue, he should not pay the slightest attention to whether people are talking a lot about him, for a respectable man desires to be good for the sake of God, rather than for the sake of fame. Good for him if he does so! I know well enough that a worthy man, who pays attention to right behavior, does not wish in his heart that people should talk about his goodness. No man can alter the sun's rays throughout the day, and if I were to say that it was bright, my words would be superfluous. One should not relate things that every man can see for himself, and the man whose own deeds praise him is justly praised indeed. No one can criticize the man whose own deeds accord him praise. Moreover, it is completely unnecessary to praise the man—this is the truth—whose own deeds praise him, for his praise is evident enough. A man eager for renown is always miserable, for he is wishing to do more than he can and worries all day long about how he should go on living. Whoever observes him correctly can see that he is never happy with himself. His name is good for nothing other than to bring him with much prattling and bragging to hell, and to cause people to clap their hands when he comes to a bad end and shout out all over the place that he is dead. That is what the name he labored to achieve throughout his life has brought to him. I would rather ascend quietly to heaven than go to hell with a fanfare. The man who wishes to ascend to heaven should be very wary of fame. My advice is that one should conduct oneself well without making a big noise about it, for it will be clear enough in heaven. However, there are many lords, it's true, who consider themselves maligned if people deny them their recognition and praise. I do not think that they are wise in this, for if a gentleman behaves well, he diminishes his goodness if he does so because he wants other people to talk a lot about him. (3718)

Whatever does not derive from virtue is always vice. If a man behaves correctly, his heart should be motivating him to do so, for if he is motivated by worldly fame, virtue will bring great vice with it. Regrettably, however, there are many people—and I want to tell you this for a fact—who do more for the sake of fame than for the honor of virtue. I can honestly tell you that a man may be able to refuse a penny to a poor man yet straightaway give a horse to a man who could well get along without it, because he will go around talking about it. Alas, avarice, what paltry honor! He gives nothing to the pauper who walks about naked but always gives clothing to the one who has enough clothes already. The gift arises from the complete lack of virtue, by means of which, however, he strives after virtue. (3740)

The branches wither if the roots are rotten. If a man constructs a foundation from straw and wishes to build something on it, the building will not be firm. Likewise I say: if a man behaves correctly, not out of goodness but for the sake of worldly fame, this cannot be called virtue, since it does not come about as a result of virtue, and if someone believes for a short time that vice is virtue, it cannot last for long: to be sure the bragging will soon be at an end. Fame has very weak legs and tends to bring up the rear on its own. However, what one does out of virtue is steadfast and good, for God does not forget this. Thus it often comes about that a simple man is recognized over and above the kings throughout all the lands. (3760)

Those who have always striven for fame and labored all their lives for the sake of fame and have always given gifts in order to achieve fame will never live to see the day when their bounty was so widely dispensed that people would talk about it. Alexander gave away many lands where he is scarcely mentioned these days, and he gave away many fine gifts but has no praise to show for it today. For, just as I have said, whatever is done for the sake of fame cannot have very long legs, for it must remain behind on its own. However, anything that is done for the sake of virtue, even if a simple man does it, will be spread far and wide. It should always be related how a virtuous poor knight, of little means but rich in spirit, gave away a portion of his coat and how this portion assured his complete salvation. Look: he gave little enough but for the fact that his heart was so pure that he gave it out of virtue. As a result his name is known for all time. Thus every man who conceives of doing the right thing should not overlook the poor. Those who give to wandering singers so that they tell lies about them also have the sense not to forget the poor people altogether, for these tell the truth about them. But now it has come about that we give more for the sake of worldly honor than for the sake of God, and because of that our praise cannot endure. No man should look for pears on a cherry tree, even if he wanted to, nor do I think the man is very wise who believes he can acquire glory when all things come to an end. He has landed on good counsel who seeks to acquire praise where much praise is to be found and where nothing has an end, for that world does not pass away. (3808)

Now I have told you enough about what misery the idea of avarice causes the famous man. It always troubles the man who is not famous too, for if he also wishes to become famous at some time, he thinks day and night about how he should set about ensuring that his virtue is much talked about so that he actually seems virtuous. He does not really want to be good, for anyone who desires to be a good man does not need to be accorded much fame. And so he thinks: "If I do this, people will speak more favorably of me." The man who is always desirous of fame does not think about what would be a better course. He often thinks how he would like to give much at court but does not give much thought to how he should act in order to dispense gifts well. (3830)

So in his mind he arranges a tournament to which many a good knight will travel, and he wishes to perform very well there. Thus the spear of his foolish fantasies empties many a saddle. No one can compare with him: they must all give way before him. Just look, how his courage is bruited abroad in the world! And everyone says that he has such fine, courtly livery. His hauberk is very splendid, and no one can compare to him in this respect. His steed has an excellent gait. His armor fits him to perfection. His greaves are neither too big nor too small around his legs. My! How that man uses his legs! No one there rides as he does. He has a wealth of attributes at his disposal. And so he thinks to himself: "That was a super dream!" (3854)

The idea of nobility can make us dream like this. If a man is nobler than someone else, he thinks he is always superior, but he is deceiving himself: no one is noble except the man who has directed his heart and his mind towards true goodness.[19] (3862)

If a man is highborn and yet has lost the nobility of his mind, I can tell you for a fact: his birth actually brings shame upon him, for if someone is highborn, his birth demands at all times that he behave well and do the right thing, but if he does not force himself to this, he will disgrace himself all the more: his birth will diminish his honor. (3872)

For that reason I am very surprised that any virtuous man would wish to demonstrate overweening pride because of the wealth and nobility of his forebears. It would seem to me a better idea that he should himself do something because of which he could be called noble, rather than rely on what they did. (3881)

Every man achieves his nobility from his father's side. If people can understand this: anyone who wishes to maintain his birthright has a great

deal of nobility. They are all the children of God who obey His command-
ments. The man who does not obey His commandments has deliberately
forfeited the nobility that God gave to him and has also chosen for himself
a father who, by his evil doings, is forever ignoble. Anyone who forsakes his
noble father has forfeited his nobility. (3894)

God created all of us. In truth it was His will that brought us into the
world, and because of that we are all His children, except the man who for-
feited it with his evil deeds. By this you can indeed see that no one should
be called noble, save the man who behaves properly. If a man has a false
disposition, he must live without virtue and has forfeited his nobility for the
sake of the love of vice. That was not a sensible idea. Whether he be young
or old, a man has made a bad deal if he has sacrificed his nobility through
his wickedness and evil, his lying and inconstancy, his lack of courtesy and
his vices. (3914)

If you have understood me correctly, then it is easy to comprehend
that the man who is noble in the world is always courteous: for as I told you
before, correct behavior is courteousness. If a man has a courteous disposi-
tion, he does whatever he does correctly, and be assured that the person
who always behaves correctly is noble. Know for a fact, therefore, that those
who are noble are all God's children. (3926)

Now that I have spoken about nobility, my heart longs, if you think it
a good idea, to say how it is with desire. Every man has his own desire: one
loves gambling, the other tends to be a gourmand, the third enjoys fal-
conry, the fourth lazes around in an inn, the fifth spends all his time hunt-
ing, the sixth whiles away his time with women. Those who eagerly pursue
their desires take very different paths. (3938)

Anyone who cannot easily follow his desires all day long considers him-
self most unfortunate, but I tell you for a fact that the man who always
follows his desires is a much more unfortunate fellow, for even if the latter
does gain pleasure from it, he immediately also brings upon himself such
great suffering which is, after all, the companion of joy.[20] (3948)

Understand this: the gambler is never better off when he wins the game,
without being much worse off when he loses it. The dice he has in his hand
demonstrate then and there to him that simultaneously there is joy on one
side, sorrow on the other. You should know that, when it comes to gam-
bling, there is not much separating joy from sorrow. There is only a piece
of bone between them, and a small piece at that. The gourmand never got
better by eating without that which had made him ill in the first place mak-
ing him still worse, for otherwise he would not have eaten ten times what
people gave him. That serves the gourmand right. You should also believe
me when I say that no one fared so well through falconry without doing
much worse when he lost his falcon. You should believe me when I say that

no one feels so good from drinking that he does not feel much worse when the wine goes to his head, for he can neither see nor hear, because the wine has deprived him of his senses. If a man exchanges his senses for wine, this exchange is called a loss. Every man knows that the huntsman does well, yet he's worse off when his hound is wounded by a wild boar. (3982)

There was never a man so happy when he won a woman that he did not become much unhappier, if he loved her, if she desired to love another man. For it happens all the time that, however great the joy, it is always accompanied by great sorrow. (3990)

The man who enjoys winning will always suffer loss more acutely than the man who is not good at amassing wealth. If a man has a faithless wife and if he loves her, great sorrow and great suffering are included in that love: I should not want to be that man. (3998)

Any respectable man whose wife behaves less than well should know that no man can with any virtue please his wife, if she is inconstant, so that she dismisses others from her mind, for if she were to do this she would be a good woman. A woman who does not intend to preserve her honor ignores the virtue of her husband and pays no attention to it, when she happens to behave badly. A woman who wishes to preserve her honor, even if her husband has many vices, will do what she ought to do. You should believe me on this point. Take note: a good woman does the right thing, whether her husband is good or bad, but, if he is as good as one might wish, his malevolent wife will be up to all sorts of things. (4018)

I would like to offer some advice on this. Let the man who wants to live in peace and comfort be happy, whatever his wife does. If he is himself a decent fellow, then anyone with any sense knows that it is simply something inside her that makes her behave like this. Whatever happens to her is not her husband's fault. Let him just be steadfast in doing what he ought to do. However we [men] do not do this. Such a man is himself a scoundrel if he wishes to have a respectable wife. I believe it would be a better idea for him to abandon his impropriety. How the man is duped who can make his wife good but is himself a wrongdoer! He wishes to oversee his wife but is himself a malevolent fellow. The man who can watch over himself has acted as he should, but the man who watches over his wife more than himself, take note, diverts the loyalty he owes himself, if he were so inclined, assiduously to something for which he will not receive an iota of thanks. Surveillance does not help much, for anyone who is intent on bringing shame upon himself can discover a thousand ways to do it at some time or another.[21] (4052)

I wish that everyone, both man and woman, would guard his or her person: that would be the proper thing to do. However, many [men] believe that it is courteous and honorable to conquer many a woman. Therefore it serves them right, since they regard their shame as negligible, that their

wife's misdeed soon brings disgrace upon them. Whatever a man undertakes
with regard to women should always be something good. We have estab-
lished what is right through our power and strength and cannot defend
ourselves against the injustice we experience, for if our wives go astray we
ourselves are shamed. The violence that is done to women out of arrogance
can never be so great, unless it is equal to the violence that we ourselves
must endure. I can tell you that in truth. We are guilty of great violence and
yet we consider our shame a mere nothing. Women cause more damage to
us, for their shame is our dishonor. This has come about through our own
desire, if you have understood me correctly. (4082)

It would be much better if we were to allow women to have their own
[standards of] proper and improper behavior, and if we held to ours. It is an
amazing man who can guard someone else better than he can guard himself.
I should never want to go to school to learn that: such a school would be
anathema to me if there were nothing better to learn there. Whether it be
foolishness or good sense, I prefer myself to any other man, and I am includ-
ing women too. If I were to have a wife and if she did not do what I wanted, I
would leave her to her own shame, and that would seem to me the best thing,
for no woman can bring such shame on her husband by her bad behavior
that he cannot more readily attain honor by means of his own virtue. (4105)

Now I have told you enough about the trials and tribulations that are
associated with our desires, and how sorrow goes hand in hand with joy.
However, if a man cannot check his desire, then he will suffer all the time
from thinking about it. If the gambler has nothing to play with, then, alas,
he goes backwards and forwards from one game to another, "winning"
many thoughts. When the glutton has nothing to eat, alas, how he suffers if
he comes round to thinking that there are many fine dishes! If people like
hunting or falconry, or enjoy spending their time in the tavern, these things
are all agony to them if they lack any of them. (4124)

If a man serves a woman he will suffer all the time. If he cannot get to
see her, he is beside himself both day and night. Ah, what useless things he
thinks about the whole time! And if anyone were to see the thoughts he
harbors in his mind, he would be bitterly ashamed of himself. However, he
should be even more ashamed that He does observe him, He from Whom
no thought is hidden and Who has the power, if he will not give up this way
of thinking, to send him down to where the bright day never shines. Before
Him one should take care where one goes in thought and deed: that is the
counsel of wise people. (4144)

Let this conclude the third part, and one should take note of the fourth
that follows.

BOOK IV

I have spoken on the matter of inconstancy and about how a lack of constancy can cause us to worry about our wealth, and what torture a man must endure from authority, and how authority always burdens people with its power and how it has the strength to plague a man on account of his reputation all day long, and how at all times it troubles us because of our nobility, and how that same inconstancy inflicts suffering upon us through our desires. (4160)

Now it puzzles me how it comes about that we love most of all that which causes us the greatest consternation. Because of that we are led astray to such an extent that nothing does us so much good as vice; if it were good and if vice were [in fact] virtue, then I believe we would disdain it. If we should succeed at all in the six things of which I've spoken and if there were to be constancy in them, they would be completely negligible to us. However, if vice is associated with them, everyone will strive to acquire them. (4174)

Wealth does not exist without greed, for you know full well that we would not strive so much after possessions if we did not have a malevolent disposition. Authority does not exist without pride, and out of arrogance we crazily pursue authority. Note, too, that inferiority strives for power. Vanity struggles to establish a reputation. Foolishness relies on nobility, that's true. And know that lechery is the constant companion of desire. So why should a decent man who can do good deeds trouble himself with these six things, in all of which he may prove so inept that he becomes completely bad and loses the resolve of his heart? He who has chosen vice as his mistress has lost the resolve of his heart. Moreover his nobility has vanished at the same time. He has turned from a freeman into a vassal, if anyone can understand that. (4200)

If wise Socrates were to rise from the dead, I have no doubt that he would think that many freemen today were slaves to vice, for he rejected many things for the sake of virtue, if we are to believe it. And know this: he did it in order that people might understand that possessions [by themselves] are meaningless. (4208)

Every worthy lord should guard himself very carefully against the vassalage of vice, and see to it that he does not come under its control. Anyone who wishes to protect himself from it should steer clear of riches and authority, fame and power. Nor should he rely heavily on his noble standing or pursue his desires: in this way he will be well protected, as a gentleman should be. (4220)

Know that a gentleman who turns his heart towards accruing wealth has chosen avarice as his mistress. Should I not, then, be angry if a man who himself wished to be a vassal and must himself lie down under the foot of avarice were to issue orders to me? What use are castles and lands to him, if much to his shame he is a slave to avarice and must serve her at all times? (4232)

If a man relies on power this is not good for him either, for he is a slave to arrogance and has brought much shame upon himself. How can any man be his vassal, when he cannot free himself from the vassalage of arrogance? He lacks the strength of a steadfast heart, since he talks like this and behaves as one who serves arrogance. (4242)

A man who relies on power has also lost the resolve of his heart and must, like a knave, wickedly serve Lady Shame, whether he likes it or not. This can only heap more shame upon him, if he has any sense: know that for sure. The fact that the devil[1] is riding him should certainly bring disgrace upon him. His friends will not be able to help him with what he will have to put up with from his lady. Whatever she does, he will have to consider it a good thing. (4256)

Anyone who pursues a reputation often serves a vice that we call extravagance. What use is it to him that he has made a name for himself far and wide, when he is enslaved and must also always serve a woman who is inconstant in everything she does? If her extravagance is not inconstant, then her inconstancy is constant. (4266)

Any man who relies on his nobility has [chosen] foolishness as his mistress, for he disdains to learn anything. I do not think that any land is well ruled by someone who has not learnt what he should. If anyone were encumbered in this way, then his nobility would be meaningless to me. What use is it that once upon a time his ancestor was noble, given that he himself has now become enslaved to foolishness? If anyone wants to take away the pillars, there will not be much of the roof left. Anyone who is himself a villain does not possess the nobility of his forefathers. (4282)

A man who is given to following his desires has many mistresses: Sloth and Gluttony, Unchastity and Drunkenness. They have power over him: they have just inherited him as their vassal. How can he be a lord who is ruled by mead and wine? Anyone who gets drunk from the influence of wine has certainly become enslaved to it, just as anyone who is occupied all the time with what he is eating is truly a lascivious fool, or, there again, anyone who is lying around all the time with one leg over the other is an idle rogue. He may be happy among the ladies, but is a man supposed to be free who cannot survive without a woman and who is so lacking in strength that he must submit to her authority and follow all her commands? He is making a mockery of himself, if he must remain under the thumb of a woman in everything he does. How can a man lord it over me, when he has allowed his spirit to be broken by a woman? May I be eternally cursed if I claim him as a friend! I declare that it will never come about that I would want him as my lord: that I shall never do. (4316)

Now you have taken in that one should guard against vice, and I have also spoken about how inconstancy can cause us distress all the time. I have also said how every man should adhere to his place in life. In the following I am going to write about virtue and constancy. I am going to set inconstancy aside for a while, if it does not mind. I should have much to say about it that I cannot relate at this moment. Our days are not long enough for me to say what I ought to say, even if people would like to hear more. (4332)

I have stated that inconstancy is present in all vices. Now you will also find out that constancy ought to be the mentor of all virtue, for by imbuing them with constancy one can perfect all virtues. One should always strive to be constant in virtue, both in youth and in old age. Virtue without constancy is nothing, and certainly constancy is nothing without virtue. (4344)

What is constancy? The attainment of all goodness in a steadfast spirit. Constancy is being constant in respect of all good things. No one can apply it to bad things. No man is virtuous unless he has the power of constancy. He is a virtuous man who can possess constancy in goodness. If a man behaves correctly on one occasion he does not thereby become virtuous unless he is also steadfast. In fact one good deed is of little use. However, if he remains constant in carrying it out, he is a virtuous man. One virtue in itself has not the power to make someone virtuous. Anyone who professes to be virtuous must have many virtues. (4362)

Now you should know that virtues are of benefit to both the old and the young. At all times that which is good for the virtuous is injurious to the bad, and I'll tell you how those things which bring success to the good man must always cause suffering to the man without virtue. (4370)

I have said how neither wealth nor poverty is good for malevolent people. I have told you plenty about how, if two people are seized by evil, they must be enfeebled by poverty and wealth alike. If the poor man and the rich man are both virtuous, then they are also alike, for the virtuous man does not become weaker in spirit because of what happens to him through poverty, nor does he in any way become arrogant on account of wealth. (4382)

Whatever the good man has in the way of possessions, he has the sense and the judgment to use them for good ends, and because of that he cannot go wrong: he shares them with whomsoever he should share them. If he is poor then he puts up with that gracefully, without complaining and without suffering: that demonstrates great dignity. (4390)

If the bad man becomes affluent, he does not share his wealth out equally. His wealth is certainly not common property: he wants to keep his wealth to himself. He uses for himself that which would be better shared.

We will all have enough if his sack is disgustingly full. How can we be freezing all the while he is well dressed? (4400)

If a good man becomes a lord, he humbles himself very much. That way his authority is good, if he does not become arrogant because of it. If he were to become at all overbearing, then his authority would cause him a great deal of trouble. (4406)

If a villain manages to become a lord, he no longer recognizes the people he previously knew well. He thinks to himself: "I should comport myself with pride: that is the proper and noble thing to do." He does not know what honor is: that one should notice for sure in his behavior, for if a man achieves honor he should honor his friends all the more. That is a sign of a noble spirit. The man who does this knows how to act with honor. However, if a man does not do this, it comes about as a result of his dishonor that someone who once was well disposed towards him now becomes his enemy. (4422)

If a good and virtuous man is powerful, know that he perpetrates no violence towards anyone as a result of his power, for he should just make every effort always to protect poor people wherever he may be. If a bad man who cannot see himself for what he is becomes powerful, he will wish to take due revenge for what people did to him many years earlier. He will avenge both good and bad: all he wants to do is behave violently, and he will often avenge himself on someone who is happy to serve him at some point. (4436)

If a respectable man gains a good reputation, I know that he will strive to behave better than people say. Truth means more to him than the false impression that people have. If a bad man gains a name for himself, he does not guard against boasting and becomes very full of himself: know that for the truth. (4446)

If a virtuous man is noble by birth, he will always make the effort to act in such a way that people call him noble more on account of his noble spirit than because of what his father does or because his ancestor behaved properly at some time or other. (4454)

If a scoundrel is highborn, he has no regard for other people and believes that whatever he does in the world is noble and really well done. This comes from his ignoble spirit. A good man does not rein in his desires when it is possible that he should rein them in: that is how vice strikes. A man is virtuous if he can raise himself above bad things at all times if he has the power to do so. If out of weakness he allows evil to prevail, then this is not the effect of virtue. (4470)

The man with a virtuous heart has five things that serve him well, for they open up his virtue both in youth and in old age. Riches reveal the power of a generous man if he is virtuous, and always betray his avarice if he is given to greed. Authority brings out the arrogance of a man if he is not virtuous and shows us his humility if he is good and kind. If a man is not virtuous, then power reveals his violence, but if he is virtuous his power reveals good judgment. If a man is virtuous his virtue can clearly show what the manifold vices betray in the man who is not virtuous. (4490)

I'm not going to talk about this anymore. You should just take note of this lesson and know for a fact that the respectable man turns everything that happens to him to the good, whereas the bad man will come to nought, whatever happens to him in this world, whether it be favorable or not. The lot of the pious man is salvation, whether he experiences joy or sorrow. (4500)

If good befalls the bad man it makes him arrogant, and if he does not get what he wants he goes round complaining all the time. The good man has an even disposition, whether he experiences good or bad. Why then does any man who knows anything about good things say that the bad man is blessed with good fortune? I often hear it said that the bad man fares better than the good man, but note that this is absolutely untrue. The good man always fares well, but if it seems to us that the bad man is better off, then I have not a shadow of a doubt that he is having a really hard time. A man is not doing well when he does not get his just deserts.[2] (4520)

If the bad man is faring well, know that he has not received his due, and since he has not received his due, you can be sure that things do not stand well with him, for if bad always befalls a bad man, he is not altogether unfortunate, I can tell you that for a fact. However, what if he fares well, so that he ought to be even more fearful? For, after all, the person who derives good from his evil has not received his just deserts. Since he has lost what is rightfully his, this should make him angry, for it should upset him to know that the trouble he has always deserved has been directed somewhere else. He has two misfortunes: the one that he is inclined to evil, the other that even though he sins like this all the time our Lord does not punish him with disaster. (4544)

Our Lord used to be inclined under the old law never to tolerate any sin but to punish there and then those who had perpetrated a sin. I know that I have read that some were killed and so lay dead, some were drowned and some became lepers, some were even burned alive. I know that they immediately gained absolution for their sins. At that time they were better off than we are now, for we can be sure that worse will happen to us in the next world since He does not punish us in this. Why are we less afraid than they were? That is utter foolishness, for we would be more afraid if we believed that the Supreme Judge was still alive, who avenged guilt in this way when people acted so forcefully against His grace. (4568)

If God were to punish an unjust man and if he knew how fortunate he was, that would be a happy day for him. If a man who behaves wrongfully ponders on the bad things he has done, he is a wretched man, even if he manages not to be afraid. On the other hand, if he is afraid that he will incur a great deal of misfortune, he will be plagued by calamity. So how can any man who understands anything about goodness say that someone who commits evil is more blessed than a good man who has done nothing that torments his mind? For if good befalls the good man he accepts it as he should, but if something quite different befalls him he is able to ignore it, for the time will come when it will be very useful to him. His goodness and his patience earn two kinds of blessedness for him: his good deed brings him a reward, his patience another crown. (4596)

Now you have taken into account that anyone who has any wish to be blessed with good fortune must derive it from his virtues. Thus anyone who is not virtuous is a wretched man, even if he had such great power that the entire world was subject to him. (4603)

At this point I wish to inform you—and do not doubt this one little bit—that anyone who does wrongful deeds is more wretched than the man to whom he has done such wrong, and I wish to give you a judgment about this that seems appropriate to me, and let me tell you that I think that these are his just deserts. If one of you were to think to yourself that one person were to do an injustice to another and you were at some point to become their judge, who, according to your decision, would have to make amends to the other? It seems to me that I would want the man who had perpetrated the violence to receive the penalty. Thus you should take good note that the one who is always committing the violence should be deemed more wretched than the one who is suffering it, for he who commits the violence is rendered guilty by his wickedness. So be sure of this: guilt is a great misfortune. The man against whom the violence is committed does not share the guilt, and so he should not by rights have any part in the misfortune either. He does not share in it, and you will see this when it comes about that the Judge who can certainly judge rightly stands in judgment. (4634)

A foolish man will probably say: "Our Lord is taking His time about it when He tolerates for so long a good man lying beneath the feet of a wicked man and having to serve him all the time." No: He is not taking too long. It does not help the wicked man, nor does it bother the good man, however long it happens in this world that God chooses to tolerate it, for He has many rewards which will come indeed to both of them when He dispenses them in the next world. If the one commits more and more evil, then his wickedness will bring him more and more unhappiness and misfortune: be sure of that. If the good and gentle man endures ever more affliction from people, then he will have even greater reward, for that adorns his crown. (4656)

Therefore, I wish to say that whatever happens in this world ought to happen in accordance with justice, for nothing happens without justice. Our Judge is so good that whatever He decrees or does Himself happens with justification: this I will declare with His grace. (4664)

Is it right that He permits us to sin so greatly? Yes, it is right, for our own natures have caused Him to do this. If it were not our fault He would not allow many things that happen. Thus you shall know that whether it seems to us true or false, whether it seems to us good or bad, whether He does it sooner or later, everything happens rightly and in His own good time. Since He allows good or ill to come to pass, or brings it about Himself, every man must know that nothing unjust can happen in this world: that I can certainly declare. (4680)

Now a man who does not understand me will very likely be saying: "Since everything happens justly, what one man does to another is not unjust. If he steals his property from him this cannot be unjust. According to this, if a man kills another man, you would have to say that it is a just action. Then, why should there be any court of justice if there is no injustice in the world? I do not think anyone should pass judgment if every deed is a good one." (4694)

Any man who talks like this does not understand much about what is right and what is wrong. What I am saying is very easy to understand: God sees the intention better than any man. If a man behaves correctly, his action shall nevertheless be described as good or bad according to his intention. Often a man is killed who would be little mourned if it were done in the name of justice, but, in this case, a robber has killed him for his money. By this example you can see how the intention turns justice into injustice, for he who would have behaved very justly if he had done it in accordance with the law, has not behaved justly. Perhaps the dead man has received his just deserts, but I cannot say that the man who kills another man for his money has done the right thing. Indeed, I can say truly that a certain man has perpetrated a wrong, in that this same man has previously committed the sin through which, at another time, he became guilty of an even greater sin, or so I have often heard. Injustice has justly befallen him, that's easy to understand. As I see it, justice comes quite rightly to the one who is at the receiving end or the one who perpetrates the act. Now you can see clearly from this that everything that happens can be said to happen justly and that even so judgment should be passed on him who does not do whatever he does out of goodness. To be sure, it was just that Absalom did not wish to leave his father in his kingdom, for David had done several things against God, and this made him a source of mockery by his son. Then, later, his son was slain on account of his sins. He did not exercise justice for the sake of justice and so he incurred the judgment of God.[3] (4746)

To be sure, we could build a church from such materials and that would
be evil and a sin. The intention always gives a name to deeds: it bears pre-
cisely the name of the deed, that's the truth. Deeds are good or evil accord-
ing to the intention that one has. You should know, too, that a man has not
bestowed his charity well if he knows that a man is drunk and promptly
gives him wine. Whatever happens with base intention in the world nowa-
days is not good. (4760)

Can it be called injustice when the devil harries a man with his power?
No, it is actually very just, for our Lord only permits that which is just. I ven-
ture to say [of the devil] that only that which befalls us justly can befall us
from him, for our Lord does not permit [anything else]. God often grants
him power over a man who has committed evil. We can certainly see many
examples of this, if anyone wants to. It also happens that He grants him
power over a man, but, to be sure, not without good cause. Anyone who
wishes to discover why God performs so many miracles is not wise. Yet we
can understand that the good man fares better if God does not prevent
the devil from putting his constancy to the test. Look how well it went for
Job, for he recognized that he had the favor of God at the time that he was
enduring torment through no fault of his own. Then He recognized his
constancy which previously He had not properly recognized as genuine.[4]
Thus no one should say that God allows the devil to do things unjustly.
(4794)

Gregorius, that holy man,[5] about whom a great many good deeds are
known, for whatever he said he spoke with the tongue of God, says that the
power of the devil is not evil. He even says that it is good, but that his inten-
tion is always evil, or so he says. Now see that his power is good, inasmuch
as he inflicts damage with it when God permits him to do so. Moreover, his
wickedness provides much assistance to good people: whatever the wicked
man does sharpens up the spirit of the good man. Thus you should know
very well that our Lord also allows a wretched man to have power, for then
the good man will be even more blessed if an injustice is done to him. The
evil man only ever harms someone who is himself evil. If he perpetrates
an injustice against a good man he thereby increases that man's goodness.
(4818)

If there were no unjust people I think that a person would be blessed
today who otherwise would probably not be. I'll tell you one thing, too: if it
were not for evil people, St. Paul could be alive today and not be slain. He
need never complain about it, for the man who killed him freed him from
great distress.[6] (4828)

According to what I have said, everybody can probably understand that
nothing that happens in the world happens without good cause. Perhaps
some man or other who is not very sensible will say: "I think that it is right

that a good man should always have everything he wants. On the other hand it seems to me that a bad man should never have what he desires. In that way they would both have their just deserts." But no: what happens is much better, if you understand correctly. A good man and a bad man should be alike in that in this world both good and bad should befall them, for the good man and the bad man should in their hearts have both hope in God and fear of Him: that is His will and His command. The man who at all times experienced what he enjoyed and what he desired could be devoid of fear, for he would believe he had the grace of God. Otherwise, however, no one has the wit to know whether God loves him or whether he is so guilty that he will die without the grace of God. Whosoever at all times experienced things that he was reluctant to endure would probably abandon all his hope. Believe me, this is the truth. Who is after all so wise that he can know what will happen to him in that other place? Happiness and suffering are common to it, so we should know that a person cannot know [what will befall him]. Still, someone or other will probably say that it seems strange to him that God allows someone who has not transgressed to live so wretchedly and allows someone who dissipates his life every day to live with such joy. I would like to answer him like this: no one can live in this world so completely without sin that he would not sin at some point. Therefore, however good a man is, it is right that for a time in this world he does penance for his sins, for afterwards he will have endless joy evermore. Whatever suffering is inflicted on him here will not trouble him then, if it happens, be sure of that. In fact I would like to say more about this: if a good man were to be hard-pressed the whole of his time in this world, he should not resent it, for afterwards he will be accorded happiness without end. (4892)

On the same subject I would say to you that the bad man cannot experience too much good in this world. I dare to say of him that such anguish will befall him in the next world that this world will seem absolutely nothing to him. There is no man so wicked that he has not done something that is perhaps good, and so let him have in this world for a short time what he wants, for much suffering will come to him. If he is happy all the time he is here, take note that he will think nothing of it when he leaves this joy behind him. (4908)

The good man experiences happiness in this world, for both here and in the next world he should fare well on account of his goodness. Thus I can also say for a fact that if bad things happen to him, this is so that in the next world he will nevertheless fare better. Things go badly for the bad man in order that he may improve himself, but if he does not improve, know that it will go worse for him in the next world. However, if he should get to know good fortune in this world, I have told you often enough that it is meant to befall him here but that he will never fare well in the next world. (4922)

In this regard, as I have said, it shall be known that blessedness and misfortune and whatever else happens does not happen without just cause, for whatever contributes positively is good, and fortune and misfortune do that. Misfortune is good for the bad man: in time it makes him a better person. However, even if it does not improve him, it is good, for it befalls him justly and justice is good, no matter what suffering it causes him. However, if fortune comes to him, I have told you that that is not a bad thing either, and, if he is happy all the time, that nevertheless causes him to be unhealthy at a later date. I have also said often enough that fortune and misfortune are both good for the good man. Misfortune serves to strengthen his resolve, and good fortune rewards him, that is true. Moreover, I have declared that nothing that happens in this world happens without good cause. No one knows for sure why he is visited by both fortune and misfortune, whenever that occurs. Consequently one should never be without great apprehension when God casts either fortune or misfortune upon us. Every wise man should make the effort to ensure that his misfortune in no way leads to eternal suffering, and he should also have the sense to understand that his fortune is the start of eternal blessedness, and thus he will have conducted himself in an appropriate fashion. (4962)

I have spoken of this and have informed you that fortune is a good thing for the good man, but that it is sometimes useless for the bad man, since, if he desires injustice, it does him a great deal of harm, for he can better execute his evil desires, be sure of that. Misfortune behaves in a similar fashion, know that for the truth. Misfortune is always good for the good man, and very useful too. That is not the case with the bad man, for if it does not make him a better person, it is completely useless to him: take my word for it. Look, this is how it happens: when the thresher breaks down the corn, it separates the wheat from the chaff. The bad man is often put out by things that are very good for the good man. (4984)

You should not take it amiss if I have not told you absolutely everything about why fortune and misfortune befall one man or another, for a man ought to speak only about those things he really knows about, and no man is so wise that he knows everything about how this or that happens. Such a man, I think, is not alive today, for who can know the thoughts of God which He alone possesses? Therefore any man who cannot understand why this or that happens should not believe that it does so without justification, and in addition he should be aware that God can judge everything properly. However, if a man does not understand why this man is always unfortunate and that one fortunate, what does it matter? It has all happened with justification, that's for sure. If I am not so wise as to know why sweet food suits the sick man well and why another man should, according to the nature of his sickness, rightly eat sour food, I would be behaving very wrongly if I were to say that the doctor does not know what he is doing. The master often acts in such a way that his squire does not know why he does it. Is he not a foolish man who thinks he can judge why God does so much good to one man and inflicts suffering on another? Know for a fact that anyone who wants to discover all that has set his sights too high. (5026)

As I have said, we do not know why one sick man wants sweet food and another insists on sour, and we wish to know why this one has so much, the other even more. We say "If this one had that, he would be better off. God has performed wondrous things by letting the good man live in poverty while the scoundrel is rich. God ought not to do that." This shows our stupidity. When the doctor causes us pain by opening up our wounds, we do not dare to say at that point that he is doing something bad. We leave him alone to do what he wants and do not dare to complain much. How dare any man complain about Him who can heal every soul according to how He should heal it? Many a man is of the opinion that affluence is not good for him and that he would become foolish if he were rich. Another man is different from him in desire and disposition, and for him wealth is a positive thing. For a third man disease is always very useful, for he might easily be too full of himself if he were to be like the healthy person. Then again the fourth person always thinks it good if he is really healthy, since he applies his good health at every turn to good deeds. All this is well known to God who does only what He should do. (5066)

Consequently, no one should be inclined to say that God does anything but what He should justly do, for anyone who might presume to know people better than God [knows them] would be a fool, be sure of that. Will anyone who speaks about it not presume to say that God should grant blessing to this one, joy to that one and harm to the other? Certainly, God knows well enough to whom He should grant an unhappy or a happy life. God always heals us according to our malady. If we do not wish to consider it good if He heals our minds and if we were to suggest that He could do it better, then we could easily drive the noble Physician from our hearts and never again acquire one with such good training. (5088)

A doctor who is well versed in healing often heals a sick man with thirst, with hunger, and with fire. He binds him to a wall; he cuts him and pricks him very sharply. He tugs another man's beard and hair, because he does not want him to sleep too much. In another case, he finds a way to enable the man to sleep better, and he does not let him go hungry. We can see exactly how it happens, and our Lord acts in the same way when He ministers to our hearts. The one He heals with happiness, the other with sorrow. He heals each one of us at a certain time and according to our sickness. (5106)

Therefore, every man who can comprehend what good is should con-

sider good all that our Lord visits upon him, for if he considers it good, you
shall know that that same man has no need to complain about anything
that happens to him in this world, for great blessing is coming to him. If,
however, he feels that what God does with him is bad, then know for sure
that he has much misfortune. (5118)

On this matter you can also be aware that no one should be afraid,
for whoever can bear his misfortune without great suffering can never go
wrong but will turn it all to good. (5124)

If you have understood me correctly, then you will have gathered that
the virtuous man never incurred any harm from man or woman, for, as I
have written and as I am writing, whatever wrong is done to him does not
injure him, but rather he finds it good. Some man is probably saying: "I
can easily be harmed, if someone does an injustice to me, in that I turn my
back on virtue and become immoral: in that way I have been harmed. Vice
deprives me of the kingdom of God, and that will surely harm me." But I say
that I have never witnessed that this happened to a good man, for in that
case virtue would be inconstant, whether joy or sorrow banished it. No one
can have the power to cause a virtuous man to abandon his virtues, whether
he is old or young. If anyone robs him of his property, he does not affect his
virtuous heart; if anyone deprives him of his gains, he still does not affect
his mind. In truth, no one but he himself can take from him the reality of
his virtue and his manliness: that is easy to comprehend, for what is inside
one is never overcome by the external. He who deprives me of what I am
inflicts harm on me: make sure you take good note of that. If I am a virtu-
ous man, I can certainly bring harm upon myself if I become a scoundrel,
but another person cannot make me worse. Thus it is true what people say,
that no one can harm anyone but he himself. I am talking about real harm,
and in that respect no one can harm another person. I cannot harm anyone
unless his own lack of virtue helps me to do so. If he is bad he can easily
be harmed. If the moat is close to the wall, the wall will collapse of its own
accord. (5174)

It has been brought home to us through the case of Job that all of this
can come about, for whatever the devil did against him he did with the pur-
pose of leading him into wrongdoing.[7] However, he was not successful in
this, for whatever God chose to inflict upon him he accepted as was proper.
Now you can see that no one's power can harm the virtuous man, not even
the devil's tricks: the person who inflicts the harm upon him suffers all the
harm himself. Anyone who examines it perceptively [can see that] the only
person to receive the harm is the one who inflicts it. You can see this in
the case of Cain, who out of foolishness slew Abel and inflicted great harm
upon himself, for Abel arrived at the place where he is very glad to be.[8] Now
be aware at this time that we can say before the judgment seat of God that

something we never dealt with correctly is causing us consternation, given
that no one can harm us and that Job did not deviate from the proper path,
for he was not led astray by him who worked so hard to trap him and who
knows so much and can do so much that he has more tricks than all the fish
have bones. Since Job was not forewarned and had neither heard nor read
either the old law or the new, how can anyone force us to turn our backs
on virtue or on God Himself, when we have His commandments both in
the old and in the new scriptures? We cannot be dissuaded. No teaching
can improve us if we avidly pursue wrongdoing. Now I know that nothing
can help the man without virtue unless he is inclined to wrestle with it and
wishes to help himself, in which case our Lord will swiftly come to his aid,
just as we have read of Mary Magdalene,[9] who had long lived in a state of
sin. Anyone who does not help himself will always be a scoundrel. That is
what we read of Judas who remained in a state of sinfulness.[10] Pharaoh was
often tempted and would not change his mind.[11] Nineveh was immediately
converted when Jonah was sent there.[12] (5230)

Now you maintain that the virtuous man can never be harmed and that
someone who is laden with vice can never really be helped. I would like to
provide you here with examples of this, from both ancient and modern
times. What help was it to the Israelites that they were better ruled than any
other race? It is written even today that God gave them what they desired
and that they did what they ought never to have done, for they fashioned
idols contrary to the commandment of God and Moses. How did it come
about that the three young people, Shadrach, Meshach and Abed-nego
remained so long in heathendom without guidance?[13] In our youth we are
not amenable to persuasion, for [after all] no one diverted these children
from virtue either with gentle means or harshness. What use was it to Judas
that Christ always treated him so well? Neither by the teaching of Christ,
nor through His miracles did he wish to move his heart in the slightest
way so that he might abandon his vices. He was a damned scoundrel. What
did it matter to Paul, that he never saw Christ in this world? For, once he
had received His commandments, he never transgressed against them and
because of that he is today in the presence of God. What did it matter to
him that he suffered misery, since he escaped eternal suffering? What did
poverty matter to Lazarus? What use was wealth to the rich man? Wealth
and poverty are of no consequence to us, if we do good, for Lazarus has
gained the eternal kingdom, while the rich man is surely burning in hell.[14]
Why should a man be dismayed by imprisonment, since the lion's den did
not bother Daniel?[15] If he was virtuous in heathendom, no one's wicked
rule can dismay us. Women will leave us alone, if Joseph could defend him-
self, as we read.[16] No trouble can afflict the good man, since death did not
trouble Abel.[17] (5278)

Whatever causes us harm or disgrace is called vice, but none of these can harm the good man, for vice which inflicts damage does not reside within him. Since nothing harms the good man he may rest assured, and a long time seems short to anyone who is always secure. Someone who must always be afraid never has any rest, and a brief hour seems long to him: that comes about as a result of vice and sin. Thus you should know that the bad man must inevitably be a coward, whereas the good man is also a brave man, since nothing can harm him. The good man fears only God, and [is anxious] that he may better obey His commands. Indeed, the good man and the bad man fear God in different ways. The bad man is afraid of the Judgment of God, but the good man is not so concerned about it, for he will be crowned in that world, while the bad man will be mocked. The one is afraid of what he is to receive, the other is afraid about avoiding it. The fear of good men is sweetened by love, as they have discovered. The fear of bad men is seasoned throughout with bitter gall. The fear of good men stems from virtue, while that of evil men stems from vice. The fear of good men provides a sense of security, while the fear of evil men manifests itself in toil and tribulation. The evil man fears all manner of things, while the good man fears only the power of God. (5316)

Why should a good man fear anything? For I have shown that nothing that happens can dismay the good man. Even if he is not wealthy, he is rich in spirit, and so his virtue shines forth more brightly, if he is careful: know that for a fact. For whoever in his poverty shuns ill gain thinks that it would probably not matter to him if he were a rich man.[18] (5328)

Nor should a good man be afraid of what happens to him through sickness, for if this man becomes ill, his spirit immediately becomes more healthy, for he is patient, regardless of what befalls him at any time. Sickness is good for the good man, for by this means his spirit is strengthened. (5336)

I venture to give the opinion that no good man should fear that anyone will banish him, for that which he loves above all must remain with him. Anyone who does not abandon his virtue is always at home, however far away his house may be. If he does not have virtue and goodness and courtesy in his heart, know that he is in fact in exile, even if he is always at home. (5348)

A good man need not fear imprisonment, if it comes to him. What does it matter if he is captured? After all, in his heart and mind he is better off than a wicked man would be. Wherever he is and however he might have his way, he is subject to misfortune. The good man is always blessed. What does it matter if he is taken captive? For in his heart and mind he has in terms of virtue and goodness whatever he wants in the world. He has plenty of things to be happy about, and even if his prison is not very beautiful, his spirit is adorned with a crown. Since his house is beautiful inside, what does it matter for the time being if his prison is not beautiful, for whosoever sees the shining light of virtue within his heart is indifferent to the darkness of his prison cell. (5370)

Now a man who does not know what riches virtue can bestow upon a good man is probably saying: "How can anyone live without fear when someone wishes to do something to him?" Anyone who says this has not made much of an effort to see what virtue is accustomed to bestow upon the man who will live according to its tenets. And even though I have not been put to the test myself, I do know for a fact that any man who is just and virtuous should not fear the power of death too much. Moreover, you should take good note: since he does not have to fear death, why should he fear any other privations? (5386)

Then you may say: "Perhaps someone will kill him." So what? He has the sense to know that he must die, for that is the way of the world, to receive us in pain and take leave of us through death. One death will bring him to the same place as any other, and however the virtuous man may die you should know that he will gain thereby. (5396)

And then you say: "Someone deals him many deep wounds." And I say that whoever dies that way can complain as little about forty wounds as about four, for one can die just as quickly from one wound as from ten, as we have witnessed often enough, but if death comes more quickly to him, then he is put out of his agony more quickly. (5406)

Then you say: "He will not be buried." So what if that is so? The sky can perfectly well cover a man who can be covered by a stone. It bothers the man a lot while he is alive if people don't want to bury him, but the body does not feel any pain when the man is physically dead. It does not worry him if they cast him aside, and if, as is likely, it comes about that he is cremated, what harm does that do? He will not be worse or better off. Has he not, after all, attained from God that this should happen to him?[19] (5420)

Why should a good man be afraid of dying? For know this: death helps him out of enormous trouble. Whatever the master gives his squire, he should keep it, that's only right, and the master should give it to him whenever he chooses. Whether we live for a long or a short time, every man eventually dies. The virtuous man is just as happy to die sooner. After all, he will be better off if he gets there quickly, be sure of that.[20] (5432)

Any man who comes into this world should certainly have the sense to think that it is right and proper that he should also go out of it. A man travels around the whole time he is on this earth, but one should know that when one dies one travels home. He should not be too much afraid that pain is coming to him, for the time will pass very quickly for him if he has a serious illness. If, on the other hand, his sickness is a mild one, he can well put up with it for the time being. Either he will leave the sickness behind him or the sickness will pass. One should certainly fear the sickness which does not leave a man and which the man cannot shake off once it has taken hold of him and which is so severe that no one wants to be near him.[21] That sickness one should always fear and it is found in the depths of hell. (5456)

A man should pay no heed to how long he has to live, but he will do better to care *how* he lives. Every man certainly has the sense to know that he must pass over, regardless of whether he does good or bad, but the man who behaves correctly has a better journey. He should not greatly fear death, but if he has not lived well in this world he should fear more the journey that he is to make after death. Nor should he take any notice of where he dies: wherever he does penance for his sins is good. He should prepare his mind and heart to make proper recompense, wherever he is, for he should pay back what he has been given. Wherever the man happens to be living, there indeed he can also die if he does what he should do. There is a path in every land that always leads to God. There is a path in every land that always leads to Hell. Wherever a man is meant to die, there he will die, whether as a good man or a bad man. No matter where he dies he will immediately be sent to rest or restlessness. However, a man incapable of understanding more deeply often says: "If I do not die at home, I shall probably not receive so much honor at my death as I deserve: that's a problem." (5492)

I tell you that a good man should not concern himself with that, for however he comes into God's presence, he is honored by His commandment. However, those who all their days have been blinded by their arrogance cannot see what will happen to them as a result of this at their death. Why should they bother that people honor them more when they die than they do another man? For that is all part of it, too. (5504)

They should make their graves beautiful, because they do not have the jeweled crown: even though they are rather common, their stones are specially chosen. He who must journey downwards often makes for himself a lofty tomb. He whose tomb is so imposing now is probably in the depths of hell. He whose tomb is splendid here is perhaps wandering about in darkness. But the person whose tomb in this world is modest is probably elevated by now. (5516)

Whatever happens to his body cannot perturb the dead man, unless he has forfeited the grace of our Lord by his guilty behavior. If he does not enjoy His grace, it will not help him much if people crowd around his grave, when they lower him into it. The honor that people accord him then and that, in his arrogance, he loved while he was alive will then be of no consequence to him at all. (5528)

Regarding this, I want to offer a piece of advice: that during his lifetime a man should strive upwards, no matter what his tomb may be like. Even if his tomb is not radiant he can manage without that, provided he ensures that he comes towards the light. His thoughts, his speech and his actions should achieve for him the host of angels: that will do him more good than friends, be sure of that. A friend often abandoned in the ditch the man whom the angel raised up. His friends may leave him behind, but I can write it down as a fact that at that same time he is with the holy angels. (5546)

Let me give a word of advice here. If a man's friend is no longer alive, he should grieve in moderation and allow him to go gently on his way, for whatever friends we may have here, let us accept that we must leave them behind and lose them so that we may gain them. If anyone can understand this sensibly, one must suffer on account of one's friends, and yet the suffering must be of such a kind that we master it, rather than it us. The person whose sorrow dominates him suffers too much. He can never be happy. If anyone is willing to understand this correctly: we inflict much more injustice upon ourselves than death can bring to us when it deprives us of the life of a friend, for we dispense with many friends. If I do not wish to make someone my friend, then I have cast him aside, if you have understood me aright. If a man has lost his coat, let him not be angry but quickly throw another round himself, for if he goes away naked because of his grief at his loss, then he has lamented his coat too bitterly. Thus one should take the advice that if someone has lost a friend he should try and find another one who will suit him very well. (5578)

I'm trying to tell you that one should not mourn one's friends excessively, but on the other hand one should not allow one's friends to depart this life without lament. One should swiftly cease to grieve for the virtuous, for you can believe me that they are much happier in the next world. Because of that a good man approaches his death without great apprehension, for then all his trials and tribulations are over. It is the wicked man who should be lamented, for his suffering begins with his death. (5591)

Although I have said that one should quickly let one's friends rest in peace, one should not understand that to mean that if it perhaps comes about that someone has lost his friend he should be so foolish as to go off straightaway and play, for it would be too much if he did that. He can leave the flowers where they are for a while, that's my advice: a garland does not suit him at all. And he should also steer clear of dancing, jousting, and playing stringed instruments. That's what I want to advise. (5604)

What does it look like if a man who has lost his wife immediately goes off and marries another? He should rather have left it for a year. A woman should know similarly that she is not doing something good if she takes another husband before a year is up: it looks very bad for her. In any case what one should do is clearly written in the law. It says there that if a woman has not been without a husband for a year she will forfeit her good name. She will not inherit her husband's estate if she behaves in an improper way. And, moreover, one should take good note that, given that one should refrain from lawful marriage for a year, it is absolutely wicked to seek out some dark corner and do something outside marriage. (5626)

When one is languishing in the darkness, one can easily say at that time: "Now no one can see me. What could happen to me since, whatever I do, there is no one around at the moment to know about it?" Now, tell me: do you not know it yourself? Alas, woe to him to whom that happens, that he regards as negligible the witness who is actually standing so close to him! There is one thing that a person should believe: that the time will come when every man must acknowledge his misdeeds, when he comes to atone before the Judge who knows absolutely everything about it. (5642)

I have said that I do not want anyone to mourn his friend excessively, for he is going to find him in the hereafter. Whoever is capable of grasping it sensibly should perceive that when we come into the next world we shall see all our friends. You may believe that. (5650)

I have often been asked about what I wish to tell you here, namely, whether one will recognize one's friends one day in heaven. Any wise man who gives some thought to this will certainly know for himself that one will recognize them there. If one did not recognize them there, there would be something lacking where nothing can be lacking. Where the light of day is always shining, how could something be hidden so that one could not recognize it? We should be lacking many things—I want to tell you this for a fact—if we did not recognize one another there. Know that there is no lack of blessedness there. Know also for a fact that one will without a shadow of a doubt recognize one's friend there. You should also truly believe that we shall even recognize those whom we have never seen, and that will be a source of joy for us. How should a man not recognize all the other people, when he sees Him and recognizes Him Who knows everything exactly? Through Him we shall see and recognize and distinguish everything that is in the world. One sees this through Him at all times. Everything that ever was or will be one can see exactly through Him. I wish to declare without a shred of doubt that whatever is useful for us to see, anyone who comes out of this world into that place will see through Him. (5690)

This is where my fourth discourse ends, but you will be hearing more from me.

BOOK V

I think I have been talking for a long time about how much joy virtue provides and how the virtuous man never experienced any misfortune. I have shown that he should not fear whatever befalls him by way of ill luck. Now I propose to demonstrate to you how virtues bring it about that one gets to heaven. Then I shall have proved that there is nothing so useful as virtue, if someone pursues it all the time. (5704)

For the person capable of perceiving it, there are two kinds of good, and two kinds of evil. The fifth [element] is made up of a group of tools,[1] and they are always the generator of evil. (5708)

The first [element] is called supreme goodness, for it does nothing but good. That is our Lord God. It is His wish and His commandment that whoever wishes to come into His presence should do the right thing. It is right that God should be thus called, for you should believe for a fact that whatever right one does emanates from the highest good. (5718)

The second thing is actually called good and these are, in truth, the virtues. Indeed I like to call them 'good,' for through the virtues many people go forward to the highest good, and know this: whoever behaves according to the virtues will certainly attain the highest good. (5726)

The first evil is the devil, for it is from him that whatever evil occurs in the world always emanates. He is not without his part in that. We can certainly call him the lowest form of evil, for on account of his great arrogance and because the highest good desires it, he should always be lower than any other form of evil. The second evil, this is true, is the host of vices, and I am quite justified in calling them evil, for they pave the way towards the worst form of wickedness and always bring us there. (5742)

The fifth element is both good and evil, or so my heart informs me. I am talking about the [following] six things: nobility, power, desire, reputation, wealth and authority. They are not entirely good, for in truth it can happen that an evil man possesses them. On the other hand, they are not altogether evil, for a good heart can often contain them. Thus they are both evil and good: it seems to me that whatever causes trouble and on the other hand helps a great deal should be called both evil and good. I have demonstrated by reference to the six things that neither the good nor the bad people may benefit from them, for harm comes to them because of them. Accordingly, they are evil and good, as is the heart of a man who is powerful and rich, and you can believe that for a fact. If anyone takes proper note of this, desire is rarely good, for it is deep inside the body and always leads to bad acts. If, however, you would let desire take over from your will, then it would accordingly be considered good and would reflect the man's intention. And so a person should reject it, for desire is nothing and yet can often improve a man who is able to withstand it. (5774)

These six things are the agents of the most despicable form of evil. He has the power at all times to pull the bad man down to where he himself is lying. Now pay good attention, as I propose to tell you how all this comes about. (5780)

Both my mind and my heart inform me that whatever can attain the highest good must in truth be specially chosen. The ladder that can reach up there must be very sturdy. The bricks that are placed in it must be absolutely perfect. The rungs must be unbroken and sound bricks must be selected. The ladder must be composed of virtues. If anyone thinks I am lying, let him say what is absolutely good, for if he does that he must declare in truth that the virtues are quite perfect, for there is nothing else in the world that is always absolutely good. Thus nothing can better attain the highest good, know that for a fact. What is heavy must be pulled down and cannot get up again by its own strength. Evil does not reach the goodness that has its spirit somewhere else. What is light always rises up. One good belongs with another, so it is also right and proper that one evil is always to be found with the other too. (5808)

Now you have heard precisely how a man should construct a stairway that can lead up to the highest good. Anyone who intends to climb up there must think very hard how he is to construct the stairway so that he can mount it properly. (5816)

Every step must be made completely of one virtue, that's my wish and my advice, too. Then, if one treads onto it, one can have a firm footing, but even so one should proceed with constancy. (5822)

Anyone who wishes to construct this ladder must also pay good attention that no vices are included, for, if that happens, be aware that it can certainly never attain the highest good. Indeed, night and day should never mingle with one another, nor have I ever heard that there was daylight around midnight, for the darkness would have the power to radiate brightness, which after all should not be. Likewise virtue, it is true, cannot fit together with the whole host of vices. Let the person who is to build the stairway that leads up to the highest good have such a pure spirit that there is no ugliness to be seen in those steps. Whatever material one uses for the stairway should be absolutely pure and good. (5846)

Now you have heard precisely which stairway should lead up to the highest good, and now my heart wishes to say which stairway always leads down to the greatest evil. A stairway constructed entirely of wicked things must lead to that place, and anyone who constructs that will receive a bad reward. The reward he will receive for his troubles will be pain and suffering. Whatever one does out of vice can never be good, so take my word for it that vice is thoroughly evil. Similarly, badness within any man's heart is not without vice which is always absolutely evil, so it rightly leads at all times to where the lowest evil lies. (5868)

In youth and in old age one fashions a stairway out of vice. This is rooted partly in this world and partly in the next. The rungs are all fashioned, it is true, of vices. Each vice takes its cue from the worst evil. The rungs are facing downwards, for everyone who treads on them is electing to fall down and never come up again. You should know that the man who cannot prevent himself from doing so soon comes to where the worst evil resides, for the man who sets his foot on this stairway must inevitably slip. One is always slipping down from there into the depths of hell. Alas, how swiftly one can come to where the bright day never shines! One does not get into heaven so easily. I think this comes about because something heavy drops down more quickly than it can rise again. A man's sins make him heavy, so that it is always easy for him to fall. If he wishes to climb up to the highest good he must have a constant heart. And you must believe me that he must labor to arrive there. However, the labor is nothing to us, if we manage to get there. In fact, it is only right that the person who is to experience such happiness should have to struggle. (5904)

Now I have told you enough about these two stairways. One of them takes us up to the highest good, but know that the other one tries at all times to take us down to where the worst evil resides. In truth, the one is composed entirely of virtues, the other of vices. Because of this, as I see it, vice is all evil, virtue all good. (5914)

Now I'll tell you what is always both good and evil. Those things which should confuse us and help us, too, are called good and evil. The devil's hooks do this, for he is better rewarded who always deports himself in such a way that he is not pulled back by the hooks to where the worst evil is lurking. On the other hand, know that whoever does allow himself to be pulled there has chosen the hooks to his lasting misfortune. They pull him towards great misery. These hooks are wealth, power, nobility, reputation, desire, authority. Know that a fool can go wrong on account of these six things: they easily pull him to where he is completely disgraced. Because of that they are the purveyors of the greatest evil. He has the power to pull a man who cannot protect himself to a place where he should not travel if he wished to choose the right path. Whenever a good man wishes to climb the stairway that is made up of many virtues, the hooks are always there and wanting to pull him back again so that he falls down onto the other stairway. When someone wishes to climb up to generosity and humility, authority and wealth quickly pull him down again: then he must fall down to greed and arrogance. Possessions say to the man who wishes to be generous: "You will become a complete nobody; a man is nothing without wealth." To the man who is humble, authority says: "You do not have the strength of a lord. You should be thoroughly ashamed," and this causes him to become arrogant. Whoever becomes arrogant on account of his honor will be viciously cut down by his honor. I have also surely heard that if a man wishes to come to the third rung, his nobility pulls him away, for you should know that any man who thinks he is noble will become envious because another man thinks he is better, be sure of that. Thus nobility always draws him away from love towards hatred. The man who hates what he should love is given to bad thoughts. If someone has arrived at the fourth rung, his power is always egging him on so that he cannot tolerate anyone and thus it jerks him from gentleness to anger, so that he has lost the battle. Whenever he wants to advance towards righteousness, his craving inflicts great damage on him. Anyone who wishes to follow his craving must turn his back on righteousness. Desire paves the way from right to wrong. The man who would aspire to truth must guard against the blows of fame, for if he is a famous man and enjoys being so, he will always be content to allow people to lie about him far and wide. He must abandon truth to falsehood and perjury, for he is not at all bothered about lying. Thus his reputation pulls him down from the stairway of virtue, so that he falls down on to the other stairway. He is very happy about this, even though he will not escape from suffering: I'm talking about the devil himself, for it is his strange custom to rejoice at the misfortune of people, even though he himself is suffering. Perhaps he thinks it will be better for him if evil and no good befall all of us, but he is deceiving himself completely. He does not burn any less because there is a man burning alongside him. If there are more of them in there, I believe the fire will always increase. The man who wishes to have a large fire puts plenty of wood on it. For this reason no man who can understand anything says: "Wherever I may go, I shall certainly find companionship," for he will not benefit by burning alongside other people. He will not be better for it, believe me. Even if he sees the others being killed, this does not take away his own suffering. His fears will simply increase if the others are hideously martyred. (6026)

I have rightly demonstrated that no one should believe that vice and arrogance will lead us to the highest good, for it must be goodness alone that rightly takes us there. I have also demonstrated very correctly that it is only vice and sin that always smooth the road to hell for us. If anyone cannot grasp this, I propose to demonstrate it another way, for I want everyone to have available the means to understand better. (6040)

You should know right now, that anyone who has got to heaven had to climb the stairway of virtue. If anyone thinks that I am lying, let him show that anyone ever arrived there without being completely virtuous. If he cannot show me that, then let this same man believe that neither in youth nor in old age can anyone enter there without virtue. How did Abraham get there? Through his obedience, that's the truth. Moses came to the highest good through his humility, Job through his patience, Phinehas because he was distressed that his people were breaking God's commandment.[2] How did Isaac come to God? In truth, through his chastity. How did Jacob come there? Because of his modesty. Enoch, too, was led there on account of his purity. Joseph let good hold sway over evil and came to the highest good. Look, they all came there, not because of a single virtue, that's true, but each one of them appeared better in respect of the virtue that I have just named to you, know that for a fact.[3] However, if anyone wishes to go to heaven, he must have these virtues, believe me: he has to possess them all, even if he does not possess them in full measure. (6074)

Every virtuous man possesses one virtue to a greater degree than the others. This is because we cannot possess all the virtues to perfection. Who can compare himself with God who has all the virtues in full measure? It is true that He was more obedient than the obedient Abraham, and He had greater humility than the virtuous Moses. He was more pure than Isaac; He possessed the simplicity of Jacob. And know for a fact that He was more patient than Job. Joseph was never able to avenge himself better on his enemies than He. Since He has all the virtues, know too that anyone who goes to Him must have many virtues. (6095)

Anyone who intends to go to hell must be wicked. Vices certainly have the power to deliver him right to the place where no good man should go. Whoever landed in the depths of hell save through wickedness and sin? Now, tell me, why did Nimrod[4] and Cain[5] come there, if not through wickedness and sin? Anyone who consistently commits evil shall by rights have evil befall him. We have often seen, too, that damnation frequently befalls him, and yet we do not improve ourselves because of that. (6110)

We believe that we can ascend to the highest good through wealth and material possessions. We believe that authority, noble birth, reputation, and power enable us to come to God. We are making a mockery of ourselves. You must believe for a fact that we are completely deluded. Nero would not at this very moment be languishing in the depths of hell if his wealth and his authority had been able to release him. He will not be taken out by those means, for even if someone were at this time to offer whatever material goods there may be in this world, the devil would not surrender a single soul that he has managed to secure for himself. Therefore no man should console himself with his wealth. (6130)

I have heard a man say something very foolish: "I can do just as I like, for I have so much wealth that I can always atone for my sins with almsgiving." Anyone who then goes off and sins will not be much helped by his offerings. God does not refrain from passing judgment according to a

man's wealth. After all, heaven and earth are all in God's hands: He does
not need anyone's possessions. Why would He, then, refrain from passing
judgment? He does not do it, God knows, not He. He is not one of those
judges who make wrongs into rights on account of masters or servants. He
does not act any differently than he ought to because of anyone's wealth.
However, you should know that one ought to make offerings in God's name,
but one should not pursue wicked ways and hope to buy one's way out with
God when one has perpetrated many an injustice, for then we would be
acting as though God were not wealthy enough and as though He did not
own anything, He who provides everything that brings us joy in this world.
(6161)

At this point I wish to inform you that the richest man who may ever
live can never give away so much that a poor man cannot give just as much
if he wishes to: I mean that it will be just as good for him, for God sees only
the intention that is behind it. If one man has ten thousand marks and
gives away one thousand for the sake of God, and another gives away one
penny of the ten pennies that he possesses, the latter has done just as well,
for he has surrendered one-tenth, too. If any man behaves according to his
means, God certainly deems that to be good. Whatever the poor man gives,
and the rich man, too, both are equally pleasing to God. If they give with
a pure intention, both seem good to Him. You should believe that a man
who never gained any wealth can in truth give away the whole world for the
sake of God. Whatever a person gives away from his heart, know for a fact
that he has given it away as if he were giving it out of his coffer: this God
demonstrates with an example. (6188)

Whereas King Solomon built God's temple, a poor woman had a greater
reward from Him than he, for she gave away more in her heart.[6] Look, one
thousand marks were weighed against one penny: the rich man gave much,
yet the poor woman with her little gift became his equal, for her heart was
very pure. Our Lord looks more closely at the intention than at any riches.
You must know that God always gives wealth to the one and poverty to the
other, and because of that he does not permit a man to suffer because
he is not rich but sees to it that this man is aided by his intention as that
one is [aided] by his wealth. You must know that the fisherman would not
have climbed so high if wealth were the condition for admission, for how
would he have acquired so much that he might purchase that kingdom to
which no kingdom can be compared?[7] If any man could buy it, then the
emperor Julian, who is burning for all eternity in the depths of hell, could
have bought it.[8] (6216)

Thus you should know full well that no one can console himself and
no one entertain the hope that his wealth can bring him to God: a host of
virtues must bring us there. The emperor Constantine was very rich, but he

was saved on account of his virtue, not his wealth. While he was of a mind to desire the deaths of the children, no one helped him out of his trouble, but when he was prepared to endure sickness before he would put the children to the sword, God very quickly came to his aid. Thus we should observe that he did not come to God on account of his wealth, since at no point could he survive because of his wealth, as we read in the books. So what brought him to God then? The fact that he heeded His commandments and that he became virtuous. On account of his virtues, God bestowed upon him the strength to come to Him, as we have often heard.[9] (6242)

Now I have told you clearly why one should love virtue, for the Lord of all of us loves virtue very much. Any man who does not wish to follow our Lord should be thoroughly ashamed of himself, but the man to whom God has granted power and honor should be even more ashamed if he does not choose to follow the Lord who has bestowed much honor upon him. (6252)

Our Lord often dispenses honor to someone who brings great shame upon himself, thus preventing him from becoming a lord. It has indeed become apparent that he does not wish to follow the Lord who bestows much authority upon us. Since he deprives his Lord of what is rightly His, he cannot by rights receive justice from his servant. So how can that same man rightly be the lord of a land, if he has behaved so badly that he cannot rightly have justice from his own servant? (6266)

Anyone who exercises his authority in such a way that he does not observe justice at all does not deserve his authority. Moreover his power inflicts violence upon us. (6270)

Anyone who sets out to separate us from God inflicts great violence upon us. This is the action of an unjust lord: he puts a great distance between ourselves and God through the power of his wickedness, for he makes us wicked, too. God knows that there are too many lords—I'll tell you this for a fact—who make us wicked with the power of their own wickedness. (6280)

How is it that nowadays one does not find so many virtuous people as one used to find? I can tell you straightaway. The lords were virtuous and the power of their virtue so pleased the other people that they behaved virtuously both in youth and in old age. Now they have changed their ways completely and we must go along with that, too. (6290)

Every man likes to behave in such a way that people treat him better. In the old days virtuous people were better treated than today and because of that they strove hard for virtue. Nowadays vice is better treated than virtue, that's a fact, and so we are all headed in that direction. (6298)

If a decent man comes to the court, the lord does not wish to look at him, but if a villain comes there, he will not depart without honor. If a good man were at that court and then a money-lender came along, people would regard the worthy man as a nobody. To be sure, when the wicked lord sees the money-lender, the respectable man must fade away. Thus a man can easily be thinking: "If I could be as rich as that man people would respect me too. As it is, people think I'm a fool, no matter how decent and wise I am. I must turn my thoughts and my heart towards profit. I can see well enough that the man who has wealth can do what he likes. People are happy to listen to his advice. I must become a villain, since I'm not going to get anywhere by being good." (6320)

Look, that's the fault of the masters. I should not be out of favor with them because I say this: I just want them to behave better. (6324)

Where are Erec and Gawain, where are Parzival and Iwein? I don't know that they are anywhere, and this has come about because we do not have Arthur in this country. If he were alive, we could immediately find plenty of knights in the world who were so decent and just that people could call them Iwein, or so it seems to me and so I believe. Indeed, I want to say to you that many knights could still be found who through their virtues could easily take the place of Erec.[10] (6338)

So where are they hiding, that they are nowhere to be found? The virtuous people are all hidden away, that's for sure. Now anyone who is not hidden is always being abused. There are so many bad people that the good person does not wish to show himself. Know that the virtuous man is always an owl to the bad men. If they were to see him some time, they would all shriek at him and trample him with their feet. Now see whether he needs to hide! If they want to find the lords, then I tell you that they should respect virtuous people, for perhaps they would even today find those who were worthy of being respected all the time. The wicked people would desist from their wickedness if their lords were to harm them. A man would often do what he ought to do if he were to be respected because of it. The lords can easily see to it that people do what they ought to do. How can they do this? By respecting the good people more than the bad. Know for a fact that they would abandon their wickedness altogether. However, if that does not happen, then they are not without fault. (6370)

What I have been saying about knights one can also understand in relation to the clergy. Not one wishes to strive for education. Now, why do they act like this? They would be treated all the better. If they wanted to acquire an education, they would not be able to live well according to it while their master spends his life striving for nothing but vice. Every man must travel in the footsteps of his lord's vices if he expects anything from him, or he will give him nothing. Why should a man go to school since he can easily become corrupt? Who is going to read about this in school? One can learn delinquent behavior well enough at home, so that one can achieve a parish and a stipend at court. Look how well the bishops behave, whoever they may be, when they assign churches to people who live like that! Look, in that way they have arranged it so that no one loses any sleep through studying. Any man who heaps praise on his lord, no matter what he does, may sleep whenever he wants. He is courtly and just, and he should receive his due. A man who can say "Yes, my lord," may well be a decent man. Take note: that has made all the priests lackadaisical, that's a fact, so that they cast their knowledge aside, since they achieve little by it. You see, that is all the fault of the lords, and I say this by their leave. (6408)

Where now is Aristotle? Where are Zeno and Parmenides, Plato and Pythagorus? Where, too, is Anaxagorus?[11] Know this: it seems to me that if Aristotle were alive today no other king would accord him the honor that Alexander did while he was alive. (6417)

Anyone who himself wishes to strive for honor loves honorable people too. Wise and decent people do not receive praise and renown today. The fool has devoted his power to greatly denigrating the wise people. There are so many more bad people that the good people are as nothing. The bad man is valued, and this has come about because the tall pine trees have landed in the swamp because the moss has climbed up over the mountain. Now the felled trees must lie flat on the ground. This happened a long time ago and since then the world has been without justice and without honor. This has happened because people show favor to the wicked. False gems have invaded gold and rings, and precious stones have been forced out. The stools which were supposed to stand under the benches have climbed up on to them, and for a long time the bench has been standing on the table. (6442)

The foolish man has the tongue of a wise man. The wise man cannot offer advice. The young man pushes his way in front of the old man. The cow has acquired the tongue of a man and thinks it can actually speak. Every man should hold his tongue and allow the cow to speak: that's become the right way to behave. The lord should accord honor to the servant. Knights should go on foot: good-for-nothings must ride. The holy preacher said that he saw the rogues on horseback while the lords had to go on foot.[12] This one should understand to mean that the wicked are respected and the good terribly demeaned. And now all this has come to pass. Why should it be like this? Now the nonvirtuous have gained the upper hand. How? Have you not heard me say that the mountain trees have sunk into the swamp? Understand this: when the moss was down in the swamp and the stools were standing on the ground, and when we had high tables and low benches, the world was in a better state. Then the master and the servant behaved as befitted their station. Everyone had a tongue: both the old and the young. Cattle and man had what they were meant to have. Both the wise and the foolish received their rewards and their penalties respectively. The precious stones had to be in the gold rings, and the false stones were despised everywhere. You see, then all was well with the world. Anyone who wishes to be upright in the world and not diminish his honor should love wise folk. (6488)

One cannot achieve anything which is constant without common sense. One should love good sense and the person who possesses it. That is my wish and my advice. Alexander was very happy when a wise guest came to him. He very much liked wise people, and because of that he is still talked about today. His tutor Aristotle showed him everything that he should do to achieve grand results. How could that man not succeed who has wise people about him and only does what they advise him to? Nowadays the lords do not do this, and as a consequence harm often comes to them. (6504)

If the lords were to strive harder after honor, they might justly be of great assistance to those who wanted to go to school. Know for a fact that in the youth of a man who cannot attend school good sense and virtue often come to grief. If it would help, my advice would be that people should assist the schoolboy who wants to go to school and learn. Regrettably, people do not do this, for since the lords have been disinclined to see wise people about them, I can declare for a fact that they are not going to watch out that they make wise people. (6520)

I am referring to the lords in general, but you should know for a fact that I have said this more in respect of the bishops who have received from God the distinction of fulfilling His commandments and obeying His law: for this has been bestowed on them from on high. If we are in any way lacking in faith, this probably comes about because we do not have preachers. Therefore, anyone who would be a good bishop should see to it at all times that, whenever he is giving away something he no longer needs, he should be giving it to the man who would like to go to school. You see, it would be good if he did that, for what he himself does not do, the other man could well achieve if it were perhaps suggested to him. (6540)

Look how the bishop who cannot himself preach has guarded his rights and his wealth too, and, if he knows of a man who likes to learn, he does not offer him any help. Do you know how that comes about? He just wants his priests to be ignorant, as he is, and that is the truth. A blind man does not behave like this, for a man who cannot see always likes to have someone who can see with him. The bishop gives what he should be giving to those who have a poor life at school to those around him who are greedily striving for gain, and he takes absolutely no notice of what is happening to the poor fellow at school. (6558)

Note how those who have received the law of God observe that law, so that those who seek to acquire God's law come to grief in the schools, and the lord gives whatever he desires to the man back home who is always lazing about. The former is content with little, the other with much. The former is happy with little, because he is so hungry that he cannot study the whole day long. However, much harm comes to the latter, too: if more and more is bestowed upon a fool, he strives all the more for possessions and does not care how he is living. Look how well the lord apportions what he should apportion justly! He showers possessions on the one fellow and allows the other to be completely ruined without a proper education, even though he would be quite capable of acquiring it. Is it not, then, his fault that this one and that one both become scoundrels? (6580)

Now I'm going to tell you more about the great trouble that befalls good folk. Once they leave school, people at court treat cattle better than them. Anyone who is more wealthy must always be more highly valued. You should believe it as a fact that this has made knowledge and intellect very displeasing to us. We are all striving for profit. Look, that is the fault of the lords. If they wished to have the grace of God, they should treat every man according to what he can do, and according to his virtuous disposition, and according to what he does. Then we should all be aspiring to virtue in youth and in old age. We should be striving as eagerly after intellectual matters as after profit. Then there would be more loyalty and truth in Christendom. (6602)

It would be my advice that if the lords wished to do so, they should determine who in their land are endowed with fine intelligence and provide them with counsel and assistance, and be supportive of learning at all times, for the world should be well governed by wise people. (6610)

Why was the world in a better state in the past than it is now? Let me tell you: then people were devoted to virtue and good sense. Now every man is struggling to see how he can gain more material things. These days the man who lazes around doing nothing receives as much respect as the man who is occupied the whole time with studying. (6620)

Any man who is incapable of good deeds is idle. If it comes about that a man does not strive for virtue then he is redundant. No matter what else he does, it cannot be good. The man who can achieve anything good is not idle. Understand this: anyone who all the time does bad things is more idle than the one who does nothing. If someone achieves wealth by wicked means then he has achieved it entirely through idleness. Now know that one must aspire in the following manner. (6634)

Look: because we see that good people do not get anywhere, we set out to be wicked. However, my advice would be not to abandon virtue just because we do not benefit much from it. But look, that cannot be. If the sunshine turns dark, how can then the moon be bright? If it were ever to come about that there were no water in the sea, it would be a strange thing if the streams were full of running water. I do not think that could happen. How could it ever happen that the one being led can fare better than the one leading him? It can happen, but not for the better, I might add. (6652)

Even a foolish standard-bearer can ensure that an army performs better, but if a man cannot provide proper leadership he is likely to lead many men to disaster. The foolish lord often leads his knights into the thick of the enemy, and if they are taken captive there they immediately do more damage to their lord than to their captors, because it is he who always baits the others. The lord is better protected, but you should also know that the others are not neglected. It is only right that the lord who has led us into dire straits should fare worse, and we are bathed with him too. (6668)

However, our baths are very different. A chair is brought in, a blazing fire, so that the master can sit down. What can I do if this harms him? We do not have the same chair: *we* are sitting on a warm stone. Boiling water, pitch, and sulphur are poured down over the lord's head, and his skin and flesh are very thoroughly rubbed off him, until he is white, and then the hot bath is poured over his bones, so that he is clean. Ours is not so boiling hot, but our hair and our scalp drop off all the same. They beat us poor people with whips, until our skin falls off. To the lord they quickly bring splendid brooms, with chains attached to them, and I can't help it if he is afraid of this. They beat his bones until he has none left and marrow has to come forth in place of sweat. I guess he's hot enough. (6692)

Nothing is to remain of our wild spirits. The hot bath is meant to drive them out and wash away all our vices in youth and in old age. One can really avoid this bath where pitch and sulphur swirl around, if one does not blacken one's deeds with the black pitch of evildoing and make one's actions stink with the sulphur of one's wickedness. The person who tries to do what he is supposed to do can avoid the chain which is wrought with care and cunning and with which we are to be bound and beaten if we do not behave well in this world. Anyone who wishes to flee the chain should not pay too much attention to the fastening of that chain, and then he will escape without mishap from the chain of vice, just as a good man should. Anyone who does not wish to flee the chain fetters himself with many vices which in the end will drag him to where he is embedded in misfortune and suffering. Know this for a fact. (6720)

I recounted a long time back how this chain is wrought, and how wealth, desire, authority, power, reputation, nobility all have the capacity to ensnare vice, that's true. See, those are the ties that one must avoid. The man who wishes to flee the hand of the devil must shun these six things. They promote vice both in one's old age and in one's youth. If it were not for wealth and possessions, greed and arrogance would not be able to fetter people. If it were not for authority, what could be strong enough to tie up arrogance and ignominy so firmly? Now tell me: if it were not for power, what could have enough strength to combine vanity with ignominy? If it were not for reputation, what could then link foolishness to vanity? What could tie up desire and foolishness better than nobility does? Nothing, unless my mind deceives me. (6748)

Now we have arrived at the knot in the chain which, by its very nature, has impurity and laziness, gluttony and drunkenness at the very end of it. That chain which all our life we have wrought with bad deeds turns to steel in hell: believe that for a fact. And whoever does the bathing in hell beats hard with it. It seems to me that the man who allows himself to be bathed so well in this world that he does not come to the place where they prepare the devil's bath receives wise advice. The man who is to come to the court of the Lord must bathe himself very well: he must bathe his spirit in virtue and in goodness. The bath must be heated with love, for he must be so inclined as to love God and human beings: that is the best way to heat his bath, that's true. He must bathe inwardly, and then the bed in which he will lie comfortably forever will be prepared for him. He will go to that court a better and a more beautiful man, know that as well. If a man who is to go to our Lord's court does not wish to bathe well here, the chamberlain will not let him in unless he takes the time to bathe himself from head to toe. Then he must put up with the bath I've told you about: woe to him who bathes in that![13] (6784)

Now you must also know for a fact that the chain of virtue must be woven of six things which will bring us to God. Virtues must always be in contention with vices, and likewise their links must be unfailingly in conflict. The chain of vice drags us down, but our Lord can pull us back again with the chain of virtue. Happy the man who shall follow Him! (6796)

You have heard the fifth part. I have arrived at the sixth.

BOOK VI

It has been thoroughly related, according to what I believe, how one can come to God by means of virtue. I know that I have said how vice and sin bring us to the depths of hell. I have said that God—and anyone who wishes to fulfill His commandments—loves virtue, and I have also said that people do not think much of a person who wishes to follow the counsel of virtue. (6808)

Now today I propose to admonish all virtuous people not to despair of virtue, for if it happens for a while that people do not regard it properly, then nevertheless know for a fact that anyone who walks righteously will on the Day of Judgment press his way forward to the door of blessedness. (6816)

A city was once captured by its enemies, and those who were in the city fled as quickly as they could, taking their money and their clothes with them. Now there was one man amongst them who had the wisdom and the good sense not to want to carry anything along with him. The others were traveling with an enormous load. Someone asked him why he was doing this, and he gave him an answer better than the question, saying: "My heart is carrying my money and my possessions." He was referring to his virtue, his wisdom, and his fine manners, but they all mocked at him for that. Then the messenger of the lord who had taken the city came riding up and captured them all on their journey, for they were heavily laden. The one who was carrying nothing on the journey was lightly laden and easily got away, for wisdom, virtue, and good sense must go forward in the end, no matter how long they stand before the door. (6840)

The power of vice will for a time cause the virtuous ones to endure danger, suffering, toil, mockery, yet God transforms all that, for if anyone wishes to travel with God, He will bring him to where he will achieve much authority. To be sure, blessing will not elude him. Be assured that even if he is not completely blessed in this world, he will be in the next where he will receive his just deserts. I can also say that in this world our Lord God has bestowed much authority upon the man who obeys His commandments by leading a virtuous life, for, on account of a man's gentle disposition, He often rewards him with great wealth in this world. To be sure He compensated Job twice over for what he had lost. If a man is constant in virtue, good will come to him in time. It showed great virtue in Joseph, when he was a young man in Egypt and his lord's wife, who was very beautiful to look at, invited him into her bed, that he refused to be unfaithful. Because of this, he later landed in great danger, but God saved him from death. It is true that he endured danger and tribulation for a long time, but this was all made up to him later, that's absolutely true. He became lord over him who once did not wish to purchase him so that he might become that man's servant.[1] Nevertheless he was wrongfully sold and subsequently bestowed honor and wealth on those who, on account of their jealousy, had sold him and sent him far off into another land. Look how even so he eventually went forward through the door of blessedness. (6886)

The same happened to Moses, for when he saw a child who wished to kill his brother and told him that he should not do it, the wicked child said to him: "We don't need you to tell us what to do. Who gave you to us as our master, as if we couldn't live before you came on the scene?"[2] In fact, as we all know, the man whom those children did not wish to have as their master became ruler of all the Israelites. The children despised his authority, but through the power of our Lord it came about that he was given to their fathers, so that he ruled over their lives. The man whom the young and the foolish did not wish to follow or to listen to found a following among the old and wise folk. Take note: that is what is written down today. (6906)

Because of this any man who can take heed of virtue should think and be aware of how he can bring it about that he can gain great authority. One should leave it to God to aspire to that and concentrate on doing the right thing. Anyone who applies his thoughts to how he may gain authority diminishes the effect of his virtue. He should leave it to God to act, God who took David away from his sheep and chose him, if he was willing, to attain the honor that was his due.[3] Anyone who puts himself forward thinks he is very virtuous and is actually corrupt. I believe that a person who is keen to aspire to power elects himself, if you can understand me correctly. Anyone who acts in this way thinks he is either not suited or well suited to the task. If he thinks he is unsuited, he should not desire authority, but if he thinks he is useful and well suited, let him nevertheless realize that God may not permit a useful lord to be there. This the people have probably completely forfeited. Therefore, let no one strive so hard as to leave the path of virtue and transgress against God. It is His wish and His commandment that one should await His will, for if He so desires it, He will indeed bring it to pass. Moreover, I tell you that it often happens that someone is useless yet thinks he is very useful. One folly leads to another. It is the way of the unwise man to believe that he is wise, but it is the custom of God to guide the good and the wise to honor and authority Himself. He has the skill and the power to effect this better than any man, and you can know that the less courage a man has the more swiftly does He do it. Do you see how much authority He bestowed with His power on Joseph, so that, as you have heard, he was taken out of prison to become a lord? Since God loves His faithful servants, He gave him his reward. (6962)

Moses really became a lord when he returned to the place from which he had previously been driven. These miracles of God are written down. Therefore, let every man behave in such a way that he may come to virtue and allow God to take care of his honor, and may he strive for virtue himself, that is God's commandment. (6970)

King David, too, endured many trials and tribulations before he came to his kingdom. He was treated with contempt by his forefather King Saul, who always bore anger and hatred towards him. He suffered greatly at his hands, yet after his death he became king. See how he, too, achieved good fortune by means of his patience. He did not wish to take revenge, when he might often have done so.[4] Even God does not wish to avenge Himself right away, and, if a man is gentle and patient, he will follow God at all times. (6986)

To be sure it's only right that the foolish man who himself has no reputation should not praise good people. Anyone who can really praise a good man—be sure of this—must himself be very virtuous. Otherwise he cannot distinguish between the good man and the scoundrel, for a man without virtue cannot take account of anything other than what relates to vice. His master has confounded him in this way. He himself is a scoundrel and he does not recognize goodness. How is a man supposed to recognize what he has never had? The best he can do is watch over his possessions and his gains, but, to be sure, someone who has always been a scoundrel does not even recognize himself. He thinks he is a decent man when he can say: "This is all mine." Note that his possessions have blinded his senses so that he cannot recognize what a virtuous man should do. (7012)

Now you can clearly see every day that the rich man mocks the poor man. A rich and corrupt fool goes ahead of a virtuous but poor man. However properly the latter behaves, the foolish beast has absolutely no regard for him. Know this: the money-lender thinks he is better than the man who has not a penny to his name. His foolish counsel is deceiving him. (7022)

The money-lender is very happy when anyone complains of some shortage, for then that person has to ask him [for a loan]. He considers himself to be very bright and says to himself: "I am a fine fellow to be able to arrange my affairs in such a way that people have to plead with me. I shall gain even more." Foolish money-lender: you are completely deceived by your cunning. You think you have a fine plan, yet what you gain is foolishness. Now tell me: how did you come by your possessions? It suits me better if you lend them to me. You dare not right away eat what you have, whereas I do indeed dare to consume your wealth as I can. Wicked money-lender: you must really be my chamberlain. I am happy with your wealth, and that way, scoundrel, you are my surety. Now—by your eyes!⁵—take care that you touch my possessions neither openly nor in secret. I want them all and I am disposed to do with them exactly what I like, since they are mine. You are probably saying: "You must pay me back what I lent you," but I can say in truth that I will not give it back to you. I will give it to you to look after, for you will always be my chamberlain. And if it comes about that you do not live the length of time I give it to you to manage, then I shall have to assume the responsibility myself and look after my own coffers. But I shall leave that as it is. You say: "If I do not live to see it, then you must give it to my children. Whether you want to do so or not, know that this will happen to you." I'll give it to them to look after, too, if they follow in your footsteps, you fool you! For if they want to be money-lenders, they will become my treasurers, too. Perhaps they won't want to be that but will benefit from what I have gained. Now tell me, you foolish man: what use is that to you? You'll be neither better off nor worse. When you get to the depths of hell you would rather a thousand times over that you had never acquired what has called the wrath of God down upon you. (7080)

Whoever has compassion for his child, even if he does not gain much for him, will regret, if he has any sense, that with his ill gains and with his evil deeds he has brought damnation upon the soul of his child. If the son does not wish to incur God's wrath, he must make restitution for his father's ill-gotten gains. Now see how the father has treated himself and his child, for if his child does not surrender what his father gained by wrongful means, then he, too, is lost. Often one suffers both before and after death on account of one's children, and for that reason a wise man said: "Anyone who never had any children, you shall know for sure, is blessed with misfortune." (7100)

The wicked money-lenders should be glad to hear what I am saying. They should be happy and greatly cheered by these stories and be very pleased to read them. I have only ever spoken about how by their toil in this world they receive suffering in the next: they are dead both here and there. It is the same with every vice: we are harried by it in this world and the next. We have a remarkable tendency to love passionately that which in this world and the next brings us suffering and sorrow, misery and anguish: idleness produces trials and tribulations for us. (7118)

Virtue provides man with a peaceful life, and it also allows us to have a better life in time to come. You can take it from me that the person who relies on wickedness has a great deal of trouble. Anyone who depends on virtue has throughout his youth and in old age a gentle life and a pure one. Now listen to what I mean: (7128)

Whoever sets his mind to being humble will not suffer many cares, for he puts up with whatever people do or say to him. He has a peaceful life in this world in order that in the next he will be given a better one, whenever that comes to pass. You should have no doubt about this. (7136)

Whoever loads himself up with arrogance has chosen an arduous path, for, even if someone is not doing anything to him, he nevertheless thinks to himself: "I'll get back at him. That man must pay for what he said last year. I cannot do anything else." But then he thinks to himself: "I once spoke out against this gentleman. I am a man who dares to do it and can do it." The arrogance he already possesses is not enough for him. It seems that what he did before out of arrogance was good and he thinks highly of himself because he previously spoke in a haughty manner. Such foolishness is grounded in stupidity. In this plight, he will only harvest even greater tribulations after his death. (7158)

If a man is not envious, whatever advances another man pleases him, for he derives enjoyment from it too. By means of this enjoyment he sees to it that in the next world he will fare better eternally. This I can say in all truth. (7166)

The man who is given to envy is always miserable. Whatever good befalls another person engenders in him no small amount of suffering. I wish he could see that whatever good happened in the world, he would be dispirited because of it. You see, with that miserable frame of mind he brings it about that he incurs the wrath of God and has lost in this world and the next. It would be better if he had never been born. (7178)

The man who is without anger has gained a great serenity which at another time will bring him even greater comfort. The man who is angry is always restless. Even if no one has done anything to him, he thinks to himself: "That fellow and this one have done this to me" and he never gets rid of his anger, for he is furious the whole time and displaying his wickedness far and wide. His complexion, and the noise he makes, and the way he is carrying on proclaim everywhere that he is a man of vice which always prompts evil talk and which at some point will furnish him with a chair in the depths of hell. (7196)

If a man chooses a chaste existence, our Lord has given to him a serene and good life. Unchaste people are unhappy both in youth and in old age. Wickedness is an abomination. Impurity is always accompanied by hatred, strife and conflict. When the unchaste man has grown old, he is always sorrowful, for he is thinking all day long: "Lucky young man who can do what the ladies consider to be good!" Whatever he then does himself, he is always thinking that his wife much prefers a young man to him, and so he is sorely troubled. A foolish woman, who has led an unchaste life, does just the same thing. She is envious that a young woman is more appealing. Look, that's how they have tormented themselves their whole life through with wickedness, until their deaths, and then they fall into an even worse plight. (7222)

Whoever treats no one unjustly often has much comfort and with his gentle way of life brings it about that God should grant him a better life in Eternity. Believe that for sure. But anyone who likes to behave unjustly is often very unhappy as a consequence and also brings it about that he incurs the eternal wrath of God. (7232)

Know that the man who gives in to sloth has great distress. He is troubled by everything that he does in this world. However, the man who is not idle always does everything easily and well, just as a good man should. The man who is too lazy is inactive the whole time, and anyone who is always idle is always useless, too, and whoever is useless is completely redundant, take my word for it. Thus he is good for nothing except that he should be put on the glowing coals in hell, where he will burn, while the devil warms himself. Since he is good for nothing else, what good is then the man who does evil? (7252)

Anyone who gives in to larceny and thieving will have much misery and trouble, sorrow, fear, and suffering, and yet with all this affliction will gain for himself an even greater one when he dies. However—and take this to be the truth—anyone who does not do this will be less troubled by sorrow and fear and suffering. (7262)

Anyone who relies on lying will have many troublesome thoughts, for whatever he says has to be couched in such a way that people cannot see that he is lying. Know that he has to make quite an effort if he wants to rely on lying, and even so he will incur the wrath of God. You should believe me when I tell you this. (7272)

On the other hand, anyone who is happy to tell the truth speaks without difficulty, for the words are all available to him if he wishes to tell the truth. Anyone who wants to make up a false tale must watch out and make sure that he lies with finesse, unless he is lying openly. One has to search long and hard for a lie, if someone is proposing to speak correctly later. Anyone who wants to discover something which is not there must look for it all the time. God has provided us with the truth so that we can find it without difficulty. Because of this, it has always been His commandment that none of His messengers should think out what he was proposing to say to the Judge, for whoever is witness to the truth is master of his tongue and knows exactly what he ought to say. To be sure, God helps him to speak well. Whoever is witness to lying must be skilled in mastering his tongue, or else he is likely to say what he should rather keep to himself. (7298)

If you have taken in what I have said you will certainly have understood that the virtuous man always lives comfortably, but anyone who is wicked cannot escape misery. Therefore anyone who wishes to have joy and good fortune should never, in youth or in old age, depart from virtue. (7308)

Know that people rarely take from a generous man who can give appropriately, for he is always giving freely. However, if a man is stingy, people take from him all the time, for he never gives anything away if people do not wish to take it from him. How can anyone who, for all his wealth, leads a poor life give anything to anyone else? (7318)

I have heard it said that, out of cowardice, the cuckoo never dares to eat a whole leaf at a time. He is always afraid that he will have to do without it. When he perches in the branches he pecks very gently at it, so that he does not swallow the entire leaf. He's afraid he will not have any food.[6] That is the way with greedy people: the wealth of the greedy man, the leaf of the cuckoo, both vanish like a cloud of dust. Know that a scoundrel does not dare to take hold of his wealth, for if he ever has a pressing need of it he thinks to himself: "I may perhaps need it more some other time or at another point." Thus he lives with this strategy so he never experiences such a plight that he does not say: "I don't need it yet." The stingy man has followed too closely the example of the cuckoo, for neither of them does well with his wealth. The winter takes away the leaves, the stingy man believes that his wealth will come to the person who will dare to enjoy it. It distresses me that many people admire anyone who follows the example of the cuckoo. Anyone who does not wish to follow the cuckoo's example should not be denied a true gift. The person who wishes to follow the cuckoo's teaching has failed miserably.[7] The greed stems from cowardice: the fear of losing something makes for avarice. The man who always battles to achieve wealth is easily defeated, and so he has lost both himself and his wealth through his greedy disposition. Whatever cowardice produces in the fight is also created by avarice. The man can use his sword well who does not think wealth worth fighting for. Whoever overlooks wealth in the fight often achieves wealth from it, for it will certainly be there when he has destroyed the whole enemy. Whoever looks for wealth too early has lost, no matter what he does.[8] (7368)

Whoever is to fare well in the next world must fight in this. We now desire wealth before the battle and because of that we are often vanquished. Whenever we do anything wrong, the devil is slaying us without a shield. Thus we must apply the vast crowd of [our] good thoughts towards it and must abandon wrongdoing: that way the enemy must be damned by us in the flames of hell. The virtuous knight must act likewise: he must advance bravely with the banner of virtue towards the enemy's host of vices, and in attacking he must destroy them all. (7384)

Now, good and noble knights, observe how Arrogance rises up against you with her forces: you must defeat her altogether. Among her force are Shame, Violence, and Immodesty. Her standard-bearer is Anger. Her commander is always Foolishness. Know this for the truth: Reputation and Vanity travel with her.[9] (7394)

Look about you, good and noble knights, and observe what Greed does. She arms herself with her forces. Know that the following are her companions: Profit, Robbery, Theft, Deceit, Perjury, Lying, Envy, Frivolity. (7400)

Do you not see the crowd of Impurity which has armed itself there from top to toe? In its force travel Lechery, Gluttony, and Drunkenness too. Wretched Fortune and bitter Greeting, poor Wealth and Foolishness, rich Poverty and false Love must also make their way towards this force. Inconstancy goes there too, and long suffering after brief joy. (7410)

Sloth has also armed and thoroughly prepared its force. Know that always in its force are sleep, stretching of limbs, and yawning. The man who does not wish to lose the victory and opt for eternal death must conduct himself resolutely against them, so that wickedness does not drag him down. (7418)

Whoever is a knight, or is called one, must now prepare himself very carefully to defend himself. Every decent man must arm himself against vice, both in old age and in youth. Whoever wishes to come to God must not consider it too much, however long he has to fight in this world, if he comes out well as a result. Anyone who is given to thinking that he will gain much joy and avoid great tribulation and suffering must not consider it a labor if in youth and in old age he fights against vice, for no champion ever gained so much honor as the man who is able to overcome evil: I have noted that indeed. (7438)

What use is it if a man who has been forced into submission by vice and is ready to fulfill its commands can conquer towns and lands? Anyone who vanquishes vice fights like a knight. To be sure, I am not calling it chivalry just because a man breaks a lance. That is proper chivalry when someone scatters a host of vices over the earth and does not allow them to come up again. (7450)

As I have told you before, the host of vices is far-reaching. I have divided up the vices into four armies for you, and anyone who proposes to fight against these four contingents will certainly need the help of God. Now watch out, noble knight, watch out! They are riding here from all sides. Arrogance, to be sure, is riding at the head of the first contingent; Impurity is carrying a burning spear; Avarice is armed with dishonor; Sloth is clothed from head to foot in wickedness, and all four are followed by their army. Now defend yourself, noble knight, defend yourself! Their yells must not alarm you. You must wake up your virtues, so that they arm you against them. Good Sense must give you her banner, in order that you can lead the army of your virtues to the defense. Take the sword from Justice, in order that you can make the crooked straight. Prudence gives you her shield and Security her hauberk, for the man who is prudent is also always secure. Faith places the helmet on the head of him who truly believes. Good works are nothing without belief. The body without a head is also nothing. Hope shall give you a horse, so that you shall ride well and without doubts into the army of vices. They shall shrink away from you. May Courage provide you with spurs, for you must not pull your horse back out of cowardice. You should never flee the battle. Chastity shall give you the bridle, and you should let your life be guided by that. One must rise above that which one should not do. May Constancy give you the saddle, for neither joy nor sorrow must cause you to lean this way or that. With the spear of Humility you must be in the vanguard of attack, so that you, knight, allow yourself to be seen. (7500)

You must unseat Arrogance [with your spear]: that way you can soon smash the army of vices. In fact you should trample them underfoot. With the spurs of Courage you must make the horse of Hope leap over ditches and thorns. You shall control him in such a way that mountains and stones and swamp are all the same to him. (7510)

Jerk your horse round for—know this—the broad army of vices must yield before you and behind you. Wherever you wish to direct your horse with the bridle of Chastity, many vices must fall, that is the truth. Indeed you must trample underfoot Licentiousness and Idleness, Avarice, Envy, Anger, and Foolishness. If you have need of it, you must not forget the sword that you received from Justice and with it you will make the paths straight and wide on either side. The good man must in the fight deal blow upon blow without number. Whoever wishes to live in eternity must always fight, as it is written here. (7530)

The man who has vanquished the vices should at the same time take care never to become too full of himself. The man who seeks to have a reputation for having overcome vices with his strength will fall victim to arrogance and will revert to being corrupt. I have read and taken to heart that the man who does not seek to gain a reputation for having defeated them robs the great army of vices of victory. On this matter a certain man may say: "Our enemy can always draw us and our desire towards bad things and towards sin. The desires of the flesh crave that which is better for the body. The mockery of the world draws us too, for anyone who wishes to serve God is always mocked. Because of that it is very irksome to fight against the army of vices. These three things lead us completely astray." I will respond to anyone who speaks in this way: our lives are well equipped with the armor of Good Sense with which one can counter this. Prudence shall provide us with five things to use against the three which always make the battle hard for us. Prudence must provide us right away with proper faith against the devil, so that one really believes what one should believe. If anyone has proper faith, that faith advises him to fear God and to love Him. That way, if he fears and loves God, he will certainly never be inclined to be frightened of the devil's message. If a man fears God and enjoys His friendship, the devil's power can do nothing to him. Prudence shall also provide us with the fear which one must have of hell's bitter cavern and use to counter desire. This must make desire bitter for us, if we wish to remain alert in our thoughts. Hope, also, shall be led to heaven by Prudence. Heavenly sweetness must banish the sweetness of desire. Whoever gives any thought to sweetness must consider this sweetness a mere nothing. In contrast to the mockery of the world, one must surely fear the mockery of the devil, which anyone who receives the devil's greeting must endure in hell. One must also be sure that to anyone who ever gained renown in heaven the mockery of the world was nothing. Anyone to whom it happens can see that clearly. If anyone can assess it sensibly, the three things cause him less dismay. (7596)

As we have it in writing, if our forefather had remained on the side of God, we would not have had the suffering of conflict and we would have lived without death. Whoever comes there and whoever is there is always well protected in advance from sin, for he does not have to fight there. (7604)

The ancient scriptures do not lie: the first man allowed himself to be deceived, for the enemy put pressure on him out of envy. Then he did not have such an enormous battle with sin as we have: corruption was subject to him. You should know for the truth that idleness did him no harm. His desire allowed him to live in complete comfort, that's a fact. The mockery of the world did not touch him. God had given him this peace. Know that he would have been able to overcome better, if the enemy had not deceived him like that. The scriptures have not lied to us. Because he was defeated by the vices without a great battle so that the vices overcame him, as we have often observed, we must always wage a great battle with them, if we wish to enjoy the grace of God, from which the guilt of the first man separated us through his own decision. The child is harmed by what the father does.[10] (7630)

The enemy was expelled by God on account of his sinfulness, as it is written. And the first man, too, was banished from that place because of his lack of virtue. Therefore, no one shall say that God would have done better if it had been His will that people should come there without trials and tribulations. In addition, we have been guilty of acting against the favor of God, so that in youth and in old age we must fight strenuously against sinfulness. How can the man who has given himself over to the enemy live as a free man? For the enemy is at all times the vassal of sinfulness. Any man who bears a great sin is always fighting hard. Since the enemy was banished—or so we find it written—on account of his wickedness and the judgment of God, it must not seem unfitting that goodness and the grace of God should bring us there. Our goodness is always in opposition to the evil of the foe. And then again, the mercy that is accorded to us through His divine Goodness stands in contrast to the judgment of God, for we are less afflicted than the sins that we commit all the time warrant us to be. If it were not for the grace of God and our goodness, the foe would say: "They are doing me an injustice." He cannot say that, for he has left that place because of a judgment and because of his own wickedness, while man has ascended there through the grace of God, for God sees to it that a man has good intentions. If it were not for the judgment of God, the devil's wickedness would not have brought him to hell, that's true. He had to come there because of both these things. I can also declare quite truthfully that, without the grace of God, no one can come into His kingdom, for His kingdom is incomparably more splendid than our good deeds, as anyone with any sense knows. Heavenly nature, as we can see now, fell down into hell through the judgment of God and his own arrogance, if anyone assesses it aright. Earthly nature must ascend again through the goodness of God's grace and through humility. The devil made worse that which God had given to him and because of that he fell into the abyss. Whoever improves on what God has given to him will be given more by Him at another time. (7692)

Whoever does not enjoy the grace of God is always evil. If the devil had stayed within it he would still be there, or so it is written down. Since one can really come to God through true goodness and since no one can possess goodness unless he is prepared to take up the conflict that one must wage with vice, you can see clearly that there is no help for it but that we must all fight against wickedness throughout our lives. (7704)

It was given to the first man to live eternally without distress, if he were to guard himself as he should, and at the same time he was accorded the power to commit sin. In contrast, God granted us in truth that we might come to that place with great effort and that we might not sin if we managed to reach it. Our battle must take place in this world, for we are rewarded in the next. We cannot depart from there as the first man did. Therefore, we must always have a greater battle to fight than he did. Since wickedness brought the first man away from that place through the advice of the foe, we can clearly understand that whoever wishes to come there must fight resolutely with both of them, believe that to be the truth. It is no wonder, since the devil was greatly envious of God, that he wishes to drag us away from that place from which he dragged the first man and out of which he himself has been banished, as we find it written. Now note how foolish we are: if a man inflicted a small injury upon us, we always took great pains to pay that same man back with greater damage, or at least with equal damage, and it is laziness on our part if we do not resist the very wicked creature when he wishes to drag us down to hell, where one finds plenty of suffering and where one must ever die a living death without atonement. I have read and taken to heart that anyone who wishes to defeat the devil must live well alongside other people, as he should live. He should not weaken his strength by engaging in any other enmity. Whoever has triumphed over him alone has put an end to all conflict. I counsel every noble knight that as long as the devil's battle lasts he should do nothing else, for that way he can fight well. If anyone were to fight against a bear, I do not think he would wish to be counting pennies at the same time, for he would probably be overcome. Whenever we should be fighting better, wealth very often diverts us. Then the devil is happy, if he deceives us like that. The man who slays the poor man is not fighting according to the law of knighthood and then when he robs him of his possessions he displays an unknightly disposition. Think of your orders, you knights: how did you become knights? God knows, you did not do so by sleeping. Shall a man become a knight by enjoying lazing around? I have not read or heard that. Do you think you will be knights by means of good food and good wine? In that matter you are very much deceived. To be sure, it is true that the beast eats a lot. You are not knights because of your clothing and your fine trappings. If anyone were to give them to a peasant he would not throw them away, and to be sure even the fool is wise enough to know that if one ties a bell to his foot he must carry it away with him. (7784)

Anyone who wishes to practice the office of a knight must certainly pay more attention to his whole way of living than to eating. He shall have more to do than wear fine clothes and go along gesticulating with his hands. The man who only wishes to live in comfort cannot fulfill the office of knighthood. The man at leisure is busy all the time, for he probably thinks that it would be easier [now] for someone to attack him. (7796)

No man should be inactive: anyone who is at leisure makes it look as though leisure often brings unrest along with it, whenever he tussles with bad thoughts. (7800)

If a knight intends to practice what he should by rights be practicing, he should work day and night with all his might for the sake of the Church and for the sake of poor people. There are very few knights these days who do that. Know this: if anyone does not do this, it would be better if he were a peasant, for then he would not be so displeasing to God. You should know for a fact that the man who handles his chivalry in such a way that he dispenses neither help nor advice will be reproached for his chivalry. Moreover, the man who treats someone else unjustly will also be afflicted as a consequence. You may also know exactly what happens to a man who himself commits an unjust act. I believe he will be even unhappier. (7820)

I want to say similar things about the priests. A priest has a great deal to do if he wishes to fulfill his office properly and without disgrace. Moreover, he has more to do than just sing or shout at the top of his voice. He must provide good examples through a chaste body and a pure life, with good deeds and eloquent preaching. He must wear the crown of virtues. (7830)

It is also beholden upon the knight to live as he should, kindly towards his wife and trusting towards his people. In this matter, knight, you must follow me: just as you desire your lord to live with you, so shall you live, and the man who is subject to you, too. I want to offer another piece of advice: that if a man has a master he should do what he commands. Know that he diminishes his servitude thereby. His good will gives him strength, so that his burden is less if he always does this gladly. (7846)

It seems to me that the person who happily does his work throughout the day and has nothing left over has good sense and is all the less troubled by it. The man who likes to do what he does has a free spirit. On the other hand, know that he who always does grudgingly whatever he does in the world is a rogue: both his mind and his body are enslaved. (7856)

If your master brings grievous shame upon you, that is not such a great dishonor that you constantly occupy yourself with trying to make a free man subservient to you as if he were a beast. Anyone who does that is displeasing to God. (7864)

Indeed, one should permit one's servant to live according to the right of a vassal. One should honor God through him and should keep humanity, which is [to be] exalted, in mind when one demands service from him [i.e., the servant]. If you wish to trample underfoot the man who will perhaps be sitting above you in the kingdom of our Lord, that is not in keeping with chivalry. (7874)

A man is simply not a chattel: one should certainly know that for a fact. Anyone who believes this has not understood that the best part is exempt, for no man ever conquered the soul and thoughts. Therefore, never command any more than you would like your master to command you, for if you have the right to command your servant, your master has the same right over you. Therefore, follow my advice. (7886)

You are probably saying: "I have no lord." Bear in mind that it could well happen that you acquire one. Thereupon you say: "I am a lord in my own land," but then I can say for a fact that you can never climb up there unless some feckless man is afterwards able to make you his subordinate. No one, great or small, is without a lord. We all have one lord in common, and that is our Lord God. One should fear His authority indeed. From Him we derive body and soul, people, property, wealth, our children, and our wives, and He asks nothing of us but that which it befalls us to do with honor. God commands us to behave justly, but this is the way I command my servant: "Do violence to this one and to that one." God bestows upon us all manner of virtues, courtesy and goodness, but we say to our people: "Do what you will; I'll support you, whatever you want to do." Wherever there is a powerful knight, he draws the wicked gluttons into his vassalage by means of cunning. The vassal very often does what he does by virtue of his lord's power. Because of that Our Lord is more displeased over the sins of the master: both of them will greatly regret this. (7918)

Nowadays it has come to the point where we protect our vassals so that they can live devoid of Christian things and will give nothing up to have spiritual masters. Whatever the servant happens to do, whether it be good or not, is rarely displeasing to the master. He simply strives at all times to defend him against his sins and his desire, and, as I have said, if he were to prefer to foreswear him to avoid doing an injustice, he would ruin the servant. (7932)

In fact, I want to go so far as to say that if anyone does not want to compel his servant to behave in a good and correct manner, he must stand before God and answer to Him with absolute justice on behalf of his servant. (7938)

Eli, we read, had been a very good man and paid for the sins of his children because he did not put a stop to their sinful behavior at any time.[11] (7942)

Any man who is himself good should apply himself the whole time to seeing that those who are subject to him behave in such a way that justice is done. However, anyone who does not wish to do this has much to answer for to God. In this regard you should know well what will befall the man who always wishes to lead his people into sin. People are not ashamed of that sin. Whatever the master is ashamed of immediately falls to the servant to do: we consider that to be just. We make our own people into robbers, thieves, and money-lenders. We wish to share possessions and yet we are so foolish that we wish to be without the stain of sin and without any trace of disgrace. That cannot be, for if a servant is required to do on our behalf something that is wicked and against proper behavior and contrary to the grace of God, then we share in the guilt. After all, we have many sins, for very often one does not mention the hounds when the reward is given to the huntsman for directing them in the chase. They say: "The man caught the hare," but probably it was the hound that did it. Thus the sin is entirely ours, for we are always giving the commands, and the sin also falls on the servant who follows us along the unjust path. (7978)

If I order someone who is subject to me to kill a man we are certainly both guilty. You are probably saying: "I dare not ignore my lord's command," but I say that you should fear God more: He is the Lord of your master, and for that reason you should fear Him more. Your master may well do harm to you, but even so every man should fear more than any human being God, who can dispatch body and soul to that place where restlessness never has an end. Therefore take my advice and do your master's bidding as long as it does not go against God. (7994)

I also advise the lords that any of them who has good sense should never command anything unless it can really be properly carried out. You should know that if anyone issues a command that goes against God, his command does not destroy only the one who commands: those who carry it out are all destroyed too. (8002)

Similarly, I say that one should remain true to friendship, so that no one demands that another should do anything that is contrary to God and contrary to honor. A person ought to be of such a mind that if anyone asks him to do such a thing, he should definitely refuse his request. He will thereby be doing his friend a service. We tend to do something else, [however]. If our friend does not ask us we put ourselves forward and say: "You could acquire someone's possessions. To be sure, you do not have the heart of a knight." In that way we urge our friends on to do evil when we ought to be forcing them to do good things for the sake of friendliness, even if they do not wish to behave properly. (8020)

We say: "There is a woman there who has a very proud bearing. Do you want me to get her for you? She is a veritable mirror of courtly love." And if he replies: "I don't want her," we say: "Go away, you villain! You are not worthy of any respect, since you do not desire her." Woe to the man who continually wishes to follow bad advice! Bad advice will not get any better, you can believe me. (8032)

Very often masters love the thieves of their honor and their soul. Very often the wicked counselor betrays the soul of his master with his bad advice and sacrifices the honor of his master for a pittance. It takes an effort for the man to protect himself from this underhanded thief, yet the master should have enough sense to know [how to do that] if he realizes that he is being advised against the will of God, that the counselor is the messenger of the devil. The devil has dispatched his messenger to the lord. The good master should receive the servant in accordance with his rights as a lord. He should say to him: "Go away from me into the kingdom of your lord, for I do not wish to follow you, you complete and utter scoundrel!" (8052)

The counselor who instructs his lord to apply his free spirit to wickedness and to how he may relieve people of their wealth is not counseling honorably. He should not allow himself to become so weak that he follows such advice, which consists only of greed. Wherever he can justifiably take something, let him take it; it is not appropriate that we should take unjustly, even from our vassal. (8064)

One should pay little heed to wealth, for it is the whetstone of the devil, his fishing net, and his hunting bird. With it, he catches many birds that should be flying up to heaven, if they do not want to drop down into hell. Wealth: you sharpen us with your cunning, so that all the time we are slicing you, wealth, with our knowing ways. You give us a very sly disposition. Know that whoever sharpens his knife cuts better for a while until the blade falls out completely. Thus I tell you in truth that anyone who relies on gain sharpens his senses so much with his greed for riches that the blade of his mind slips away completely. Then he cannot ever again think of honor or of God. He may become a source of mockery to himself. In the end he rubs his senses so much that he smoothes them away completely and cannot direct his mind to anything other than dying of hunger and frost with all his possessions round him. Is he not a wise fool, then, to lead his senses astray to the extent that, in this world, he brings it about through his efforts that it will be worse for him in the next? For, as I have said, whoever has set his mind to profit has trouble in this world and in the next and is a living dead man. And yet the tax-collector and the money-lender think they are wise! My dear fellow, you have a poor mind if you believe you can apply it to gain. Now tell me: where are your wits? It certainly looks as though the cutting edge of your senses is completely worn out, for your gain comes to the point where it can be called loss. We can see that clearly the whole day long. If you boast about your profit, you should also have the sense to recognize your loss. Then you would give up craving for fame, for you have forsaken your generosity and chosen avarice [instead], given up virtue for the sake of vice, and believe that you are striving for gain. (8118)

Alas, poor hoarder: you are a foolish money-changer! You are devoted to gain and yet you give up gold for the sake of copper. Whenever you take away someone's property you put a fright into the virtues in your mind so that they run away, and then you have an evil gain. (8126)

If you wish to become rich quickly, then let wealth and poverty be all the same to you: that way you are rich in spirit. A poor man can do without far more while he is resting than a lord can gain through constant fighting, even if he applies himself heart and soul to it. He who wants no more has enough. The rich man never gains too much, for the nature of wealth is that it makes a person greedy. Greed grows with wealth, and so do wickedness, fear, anxiety, distress, and suffering. Anyone who cannot understand that is really a foolish man. I know well enough that the usurer, along with every tax-collector, does not wish to understand it, for he thinks he is only worth as much as he possesses: that is the counsel of avarice, and avarice is a wretched form of nobility through which a thief can harm us. (8150)

Whatever nobility comes from virtue lasts longer and achieves more than that which comes from wealth into an evil mind, for it lasts a long time. No thief is clever enough to be able to steal some of it, and, therefore, we should choose it. (8158)

You are probably saying: "Your teaching troubles me greatly, for the advice you give is too hard for the man who has nothing. I cannot live without possessions, and so I must strive for wealth, for I am a man without a trade. I must gain by whatever means I can, since I cannot live properly for a single day without possessions. So you must forgive me for that." (8170)

Then aspire for this without greed, be aware of cleverness, and do not tire of acquiring skill. Be courteous and tolerant; do no one harm with what you say; keep silent about what one should not talk about. Whenever you come before a lord, serve him gladly and behave in such a way that you are available to everyone. The poor man who has no trade should deport himself with this kind of adaptability. (8182)

It is more honorable to serve the noble lords than to serve evil; the person who relies on worldly goods has evil as his mistress and must always serve Avarice and lie beneath her feet as well. (8188)

To be sure, a man should not despair—this I dare to say—[and believe] that God may be leaving him to perish. A man can achieve wealth and honor if he is good and virtuous, for God grants him the strength to maintain good things: indeed he can never fail. God can well bring it about that a virtuous man attains honor and possessions. Moreover, he is so inclined that, in things great and small, he allies himself to the rich man. It is a virtuous man who can be just as happy with lead as with gold. He is the one to whom both great and small give their hearts equally. He has indeed separated virtuous day from wicked night. The man who is either happy or sad cannot stumble too badly, for he has light on his journey. I have seen many people who, when some harm has befallen them physically or materially, are so foolish that they believe God does not care about them. This results in great misfortune for them. Let them think what suffering the saints endured, and what pain and what martyrdom, and what manner of death, and what poverty and what shame! In that way one can immediately understand that misfortune is great fortune if someone always accepts it positively. To be sure, even our Lord God chose to endure poverty and mockery, thirst, hunger, frost, and other affliction. He who gives life to all of us chose in the end to die. If He does not choose to give wealth to someone but permits him to live in poverty, as He did Himself, that man should surely be happy about it, if he chooses to believe what we read. Yet it amazes me if the person whom He treats like Himself becomes angry. Whoever is willing to suffer with Him in this world will certainly live with Him in the next. (8240)

Now I propose to advise all the noblemen not to drop the lantern, for they should light the way ahead for us until they bring us to the gate where there is always sunshine. They would very much like to be inside. However, if someone's light has been extinguished, let him straightaway light it again and hold it up very high, for then both he and we, too, will see better, and if he does not do it soon he will fall, and we shall, too. He who did not lift his light up high quite rightly fell into a ditch, and it is only right that the person who rides around all the time in the [pitch black of] night will end up in his grave. (8256)

Enemies love the dark. The thief steals in the dead of night. At night people do much that they do not want to do in the daytime. The bright day reveals what one does at night. Often enough one discovers during the day the shame of the night. (8264)

So I tell you in truth that the Day of Judgment will reveal what one has done now. It will be a day of shame, for all the sins one has committed and for which one has not confessed will then be revealed. Thus one should more easily and with less shame confess one's sin to someone now. (8274)

I think it's a good idea if a man who wishes to atone keeps three things before his eyes, both openly and in private: fear, trust, and love. For whoever wishes to make a meaningful confession should have trust in God, as well as fear and love in accordance with His commandment. Firm faith always provides us with these three things. If we believe in His great agony, and that He suffered death for our sake, this can bring us great love, if we apply our thoughts to it. If we believe that He harrowed hell and afterwards rose again, this can really give us the hope that He will grant us a happy life. If we believe, as we have heard, that He is to come to judge us, then know that at all times this instills great fear of Him within us. His goodness and His humility bestow love upon the man who acknowledges it. It always gives us hope that He is merciful and powerful. His justice and His judgment do not release us from fear. His humanity gives us love, and His divinity hope, and His judgment fear, if one believes the scriptures. We should repent our sins and always regret them out of fear, hope and love, if we have any sense. The man who does not wish to atone for his sins while he is alive and well does not love God, who had no need to choose to die for our sake. However, if someone does not love God, his faith is as nothing, since he cannot believe that God has done so much for us. Love comes, so I have said, from faith. Whoever believes in His humanity and His humility must love Him, unless he lacks the spirit. If he loves Him, know, too, that he will serve Him as long as he can and not wait until his last day. Whoever does not wish to serve God does not greatly love Him, and, as I have said, anyone who does not love Him, does not believe in His humanity. If he does not truly believe, then you know very well what will become of him. Whoever leaves it to his day of judgment without confessing his sins must out of fear make the atonement that he should have made out of love. Whoever serves God through fear and love has virtue and good sense and is a veritable child of God. Similarly, know that those who confess only when they are facing death are rogues. Even so, I wish to urge the man who has remained so long in a state of sin to make his atonement on his final day, for even if he only does it out of fear, nevertheless God is so good that He will grant him the sense to do it also out of love. If he does that, then I really have the hope that God will bring him into a state of grace. However, I wish to make it known to you here that he must do penance for whatever wrong he has committed in this world before he sets a foot in the next. Therefore it makes good sense that one should confess one's sins and atone for them in this world through fear and love, for in the next it will be a thousand times worse for us. Yet, grace will nevertheless befall us if we attain the kingdom of God when we have confessed but before we have done penance, as you have already heard. Yet we will have erred by not doing so. Therefore it is better that we should do it when we are fit and well, for we do not know how close death is to us at any time. Some man may think that, whatever he does, God's goodness and God's grace will completely forgive him, but he is deceiving himself, that's for sure, and he is lost because of that belief. Should God not be angry that he has taken His judgment away from Him? He does not act with mercy in defiance of justice, for His mercy is always mixed with justice, and similarly His justice is in no way devoid of mercy. One must have fear and trust in God, that is the proper way. Whoever does not fear our Lord does not trust His judgment, and whoever does not trust in Him should not believe in His mercy. Whoever wishes to make a proper confession should repent what he has done by way of wicked things and sinning and promptly tell a priest about it and do whatever he tells him to do. The anger of God will immediately be lifted from him, as I have read and heard. He must confess his sin to someone, that is true, but he must not share his confession with anyone else for that one person should know him well. A man may say: "I am ashamed," but he would be even more ashamed if he were to behave in such a wicked way that he did not dare tell anyone about it. Yet it must be sweet to us that shame helps us to do penance. Afterwards, as soon as one is reflecting on it, one must say what one has done, where, when and how and why, so that the priest can see whether at that time his sin is great or small. That way he can give advice: otherwise one has achieved nothing. (8414)

No one would want to steal at night if he believed he would be hanged by day. We would not perpetrate evil if we knew what would happen to us and what should happen to us, given that good befalls the good man. However, by not having faith in our Lord's judgment we are behaving very wrongfully and in doing so are turning our justice into something worse. If we believed more in God and honor, know this, we would do well indeed. How are we to thrive and how should our lives be, for those who are supposed to supply us with medication are themselves sick. Those who are supposed to be carrying the lanterns in front of us enjoy walking in darkness. The right hand has become the left. The lambs have turned into wolves. Not one of us maintains his proper order. The priest is not guiding as he should, and the layman is not following properly. The one is unwise, the other foolish. One falls backwards, the other forwards. No one picks anyone up. Everyone is stumbling along towards a fall. (8442)

The priests are hurrying off to hell. The laymen are just as quick and want to push their way forward. There is a great crush at the door. They go there without anyone leading the way. They would not go so far in a day if they only knew what was inside. (8449)

What has happened to our senses that we cannot understand that everyone must go where he has deserved to go? There is no help for that, for if God were not intending to pass judgment, His judgment would be as nothing. If our Lord did not wish to judge, tell me, what would be the point of His judgment? To be sure, He wishes us to exercise good judgment, which is not to say that anyone should think that He is abandoning His [own] judgment. However, if anyone does not believe that our Lord should punish the bad man and reward the good man, then know that he has faith neither in God's mercy nor in God's judgment. In that case he must be lost and it would be better if he had never been born. (8468)

The sixth part has now been told, and I must not neglect the seventh.

BOOK VII

I have told you why, according to my understanding and my opinion, a person should adorn his youth and his old age with virtue. I have said what trials and tribulations one can have on account of virtue and how it all turns out well for us. Along the way I have also not neglected to write that a man should treat his wife and his children and his people well. Now you should know that I am writing about the body and the soul, and I will tell you about the strength of the body and what control the soul can exert over the body. You must graciously forgive me and allow me some time if it does not all become quickly apparent, for I must interject certain things in order that I can undermine vice and wickedness. My heart has guided me to the point where, if I can do so appropriately, I can slip out of my subject matter and treat vice in such a way that it will upset wicked people. (8498)

At this point I want to inform you that every man is made up of a body and a soul, and as a consequence he must always derive from both the qualities that are subject to both of them. Virtues are the qualities of the soul; strength, speed, and agility all appertain to the body, know that to be the truth. Thus the soul is always more valuable than the body, and consequently the strength of the soul is more valuable than the strength of the body. Every wise man will say that common sense takes precedence over physical strength, and likewise the power of thought is always superior to speed. Common sense achieves more for us in terms of wealth and honor than physical strength does. Our mind works more quickly to complete a large project than does the agility of our body. Thus you can know for a fact that one ought to value the power of the soul more highly than the strength of the body: the powers of the soul hold sway. Strength and speed should be guided by mind and good sense. Strength and speed are nothing unless they are guided by the mind. (8530)

In the forest one can come across wild animals that are swifter and stronger in the open fields than any man and yet cannot defend themselves because man's common sense has swiftly devised nets which are so ingeniously twisted and entwined that whatever lands in them must endure the authority of man on account of the strength of his soul. Whatever flies, or walks, or floats, and whatever lives in the world is subject to the authority of man, and this is not because of his physical strength.[1] (8544)

It is true enough that even if a man were to fight with great strength he could not force a lion to do exactly what he wants it to do. There again, one would have trouble catching birds in the air with speed: one might as well just have a nap. A bird would not be caught except by some unfortunate chance. Now look how our intellect allows everything to be subservient to us. Everything that lives stands at our beck and call: God has honored us like this. Intellect and common sense easily accomplish what physical strength and speed cannot achieve for us in a million years.[2] (8562)

Whoever believes that a man's reputation rests on his strength is foolish, and if anyone thinks that he can find a man's goodness in his agility he is also a complete fool: believe me, that is the truth. If strength and agility were to produce virtue and goodness, then an ox would be virtuous, for that is strong, and a fool's child flees quickly, so that same fool would also be virtuous. However, you should know for sure that one should not believe that, for goodness should come to us as a result of intellect and common sense. If anything lacks the soul of a human being, then, believe me, it is also lacking in intellect. Therefore, be sure of this, beasts are completely devoid of reason. And on this matter, too, you should know that understanding should rightly be called the power of the soul. If the body had control over the mind, then a beast and a fool would also have a mind and comprehension. (8588)

Now see how God has honored us by granting to us that with which he has also clothed the angels: intellect and common sense. It is because of our sins that we cannot have them[3] in our lives as fully as he has granted to the angels. Nevertheless, it is a great honor to us, even if we cannot have more of them, that we possess them to some extent. It will bring us to complete salvation if we just apply our thoughts to the acquisition of virtues. (8602)

God has granted us intellect in order that we may thoroughly adorn our lives with it. It is only right and proper that one should use it to seek out virtue and fine habits. Our intellect makes the way smooth for us, so that we can most certainly be virtuous, if we wish to be. So how does it come about that we apply our thoughts more towards vice and dishonor, avarice and gain than towards honor? It would be my desire and my advice, too, that we should consider how God has ennobled us by giving us common sense, for take it as the truth that there is nothing in the world than can have the adeptness of mind other than man, the angels, and God Himself. That is by His commandment. (8622)

God made us in His image when He gave us the power of reason. If, then, we were to apply to evil and dishonor that which we have of God's own image, we should not be following wise counsel. Whoever wishes to turn his thoughts properly to honor and gain should be directing his mind to where they came from [in the first place]. He should turn his thoughts to God as much as he can: that is His command, and then one cannot criticize him for it. Everyone has enough sense to know that God wants him to do what he ought to do. Everyone knows this well enough. (8640)

We have plenty [of sense] when we want to have it, but when we do not want it we do not have much sense [at all]. We have plenty of thoughts when it comes to bad things and profit, and avarice, and wealth, for then we have a very crafty mind, and we sharpen up our senses and our bodies as to how we should deceive women, but then we have no inclination to acquire virtues. (8652)

Anyone who wishes to deceive another person does not hang about with it for half a day. Priests and laymen have now for the most part become blind in their pursuit of wealth, for greed does not have the eyes of modesty. Their shame has been extended far and wide in our own times. The priest is supposed to give a good example, and the layman is supposed to live according to it. As it is, the priest proceeds with an injustice, and the layman is not far behind. The priest is supposed to carry the shield with its good example at the head of the first of his flock: this is meant to be his good instruction, by means of which he converts the wicked every day. With this shield he is supposed to afford us good protection against Satan, and likewise the noble knight is afterwards supposed to employ his sword in the service of good things and of justice. He is supposed to risk all that he possesses and his very life for the sake of poor squires, wise folk, and impoverished women. Now that has all been turned upside down. The priest wishes to have the knight's sword serve his interests so that he may increase his profits. He needs more than intellect to rob the people. He also needs power in order to acquire wealth through all sorts of cunning and force, in accordance with his greedy disposition. Nor does the layman think he is good enough unless he has books alongside his sword, for he wishes to gain profit by being able to read. He has written down for himself the interest that people are to pay him. Whatever he lacks in strength, he makes up for in cunning and deception. (8694)

Now look how a fine knight benefits by applying his thoughts to sharpening his mind for gain as he lies awake at night, when he should only be furthering chivalry and virtue and justice. It would be much better if a knight who behaves like this and is a knight only because of his wealth remained a squire. Is not a knight who only engages in legal arguments for the sake of gain a mere nothing by virtue of his possessions? When he should be applying his thoughts to the practice of courtesy and fine behavior, he sits with one leg crossed over the other in a corner all by himself, thinking up many ruses, and his mistress, Lady Avarice, is helping him to find a way of depriving so and so, and robbing someone else of his possessions, a plot of land perhaps, or a field. Then he thinks he is very smart when he has thought up some sly trick. (8720)

Then, whenever the worthy and high-spirited knights are ready for chivalrous activities, a nasty fellow calls out for an ox: "Sir, you must hear more from me. Our rights demand that this man should have his ox, that's only right. They are lording it over the lad." And when he has done with all his shouting he does not care who gets the ox. If the tail comes to him, he thinks he has what he deserves.[4] If we wish to think in a righteous manner, let us see how we might apply the mental faculties God gave us so that we may come to know Him better.[5] (8736)

What He gave us for the benefit of mankind, we apply today towards injuring them and causing them to suffer, and we brag about our foolishness whenever we have deceived Him—what stupidity! If someone achieves a reputation through good things, his good deeds do not help him, but if someone wishes to gain a reputation through wicked things, this must cause him great injury. We bring it about that a poor man loses much without being able to do anything about it. Look how we put our mind to winning such a minute gain and do not wish to acknowledge that we are going to lose incomparably greater riches in the kingdom of our Lord God. We have very little wisdom and we apply it the whole time to no useful purpose and to bad things, and as a result we must often fail. (8758)

All reason derives from God, and whoever places his trust in Him must certainly become wise. St. Peter became a preacher, although before that for a long time he had known about nothing except fishing. He who does not obey God's command separates himself from Him. (8766)

If a person moves further and further away from blissful ecstasy and from the wellspring of the intellect, he retains less and less of his own intellect, until he becomes a complete fool, but only then does he really believe that he is a wise man: that is how the devil manages to deceive us. If a man who relies on gain and avarice and material things believes he is intelligent, this belief derives from his foolish disposition. The fool cannot know that he is raging when he begins to rage, nor can a drunken man comprehend it. Likewise I say that anyone who relies exclusively on the counsel of the world has lost the best qualities inherent in a man, and as a result he does not know what he is doing: he thinks that evil is good. (8788)

Everybody has four qualities from which he should seek guidance. These four qualities are so constituted that all wisdom and all virtue are subject to them in youth and in old age. Now know this to be a fact: one should always apply to whatever one is able to do in the world these four qualities, or some of them. (8798)

The first is called Imagination,[6] the second Reason, the third Memory, which tends the treasure chamber at all times, and the fourth I call Intellect. Of the first, one knows only that it transforms thoughts into deeds that, prior to this, one has not witnessed for a long time. That comes about through the guidance of the quality called Memory. They have more or less the same function, for these two are sisters, Memory and Imagination. Imagination gives to her sister that which is in front of our eyes, and Memory can retain exactly what her sister conjured up before. Intellect and

Reason have control over Imagination and her sister, and they serve them according to their own properties. (8820)

Whatever Imagination perceives, whether by seeing it or in some other way, whether by smell or touch, by taste or hearing, she must bring to her mistress and that way she will not go wrong. Reason must decide what is good or bad and must commend whatever is good to the safekeeping of Memory. Intellect must be the messenger to the angels or to God. (8832)

Therefore I have said that anyone who sets his heart too much on gain will in the process lose the best qualities which he has and which ought to provide him with guidance in achieving courtesy and fine attributes, for he will not succeed by any other means. (8840)

As I have said, the power of Reason can distinguish evil from good, and anyone who turns his mind to gain foregoes it. He does not know when he has too much; he does not know, since he cannot, what is bad and what good. Intellect, which is inherent in us all, is lost, for he does not wish to acknowledge God or fulfill His will and His commandments. He is left with Imagination, for we have written that every ox has this quality bestowed on him in general by nature. (8856)

Now note what wits a man may have if he must abandon these qualities. Anyone who sets his heart on gain must thereby turn his back on greater possessions and yet he who sets his mind to gain thinks he is clever. (8862)

Alas—and I really want to say more about this—no man can ever acquire perfect understanding on this earth, even if he lives until the Day of Judgment. Instruction is waiting for us in the next world. The person who, on this earth, fashions and forms his words to the best of his ability is really a blessed man. There is no one in this world who can live long enough to learn an art perfectly throughout all of his years. On this matter a wise man says: "I know that I can never know but one thing: that on this earth I will come to know nothing." He is speaking the truth, for whatever you tell me a man knows, it can be known better.[7] One can find nothing of which one does not lack knowledge. (8882)

Anyone who can play chess well will nevertheless find someone who can play as well or better than he can. There is no lesson so small that one cannot learn it better, and you can take that as the truth. So what can remain of the great skills that we have in writing, since not one of us can ever understand the smaller ones? (8892)

We all want to be wise. A man seeks the prize of good sense through avarice. A man who can rob another man claims he is wise. If he had made the effort to think more deeply, he would have thought his gain a foolish one. We have plenty of writing concerning the arts, and seven of these have been selected. We call these arts "skills" and also call them "liberal" since no one who devotes himself to them wishes for more: one can find a remarkable lesson in them. The nasty fellow is no happier looking at his possessions than another man may be applying himself to the skills. They are also called "liberal" because anyone who relies on them must be free of worry and must even so possess wealth, but in such a way that he does not direct all his thoughts to it, for wealth forces out the teaching of the arts.[8] (8914)

The first is called Grammar, the second Dialectics, the name of the third is Rhetoric, and the next four are Arithmetic and Geometry, Music and Astronomy. (8920)

Grammar instructs in correct speaking. Dialectics distinguishes between straight and crooked, truth and falsehood. Rhetoric clothes our speech in elegant colors. Arithmetic brings the reward that one learns to count through mastery of her art. Geometry teaches us to measure well. Music, with her lovely melodies, gives us the knowledge of notes. Astronomy teaches without fail the nature of the stars and their constellations. (8932)

We do not find it written anywhere that anyone knew all seven or even one of these arts completely: this you should know for a fact.[9] The best scholars of Grammar we know about were Donatus and Priscian, and Aristarchus should also justly be included among the finest. Dialectics also has its followers, and the best are Aristotle and Boethius, Zeno and Porphirius. Rhetoric has certainly not instructed its host without good people: the best were Tullius, Quintilian, Sidonius. In Arithmetic the best were Crisippus and Pythagorus, in Music Gregorius, Timothy, Millesjus. In Geometry, Thales was the best, along with Euclid. The master of the Astronomy group was Albumasar, the standard-bearer Ptolemeus, and the foremost champion Atlas. Yet just look how not one of them could ever truthfully maintain that he had mastered his art completely! So how shall a man ever make out that he is wise, when he never applied himself to any instruction, whether in terms of good behavior or of virtue, but only in wicked wiles, and who only knows how to deceive someone? Solomon never thought he was overwise, yet those who only ever know about speaking according to some formula believe they are wise and pride themselves on this. They think the wrong they have been doing for a long time is right. I'll leave them to whatever they think they have gained. (8976)

I will count among the peasant's children those who have never been away from the farm and I liken them also to the man who has never left the dungeon and whom no one has ever told about the length and breadth of the world. How would he know if there were other worlds somewhere else? It's the same with the man who knows no other skill than his usual legal squabbling and does not know the scope of wisdom, neither its depth nor its breadth, and thinks he is perfect as he is. (8990)

He who deports himself in this world in such a way that his foot does not slip when he is climbing knows the heights, depth, and breadth of the intellect. He does not know the breadth, nor the height, nor the depth of the intellect who languishes all the time far from the heights in the depths of hell. (8998)

He who lives righteously, as he ought to, is familiar with Grammar. Even if he cannot speak correctly, he is nevertheless a wise man. He has a proper understanding of Dialectics who is straightforward in matters of honesty and knows how to guard against falsehood, so that he does not deceive anyone else. He certainly knows Rhetoric who knows how to tint his speech with the color of simplicity. Know that he is a wise man. If he does it without any evil intent I know that he is wise. He who never does other than he should nor is inclined to do less than he ought to do by rights certainly knows his Geometry. Whoever wishes to master Arithmetic should day and night, as far as he is able, do countless acts of goodness. He knows Music properly who makes his life so smooth that he causes the sounds of his words to chime with his deeds, and you should know that the man who adorns himself with the stars of virtue in youth and in old age is well acquainted with Astronomy. (9028)

If it comes about that a man can handle Grammar well so that he speaks correctly, then the man who behaves properly knows it better, be sure of that. If he who always recognizes falsity is a Dialectic, then he who all the time speaks the truth is a real Dialectic. If the man who weaves color into his speech can be called a Rhetorician, then the one who paints his speech a single color is certainly a Rhetorician. By that I mean that such a man's speech is straightforward if he does not have a negative intent. If the man who can measure an angle properly can be called a Geometrician, then the man who can judge what he should have in his life is even more of a Geometrician: he knows how to retain and how to give away. If he is an Arithmetician who can always count well, then he in whom one can count a host of virtues is certainly an Arithmetician. If he who causes the notes to sound sweetly can be called a Musician, then he is a Musician who makes his mind chime with what he does. If the man who can always recognize the stars is an Astronomer, then he who recognizes God is even more of one, be sure of that, for a star is the sun of righteousness and brings bright joy to all of us. (9062)

In addition to these seven broad disciplines that I have told you about, there are two other great arts that are superior to any other. They are, therefore, not called disciplines because they are called upon to reign over the other seven: they are their queen and their mistress. One is called Divinity, the other Physic. The function of each of them is good and sweet. Whoever turns his mind towards them can achieve great joy and pleasure in a deep and meaningful way. (9076)

Physic teaches us exactly how one should maintain one's body in good shape and in health, so that one does not become sick all the time, and it teaches a person, if he is sick, about what food and what medication is beneficial for each illness, and what the sick person should guard against. (9084)

Divinity teaches exactly how one should protect one's soul in order not to fall into sin through evil works the whole time, and that, if one does fall into sin, one should immediately take confession as a medication: that's a good idea, and that way the soul is well protected. One should prefer to remain healthy rather than have to seek medication, but if through one's own fault one is sick, then one must always search for it. Moreover, one should also rather protect oneself from sin than struggle to have one's hands freed from the bonds of one's sin. (9100)

If someone gets something in his eye he should not remain long without medical help, for if he delays he can soon lose the eye he [still] has. No one should conceal the wounds of his soul from the priest, for it often comes about that one does not make confession for one's sins. The sick man always demands that he be given unwholesome food, and the sinner, too, desires only what will increase his sin. (9112)

Now you are going to hear more about the teaching of these two arts. From Physic one shall discover the true nature of all things that are beneath the moon. Divinity gives us the means to recognize the angels and God, and His commandment. (9120)

Now note that the highly esteemed Divinity, which is the mistress of all the arts, gives us whatever there is in heaven in terms of art and skill, and whatever is beneath the moon lovely Physic gives to us, for from her one derives one's knowledge of the four elements. Whatever lies between the moon and heaven, this nature one comprehends through faithful Astronomy. Arithmetic and Geometry help out with this, too, the one with numbers, while the other measures heaven's chamber. (9134)

As I said just now, Divinity is the mistress of all the arts, for she determines how one should banish eternal suffering in this world and how one might always live well. How does it come about that one wishes to know less about this art than any other, even though it is the best of all in terms of profound meaning and fine skill? It comes about because it does not bother with worldly fame and worldly goods, whereas we are little concerned with intellect and any kind of love. Divinity has been tossed aside, though she was always the mistress of the arts. (9150)

That we elevate the Decrees and Laws results from our wish to ape the fools all the more. And if anyone says that that is not the case, let him answer this: why would we abandon the harbor of learning, namely Divinity, who was always the mistress, were it not for the fact that we have given ourselves over to profit? I am not blaming the Decrees: they are meant to be the shield of justice, but now we bring it about through them that injustice seems right to some people, but they were not made for that purpose. Anyone who lies awake worrying how he should misdirect good teaching will later regret it very much. The emperors made the law with wise advice, as whoever has read it knows, but the law can be changed: that happens every day. (9172)

The Decrees and the Law are good, if people treat them properly, for, as we have heard, the Decrees come from God. It was done for a good reason, but now we have turned things upside down by directing all the intention of the Law and the Decrees towards gain. (9180)

I should very much like to say more about the nature of the arts and their teaching and would be happy also to say how the one relates to the other, for it would be good to hear that and would surely reward us with wisdom. However, it would not suit those who cannot understand it. If I were to do it, what I said would be of no value to those who have no book learning. Thus I shall not do it: I must not exceed the target set for the layman. To be sure, there was a time when the laity was educated but now learning has become completely valueless. (9196)

In olden times every child could read. Then all the noble children were educated, which now they are not. The world itself was in a better state, too, without envy and without hatred, and then every man was respected according to his skill and his education. The lords were well educated, and they were valued for that too. Now very few lords are knowledgeable and consequently they never achieve renown. (9208)

Alexander, whom nothing in the world could withstand, was highly literate, and he always had his masters around him.[10] Ptolemy[11] and King Neptanebus[12] were educated, so that still today people say that they were very knowledgeable. Solomon[13] is more famous throughout the world on account of his learning than his empire, believe that for sure. The good King David,[14] too, is known far and wide for his intelligence. It was the skill of the three wise kings, Caspar, Melchior, and Balthasar, that brought them to where their hearts wished to be.[15] Because the star was revealed to them, they are famous to this day. It is quite true that Julius, who was the first to govern the Roman empire, was also well educated.[16] He was rich in virtue, too. If he had not possessed intelligence and goodness, as we read, he would not have had the capacity to draw such wise and virtuous people under his authority, or so we have heard. (9238)

Now what would have prevented[17] these good gentlemen from having their children tutored? Whenever they let them go and play, people should teach them to understand what is good and what evil, and what one should choose to do, and what is good breeding, honor, and virtue, and what one should guard against, and what is right and what wrong, and what is straight and what crooked, and what is true and what false: all that they should be taught. In addition, a noble lord ought to have well educated masters at his court, so that his children and the others who are there can make progress in learning: that would be good and honorable for them. (9256)

In referring to the customs of the nobility I am including also other people who are noble inasmuch as they have their beloved children tutored in their youth, for from learning one acquires virtue. Those who are constantly concerned about how they can make their dear children rich in terms of material things should also enrich their minds in terms of good behavior and courtesy. One can bequeath no greater inheritance to one's children, nor such a fine one, as a well-tutored mind, for from learning one discovers how one should be pleasing to God. Learning also tends to inform people how they should live well in this world. Moreover, it is of greater assistance to the father than if he were to bequeath his son the means to become a usurer or perhaps a wicked money-lender. To be sure, wealth does not incite us to turn our thoughts to our forebears: know for a fact that intellect must admonish us to do that, for affluence often leads us astray with its very fickle gaze, so that we do not apply our minds to our father who left us the wealth but forget him completely. For that reason you should know for certain that one can bequeath children no better riches than an informed mind. (9290)

If, for the sake of saving and gaining, someone ruins his child's mind by not sending him to school or to court, be sure that he is directing his gain towards great loss. Whoever does not bequeath intellect to his child but leaves him wealth does not know what he is doing by that. (9298)

Very likely an unwise man who, out of laziness, is neither willing nor able to learn, will defend himself with the following talk, telling me by way of answer that untutored people do better, for the one who is well tutored does not do what he should do. The learned priest always desires wicked things and sin and material gain along with ignorant laymen. "What is the point of our learning anything, when we see that this is what happens?" [he says]. (9312)

I propose to respond to what he says with a single word: Do you believe that the person who can read well is a learned man? To be sure, there are lots of priests—I want to tell you this as a fact—who can read what they see and even so cannot maintain that they understand what is written. Exactly the same thing happens to a peasant who goes into a church and stands in front of the pictures: however well he can see the painting, he has no idea what it means. He does not know what the picture is saying: understanding is not a universal experience. So how can you expect that one man knows better than another what he ought to do, when he has not the faintest idea what the writing means? (9332)

Now, however, take as an example that a learned doctor—let's assume that he is learned—often craves unwholesome food although he knows that it does him harm and yet he still follows his gluttonous urge. A man who can read well can easily do likewise, so that his greed draws him to where he achieves trials and tribulations. (9342)

We should cherish education: if he ever becomes sick, a doctor can make himself better with medication. If anyone falls into a ditch, know that he can get out of it better if he can see than if he cannot see. The same holds true for the very learned man: if he perpetrates a sin, he realizes at some point that he has acted against God and returns to His authority by seeking to confess. The ignorant man never does that. (9356)

A fool does not wish to learn, for his foolish heart says to him: "I am not going against God, since I do not know His commandment. If I did know what was against Him, I would not want to do it." And he believes he is deceiving God like this whereas actually no one can tell Him a word of a lie. The man who out of idleness knows nothing is unknown to God. Thus we have it in the scriptures: "He who knows nothing, him God does not know."[18] He who through his own fault knows nothing at all goes against the favor of God. Justice demands that a man find out what he does not know. Then when he has found it out, let him follow good counsel. Whoever can follow good advice is not a foolish man at all. (9376)

One finds out what one wishes to know and what one does not want to know one leaves alone. If anyone took your ox from you, or if anyone killed your children, you would go to another man, if you did not understand about such things yourself, so that he might tell you the right way to proceed. And if you are not concerned to learn about the salvation of your soul, then that is foolishness. (9386)

In fact, one will not comprehend anything, no matter who wishes to say something about God, for if the devil has ensnared someone, be sure that he will not allow him to pursue such talk from which he can take a good example but ensures that he makes a mockery of anything that is said to him about God. Let anyone who wishes to walk in the way of God and quickly separate himself from the enemy be glad to hear about the goodness of God, about His martyrdom and His humility, for that will certainly inspire him to serve God, and that's the truth. If, when I am thirsty, I think of good, cool water, my thirst is made very much worse: I have experienced that right enough. If someone is walking across a bridge and out of fear manages not to look down, it can easily happens to him that his foot slips and he must fall down to where he did not dare to look. Exactly the same happens to a person who does not wish to hear God's judgment, for even so he cannot escape it. If someone does not want to hear what I am saying, I may indeed take that amiss, so how may God react if someone does not want to hear His commandment? How is He to perceive me if I do not want to listen to His word? If someone closes his ears to His words He will not wish to hear his prayers. If a sick man behaves badly when he is eating then for sure that is not a good sign. Therefore, bear in mind the sick man: if it pains a man when people speak to him of God, and even if he hears anything but then does not better himself, he may well realize that he is in a very desperate state. (9432)

The layman thinks to himself: "Since the priest, who can see in the scriptures what is evil and what is not, does wrong, then it is not my fault if I act against God's favor, since I cannot see what pleases our Lord more and what does not please Him. I do not know the scriptures." Alas, how such a man deceives himself when he lies so blatantly! Where the priest comprehends with his eyes, that same message passes through the ears of laymen. How fools do deceive themselves! (9448)

In fact, every man and every woman has five doors to the body: the first is sight, the second hearing, the third smell, the fourth touch, and the fifth I call taste, and whatever one knows in this world must always pass to us through one of these five doors. Thus Imagination takes it up and brings it to Lady Reason, who must decide, just as I have said. That is why I say that whatever does not pass to a layman through one door nevertheless goes into him through another, if he has any sense. If he does not know what the scriptures are saying, then his idleness does not persuade him not to transgress against God, and he does not follow His commandment. The layman should let the good news in through the door of his ears. If he firmly shuts the door of his ears, then the guest, this good news,[19] does not come in. (9472)

The five doors are called the five senses and derive their attributes from without. The authority of the four forces has strength within. The five senses serve them with their external attributes. The five senses are the servants of the "qualities." The four qualities have great judgment and are counselors, and the soul is their queen. (9482)

Now note that no man can live without the fifth sense, which we call touch. He can live without hearing, without taste, without a sense of smell, and without sight, but without touch no one can live for long. He must give up his life without that. For this reason a wise man from whom people know a great deal said: "One lives well from the four [senses] but it is from the fifth that one shall live, for no one can live a [single] day without touch."[20] Now take care of what is particularly useful to you here, in order that later it does not become worse and much less useful. A wise man should be on his guard against this, so that he does not incur terrible pain through touching fire or cold snow. (9504)

One rouses one's sense of touch with blows, one's sense of smell with a stench, one's hearing with a din, and one's taste with bitter gall day and night. Daylight does not shine in hell, for there only darkness and night are seen. There only misery has power. (9512)

Now our senses have gone to sleep but the man who arrives at this point will surely find that his five senses are woken up in a wretched way. Our sense of touch has fallen asleep because of the soft things we touch, our hearing because of dulcet tones, our sight because of the beauty of a woman, our sense of smell by gentle fragrances. I have not omitted our sense of taste: this has fallen completely asleep because of sweetness. Everyone must have a particular sense which arouses him according to his own nature, for, as I said, they are servants of Lady Imagination, Lady Memory, and Lady Reason. They do not serve them well here, for no one serves well while he is sleeping. (9530)

Very often the rights of the lords are ignored by malevolent servants. That is exactly what happens to the four qualities, for they are not done justice by the five malevolent senses who have delayed for the sake of gain, but it is right and proper that the master should beat the servant, if he loiters too much on his lazy journey. Lady Reason and Lady Imagination should do likewise: they should chastise the senses so that they do not go crazy for gain. They are puffed up with wealth, and because of that our heart cannot see [properly]. The five senses have been so puffed up that Imagination and Reason have both gone astray, and that is what upsets the lady of the house. (9550)

I am referring to the soul, the queen of the body: since she, the counselor, has lost the four qualities, her advice must be all the worse. However, she must not lose it [completely], unless that comes about as a result of her own desire and her fault, for Reason dare not do anything in this world to lose her favor. Only the soul has total authority over the four qualities, and with them she brings about many kinds of advice, both good and bad. The body does what it does according to what it thinks, both just and unjust. To be sure, the servant often behaves wickedly, if his master does not forbid him to do so, and it is the same with the body: if the soul were really to forbid him, he would abandon what he should not do. (9570)

It is true what I have written, that the bodies of men and women are destined for a fall. Thus the soul must fight fiercely with the host of virtues against that and allows itself to be dragged down, too. It must pay a high price for that, for it fails to do what it should do. The soul and the four powers it has as its advisors should hold sway within the body, and it should nevertheless follow the advice of the body, for the body and the five senses guide the soul towards gain. The five senses are in control: the four qualities have no strength. Look how honored the advisers are, along with their queen! (9588)

No one should be surprised if the soul has to have its trials and tribulations. Since it follows the advice of the body, it is only just that it should suffer, for it should always be using its resistance to overcome the body. (9594)

As far as the soul is concerned, things are always the same as with a king. The king should always rule justly, and then his land is well ruled. If he does not exercise good judgment in his land, then his people will immediately do wrong. If he gives himself over to idleness, then his people will shirk work. (9602)

It is just the same with the soul. If it is ever slothful and does not keep the body in good order as it should, then it will be its fault if the body often transgresses against the favor of God. Therefore, no one should ask: "What does the soul do that it should be harmed by the fact that the body is always lazy and wicked?" For the king should compensate for it if his people do not live well and his people will not fail to gain some advantage, too. The same happens to the soul that has not ordered its body well. They both land in trouble, for when the body was set on pursuing calamity and reprehensible deeds, the soul did nothing to stop it. (9622)

The king must be worse off than those who are subject to him. He excels in terms of wicked deeds and arrives first at the gates of hell. The same happens to the soul: the body does not suffer any other agony until the Day of Judgment, since it dies only once, for it has not the slightest idea what happens to it in the grave. The soul that has done this to him heads very quickly towards misery. However, when the Day of Judgment arrives, the two, body and soul, are certainly brought together, as they are. Then any men and women who have delayed too long must go to hell: there is no help for that. Body and soul must go there if a man has not atoned. (9642)

A wise man says that it is easy to understand that the soul must share with the body either good or evil, since a long time ago they both did either right or wrong together. (9648)

It should not seem surprising that the damned man should be lost for all eternity, for his will did not prevent him [from sinning] and, if he had not died, he would have sinned a lot more. Because of that he will suffer eternal misery. (9654)

Nor should it seem strange that every man who goes to hell does not perish, for our Lord, who created the whole world and what is in it, has left the damned powerless, so that they must die a living death. This they have been granted to their misfortune. (9662)

A man may well be saying: "Today you've told me many profound things, about four powers, five senses, eleven arts. How could I know them all? I dare not learn them, nor do I want to. I want to live a comfortable, easy life forever from now on." I want to answer this person. (9672)

My friend, I'll shorten your idleness with a lengthy task. If you wish to become wise in a short time, then let your faith and, in the same way, your works be combined with constancy in accordance with their right. Then the way that brings you to enlightenment and to the acquisition of all kinds of joy will be a smooth one. You can easily have faith if you firmly believe in God and His power, and what great authority He has shown in this world, both on high and on the earth. (9686)

Now imagine something quite different and think of a man who has a very small body yet great authority. God granted him the strength to control everything with his counsel. Now let's forget his mental faculties, about which I should like to say a lot, and think what marvels men and women have in their bodies by way of veins and bones. You should know that not one vein is superfluous: the body is beautifully created with great skill. That the soul exists within it and yet is quite different in its nature, that is the great achievement that the power of God has applied to it. (9704)

Since He has done that for us, no man on earth should be surprised that He has retained for Himself extraordinary and miraculous wonders. However, anyone who cannot comprehend what people say about His divinity and about mankind can simply believe the manifold miracles of God and can surely come to a complete understanding. (9716)

I have revealed to you what marvels and what authority, what art and what craft the soul may exercise inside the body. I have said in addition that strength, speed, and agility, all three things, constitute the strength of the body.[21] If the soul with its common sense does not have control of these three things, they will often cause great suffering. Know that the soul should also rule over the six things I have told you about before, and it should do it with discretion. Men and women both have five things inside their bodies, and five outside their bodies. In truth, the soul must rule them all, or they will cause great wickedness in youth and in old age. People have these five inside their bodies: strength, speed, desire, beauty, agility. Outside there are five things: nobility, power, wealth, reputation, authority. Anyone who cannot rule these ten things wisely should not be called a man. If anyone cannot adorn and govern strength, speed, agility, desire, and beauty with discretion, they will bring him many vices. Anyone who does not direct wealth, nobility, power, reputation, and authority with his intellect is more primitive than an ox, if anyone can understand that. If a man possesses wealth but no intellect, he will become arrogant because of it. Even an ox does not do that. If a horse were to become more foolish, who would be so well disposed towards that horse as to make him a bridle of gold? It is true that it would not be more foolish just because someone covered it in gold. If you make a foolish man rich, he will consider himself second to none: he will immediately get it into his head that he is an emperor, and no one will be able to cope with him. Praise a dog as much as you like for catching lots of hares: he will not become stupid because of that. On the other hand, if you praise a foolish man who cannot understand, he will become so vain that he will think no one is his equal. The hare is swift, but know for a fact that the elephant is strong and yet always so gentle. However, if a foolish man is swift and strong but does not have much sense, he will keep on trying all the time until he finally succumbs. He who wants to aspire all the time without actual need requires a lot of things.[22] The dove is a beautiful bird, yet it is always gentle. If a man or a woman has a lovely, elegant body, he or she will immediately become arrogant, which an animal does not do. Therefore I have told you that anyone who cannot govern these ten things with discretion is more an animal than a man. He is much worse than a steer, if anyone can understand this properly. An animal has its vices; thus, if the fool will not desist from them, he will have all the vices of an animal in youth and in old age. Whoever does not govern his power with his intelligence will derive so much from it that he will always be like a wolf in terms of his power. Anyone who does not control his desire is too much like a beast: like a donkey in terms of laziness, a pig in terms of uncleanliness. He is as lecherous as a dog, as aggressive as a marten. And he follows the animal even more with all sorts of vices. Anyone who does not choose to have the intellect of a human being will rightly manage to become much worse than an animal the whole time, for an animal can have what it should have without any sense. If someone lacks discretion, the ten things I have told you about will cause him harm. They should really be subject to discretion. Every man, as I have said, should govern these ten things with common sense and discretion. So see what great authority the power of the soul must have, for both men and women must govern the ten things both inside and outside their bodies well, if they are not to fare badly. Five outside and five within: this comes about as a result of great intelligence. I do not wish to leave out the eleventh one: I have not dealt with it properly because it is both outside and inside, but one should govern it with common sense, too. This is speech, for it is sometimes inside and then at another time outside. It is an unfortunate man who cannot govern that. If one does not govern it properly inside, it comes out differently from how it should. It will produce bad results outside, if it is not governed with subtlety inside. Therefore I have told you that one should not apply intellect and discretion towards evil ends. We should succeed by using good sense. Whatever we possess is nothing if it is not guided by good sense. (9848)

The seventh part is now complete, and I am greeting the eighth at the door.

BOOK VIII

All along I have been talking a great deal about inconstancy and what inconstancy there is in us. I have spent a lot of time saying how people are troubled with wickedness in youth and in old age. I have also clearly demonstrated how one can recognize inconstancy in the six things in which we tend to fail, and in the three physical qualities. I have said what control discretion has over them and over beauty. That is the tenth quality that I have included in the first part. The kinsmen of inconstancy, its troops and its retinue, I have revealed to you according to my perception and my belief. I have also talked about constancy and other virtues, and I have cited their kinsfolk and their companions too. As I have told you earlier, the dynasty of inconstancy is far-reaching, for in truth a host of vices belong to her clan. Some are her children and some her nieces and nephews. Inconstancy has a sister, and I cannot refrain from talking about her ways and her power, her activities and her nature. (9884)

The sister of inconstancy is always immoderation, and immoderation cannot be constant, as has often become apparent to us. I spoke about constancy when I was speaking about inconstancy, and now similarly I cannot omit to speak about moderation, for that way one will better recognize immoderation, be sure of that. (9894)

Immoderation is the messenger of Foolishness, the playmate of Drunkenness, and the cousin of Arrogance, if anyone takes note of it. Immoderation is the power of Anger; Immoderation has no authority. Immoderation is the mouth of the glutton, the keystone of avarice, the hound of Desire, for it seeks and hunts what Desire enjoys. Know for a fact that it is also the tongue of Lechery. Immoderation is the poison of Envy, for the scriptures tell us that the person who is excessively envious will surely kill himself. Immoderation is the fear of Cowardice and the sleep of Sloth, and you should not be surprised that Immoderation is tinder to Wantonness. I want to tell you briefly, for you surely ought to know this, namely, that Immoderation is a goad to the flock of Vices, for it drives them on and wakes them up in our youth and in old age. It is the quality of Immoderation to exceed its strength. It is the way of Immoderation to accompany vices, and thus it achieves damnation and the hatred of God. Immoderation has no limits: it is too little and too much. The man who cannot exercise moderation is cursed and damned. There should be moderation in all things: nothing can go wrong if there is moderation. The man who cannot moderate his behavior is a wretched man indeed. (9934)

You should know that moderation is always the measure of the intellect. The right measure lies between too little and too much. Whoever uses moderation as a measuring stick is doing everything just as he should. One should measure according to one's ability: immoderation has too much power. One should measure great and small, and proper moderation should be the common factor. If we neglect moderation, scales, and number, that represents a great decline in justice. Moderation bestows upon us honor and goodness, while immoderation is associated with arrogance. Moderation maintains and bestows according to what is right, while immoderation makes a slave out of a master. Moderation governs castles and lands, while immoderation inflicts damage and shame. Moderation measures all sorts of things, whereas immoderation has not the ability to measure anything. It is stretched and cannot measure; it expands and contracts. It is the bowstring and the bow and cannot hit its target. Do you know how that comes about? Its arrow has no feathers at all, know that as a fact, and so it shoots wide of the mark, if you can understand that. It shoots too far on one side of the target or the other. Anyone who cannot moderate his behavior should take a look at the wolf which flees quickly if anyone chases it quickly: it has control over its flight inasmuch as it flees only according to what the huntsman does. It does well on its flight because it runs only as it needs to. Whatever a man does with moderation he perseveres with it for a long time. I want my bed to correspond to my height. I want my shoe neither too wide nor too narrow, for if it is too narrow it will squeeze my foot and one stumbles if one's shoe is too wide. I'll leave any excesses in the world to my enemies. Whatever one does in this world cannot be good if it lacks moderation. In fact, I want to say even more, that with moderation's instruction one can make a virtue out of a vice. Anyone who wished to make the effort could turn virtue into vice, though one ought not to do that. Now hear how this can happen. (9992)

Always between two vices there is one virtue, and, in truth, humility is between arrogance and stupidity. You should know that humility is a particularly fine virtue. If anyone wishes to be humble, I will offer him this advice: that he guard against foolishness, for know for a fact that if a man is foolish he is not immune from vice. Similarly, there should be moderation in humility, so that foolishness will leave us alone. If someone is excessively humble, his humility will become a vice and foolishness right away: know that this is true. Note how immoderation can make a vice out of a virtue: if a man cannot guard against excess he will fare badly. If anyone wishes to protect himself from foolishness, let him not overstep the limit of gentleness and humility lest he fall into arrogance. He who wishes to give a good account of himself should take the middle path. (10020)

Simplicity is on the one hand cleverness and on the other hand foolishness. One ought to be simple in the proper fashion and at the same time be wary of foolishness. Whoever wishes to avoid foolishness should guard against wicked cunning. No one should be greedy. However, one should take great care not to throw one's wealth about: a man who does that is a fool. Generosity takes the middle road: it retains and gives away in moderation. Anyone who wishes to avoid thirst should take care not to drink too much. Anyone who wishes to avoid hunger should also steer clear of gluttony. The man who does not wish to lead an unchaste life should not deny himself to his wife on that account. After all, if one wishes to be excessively foolish one can easily live unchastely with one's own wife. (10042)

Whoever wishes to be righteous should not vent his anger too much. One must often be angry in a court of law, but one should not be too angry, for one should not judge more harshly than the transgression warrants. If someone becomes immoderately angry in a court of law, he does not judge correctly. The court should not remain totally without mercy. However, if someone wishes to be merciful, let him not forgive too much. The person who wishes to forgive too much in a court of law also provides a bad example. The person who wishes to love tolerance should beware of cowardice, so that he may be tolerant for the sake of God, and not through the dictates of cowardice. Let him always be careful not to put up with any violence in his court, for know that tolerance [in that case] is indifference and laziness. (10066)

Now I have come to the point where you have really heard how immoderation can turn virtue into vice. The man who cannot refrain from immoderation will never fare well. Moderation can easily make vice into virtue. Whichever man subjects his anger to reason, no matter how great a vice anger is, it immediately becomes a virtue. Anger is a great vice, and it robs a man of his senses. Anger is the cousin of drunkenness, know that for a fact. Anger is the child of madness, as those who are angry very well know. Anger is cloaked in animosity, as the angry man often finds out. Anger has no power in itself and takes revenge in all kinds of ways. When it cannot take revenge on something, it turns the lash of its tongue on it. What it does not dare to speak about, its will nevertheless fully desires. Anger is a particularly bad vice, in youth and in old age, and yet through moderation it is true that one can transform it completely into virtue. If a man can temper his anger with good sense, as he ought to temper it, so that he turns it towards justice and does not become angry without good cause but rages against evil, his anger is bringing him good fortune. Vice is a virtue if someone always tempers it like this. Anger is death to the foolish man and delivers the wise man from peril. The anger of the wise derives from something good, that of the foolish derives from arrogance. (10108)

God endowed us with both anger and love, so that good sense should cultivate both of them and we should love virtue fervently and rage against vice. We have turned this completely upside down, that I can say for a fact, for we love vice much more than the teaching of virtue. We do not rage against vice, but virtue is the object of our anger, and because of that our foolishness has transformed both anger and love into vices. Believe me, that is the truth. However, you should know that anyone who subjects his anger to prudence can make a virtue out of a vice, but that must come about through moderation, as I have stated here. (10128)

However evil arrogance may be, if someone can moderate it with goodness and common sense, then know for sure that he can lead it into the company of virtues. If a proud spirit bows down and sinks beneath the fear of God, then know that his arrogance has turned itself into such goodness that he repudiates injustice. Then he will protect poor fellows against unjust force and thus arrogance can be counted among the virtues, know that as a fact. Look how a vice has become a virtue at the same time, and, as I have said, true moderation has brought this about, for it is adept at reducing it beneath the power of our Lord. Arrogance wishes to ascend to God, but it is His commandment that man, with his measured sense, should not allow it to climb too high. One should suppress it through fear of Him: anyone who does not do that has forfeited God's grace and His blessing—know that for a fact—and he will never come into His kingdom. You may also believe that this is the truth. (10158)

Know that any man who is so envious that he always denigrates the accomplishments of another man, saying they are not good and "I would have done it better," is measuring out his spitefulness, so that he will remain a malevolent man when the other man progresses virtuously. If, however, someone does not mind if another man is respectable and does not lower himself with his spitefulness and push himself forward all the time, trying to compare with him, you should believe for sure that he is tempering his spitefulness so carefully that it may be called a virtue. (10174)

Now you have heard exactly how moderation can always make vices into virtues, if a person can temper them properly. In addition, I have also told you what immoderation does, and how nothing that one does to excess can be good. However good something may be, if immoderation is present, it cannot be good, since one does it to excess. (10186)

It is good to go to church, but one could be there for such a long time that it would not be good. The prayer that one says in church when one is thinking of the market does not please God. Thus it has been written: "A brief prayer is the gate to heaven,"[1] for anyone who tries to pray too long indulges in many other thoughts. Long praying would be fine if one could keep one's mind on it, but if one's thoughts wander it would be better if it were brief. A man who has a lot to do would be well advised to remain only so long in church that he does not in the process miss out on some other good deed. That is my wish and my advice. If he chooses to miss out on some just activity, his prayer is worthless. If he fails to help orphans and poor fellows and does not wish to give in the name of God, he is leading a useless life. If we pass the day well and go to church with a good heart, then I think that is a splendid way to live. Unfortunately, we are not strong enough to dare to take upon ourselves the behavior of the saints who have owed it to God that, by His commandment, they should be the whole night long at their prayers. If we only had the power to go to church in moderation, humbly and with awe, I think that would be good. Be sure that anyone who is full of himself there, chatting and laughing, is making the saints witnesses to his misbehavior. What help is there for him then? The saints, or so we read, are meant to be our spokesmen, whereas God is lord and judge. If someone cares so little about himself that he watches over things in such a way as to make both his spokesmen and his judge witnesses against himself, I shall be surprised if he gains anything thereby. Whoever wishes to pursue the teaching of moderation has nothing more to ask of God than that He should guide Christendom along the right path and that, in His goodness, He should deliver the dead out of their anguish and direct them[2] along the path where they are saved from sin and that they should do what is just and good. That is what one should ask for. (10248)

Once he has offered up this prayer, it is my desire and my advice that he should begin doing these things. If a man is always asking and then not doing anything, his prayer is worthless. On the other hand, the prayer is good if afterwards one does something good. Whoever asks for help from God and then applies himself to wicked things is negating with his actions what he has asked of God. However earnestly I may have expressed my respect for a man, if I value him differently through my deeds, he will not thank me for what I have said, and it is the same with our Lord God. It is His desire and His command that no one shall demonstrate vanity after he has beaten his breast, or brag or make a din after he has fallen to his knees. (10270)

If I am intending to behave badly, then my prayer will not help me much. Indeed, the prayer of a good man could not help me at all, unless I wanted to behave well myself. A doctor often does what he is supposed to, yet his work is as nothing if the patient does not wish to take care of himself. I should avoid evil thoughts and evil actions with my own intentions, and then I can better succeed if someone prays for me, be sure of that. Prayer helps in this struggle, but no prayer can force me against my own will in such a way that it can get me into heaven. (10286)

Some people ask that God should turn His anger on His enemies, some that God should make them rich and that God should give them power, and some even ask that God should grant them authority. They believe they have the power of intellect and would like to be judges. That shows their foolishness, for if they were to become lords, no one would benefit from them. Look, the person who prays like that is certainly praying without moderation. (10300)

Anyone who chose to beg a nobleman for a quarter of a loaf of bread should quite rightly consider that to be wrong. He would certainly be weakened by it. Indeed, the person serving the meal would not consider it right, if he had the spirit of a noble server. Anyone who asks God for worldly gifts is making a feeble request and has a feeble disposition as well. God is so generous and so good that if anyone asks Him for His kingdom He will certainly give him riches, too, in order that he may live. Whomsoever He gives the most, to him He also gives the least. The man who wishes to do the least and leaves the most along the way is a cowardly fool. Anyone who is fortunate enough to receive a whole loaf will also get the quarter of it. God wishes people to ask for much, for He bestows lavishly from His rich treasure chamber if someone serves Him consistently. When you see that God often grants worldly possessions to the wicked man you can certainly know that worldly possessions by themselves are a mere nothing. Therefore, as I have said, the wicked and the good man both receive wickedness and good in this world, for whoever judges this correctly [knows that] nothing which is finite is completely wicked or completely good. (10334)

Now you have certainly heard that one should go to church, but do so in moderation. I shall not desist from fasting, but do not say that one should certainly fast in moderation on the days which are determined by God. Anyone who breaks his fast on those days is a complete child, and he should guard against that, but if anyone orders him to fast more often on account of his sins, he should guard against that, too. No one, man nor woman, who wishes to serve God well should fast to such an extent that he or she dies. I have read and heard that he should abandon his desires, not his body, for otherwise he will not be able to work throughout the day. He should control his body to the extent that he can strive against it and achieve mastery over it with the power of his soul. Once he has brought it under control like this, then it is my desire and my advice that he should not inflict great martyrdom on himself, for that is not what our Lord wishes. If his body is always so troubled and so vain that it brings death to his soul, then one should cause it so much suffering with fasting and with all kinds of things that it loses its strength. One should not kill the body completely, but certainly kill the lust inside the body if afterwards the soul is to flourish. One should distribute one's riches in such a way that the poor may be happy that God has given us riches: that is my desire and my advice. The man who is to be helped through his almsgiving should adhere to moderation so that he never applies his efforts to making people thank him, for one should thank God for this: it has come about through His commandment. (10382)

Now look: however good a thing might be, it should be accompanied by moderation. Talking and laughing are good; sleeping and waking are good, if anyone practices them with moderation and does not overdo either of them. Enjoying oneself is often good, if one does not do it to excess. Some people have a habit, and they believe themselves perfect in this, that they apply themselves to making people howl and laugh the whole time, but they are certainly absolutely useless to them and to ourselves. When someone has laughed too heartily, anyone present who has any sense will really consider him a fool. You should know that my ears often turn aside from this kind of frogs' singing when I am out walking. Why should the poor man who has taken this upon himself be happy? Has he gained the kingdom of heaven? Or has he escaped from the devil? Or what has happened to him? I can declare for a fact that he is laughing about what he should cry over, if he were honest with himself, for while he is chattering all over the place all the people around him are so confused that they will not be able to recognize what are good examples. He is the devil's trickster, for with his storytelling he will cause a fool to overlook the enemy, because he is not aware of him. I tolerate nice games, too, but one should not play too many of them. As I have often said, anything that is done to excess can never be good, as we have often seen. (10424)

I think it would certainly go too far if a man who bears roses on his shield wanted to carry all the flowers from the fields on his shield, too.[3] In the same way, I want to say to you that it would be a strange thing if someone who was supposed to bear the sun thought he wanted the stars and the moon and the sky, too. Indeed, I wish to say to you that what one sees on the outside is not without significance, for it always signifies what is also on the inside.[4] A person's heart is often recognized by his weapons and his clothing. Let me tell you that it is good when a man can carefully see to it that people pay more attention to him than to his weapons. You can believe me when I say that, whatever he carries on his shield, if he is brave in the field I shall tolerate that better, too. However, one must observe moderation in this. It would not appear to me to be good that, because someone is supposed to bear the waves of the sea, he should paint the wonders of the sea on his armor, and all the individual fishes. Anyone who is supposed to bear a wild boar on his armor, let him watch out that he does not have a whole herd of swine, for that would look bad, that's true. If anyone wants to have a dog [on his armor], he should not overtax himself by having a whole hunt: let him not put too much effort into that. How would it look if the person who displays a wolf were to want to include the she wolf and the wolf cubs on his armor, too? One cannot applaud it if someone does that. (10470)

At the same time as Lord Otto—who has now suffered severe defeat— was in Lombardy and had come to Rome, as you will have heard, I came there, too, and, to be sure, remained at his court for eight weeks and more.[5]

It displeased me very much that emblazoned on his shield there were three lions and a demi-eagle. In both respects it was certainly designed without moderation. Three lions were too much. If someone wants to display one lion and behave accordingly, he seems to me a decent man. Now you should know for a fact that a demi-eagle is missing something. I will not lie to you in this matter: half an eagle is unable to fly. So, in terms of too little and too much, there was a lack of moderation, if anyone can understand this. I believe it was supposed to signify what the consequence would be. One lion represents high spirits; three lions represent arrogance. Whoever has the hearts of three lions is following the advice of arrogance. Whoever has the spirit of one lion seems to me to be doing enough. The eagle flies very high, and his lofty flight signifies honor. Thus, in truth, half an eagle signifies the departure from honor. Now some people choose to maintain that Lord Otto has been separated from the empire on account of his arrogance. If anyone wishes to rise above the spirit of a man with the heart of three lions, he will soon suffer a fall, and no matter how high a half-eagle may be, he will have to fall, that is true enough. I am not saying this to accuse him of being arrogant. I do not think it would be good if I were to do that, for, whatever course he has taken, I wish to refrain from speaking badly of him, for by doing so I should be making myself weak. It will not happen, if I can help it, but in saying what I said I was repeating what people say of him, not saying it myself. However, I can certainly say that everyone should take note and take an example from what happened to him. In fact, those who can see will note that many marvelous things happened to him in a short period of time. Whoever gives some thought to this will not consider it a long time since, in the time of King Philipp, there were so many fighting on the side of Lord Otto that people were inclined to believe that he was going to take the empire. However, his power declined rapidly, and the power of Lord Philipp increased, so that people asserted that *he* must certainly have the empire. But then he died, and all the honor of the empire quickly fell to Lord Otto, who has now departed, too. Anyone who trusts in the honor of the world will be sorely deceived. Anyone who places his hope in his own power very often fails because of that. Whoever has failed on one occasion should take care the next time around. Believe me: anyone who falls into the same trap twice has no sense. Nothing can dismay the man who places his trust in God. Anyone who humbles himself before God will not be the object of shameful mockery. Whoever places his trust in himself can easily go wrong. The person who does not wish to be subject to God must have a weaker master. Whoever fears Him does not fear death. With Him one shall very well overcome all adversity. I have read and heard that the man who serves God at all times is indeed a lord. (10568)

Now take an example from the way our child has risen:[6] when people thought they knew for a fact that he was going to lose Apulia, God delivered German territories into his hands as well. Now look how the root fashioned by the power of God soon throws off its shoots. Whereas the tree which has no roots topples, the sturdy and noble branch will always grow. God shall strike down faithlessness and arrogance as He has often done. All honor to the man who is subject to Him! (10584)

You can take as an example, if you are so inclined, the way in which Apulia was disrupted on two occasions within a short space of time on account of its treachery and will not desist from showing its great treachery towards the one to whom it should be subject.[7] Now let him who wishes to do so take note that very soon more misery will come to it. (10594)

The person who wishes to note the ways of the Greeks can also follow their example. They thought nothing of other people, and now, because of their misfortune, they have become a source of mockery to strangers. This is what God can bring about. They thought the Franks were fools and now they have to obey their wishes and their commands, and all this has come about through God. The emperor of the Greeks wanted people to call him a saint. Now, in ten years, there have been seven "saints" who have died.[8] I can say that this is a pathetic little kind of saintliness which people cannot say has amounted to much, since Andronicus now lies shamefully, wherever he may be.[9] One could take as an example the fact that he was killed in such a way that no one dared lament him. As I have now written, in the meantime, there are at least seven all slain and dead: that is a wretched business. The fact that they were called holy emperors in their kingdoms and their lands could not help Andronicus when they dragged him back and forth like a villain in the mud. The wise man had become a fool; the emperor became a slave and did not have the privileges of an emperor. The saint became a thief, and this was not a game that he enjoyed very much. Pride fell, as it often does. (10632)

Now we have surely come to the end of this and have seen and taken in that immoderation and arrogance must often take a hard fall. Know that the person who is always riding about on his high horse comes to a fall. If a man climbs ever higher in terms of pride, he descends further and further from God through His commandment. When he brings himself ever further down with his humility by means of his good deeds, he is ever higher up and close to God. (10646)

What use is it if we see, as I can truthfully state, that pride always falls at the very end? We do not improve ourselves by that, and I do not know how it comes about either. If anyone had all the chronicles he would discover that all the arrogant people came to a bad end. I have heard a bit about this, but I have not read them all. It is true that every king should possess the chronicle of his kingdom, and if he does not have it, that is because, out of idleness, it has not been written. If you have read in any book that any man has come through arrogance to a good end, I will say it is [a] good [book] and I will talk about it, but this will not happen, for, as I have said, in our own times immoderation and arrogance have given rise to many a sorrowful heart and, for those who can take note of it, brought many a man to a bad end. However, if you wish to open up the old books, you may learn what arrogance has brought about in the past and can certainly take a lesson from them, if you wish to do so and are happy to take it to heart. (10680)

In the land of Persia there was a wealthy king called Khosrow, who had turned his mind towards arrogance.[10] In his country it was his commandment that people called him god. Heraclius, the brave hero with not a bit of conceit in his heart, shattered his pride and his strength with his [own] fine chivalry. God allowed this to happen, because he did not want his arrogance to continue. Then his son was also killed, much to the benefit of Christendom: what happened to him was just and good. God has always been there and always will be, and anyone who sets himself up as His equal will not live long. His heirs will also not thrive, so that he cannot endure through them. He should certainly perish completely, along with all his seed. (10702)

Once upon a time there was a mighty king, whose name was Ahasuerus[11] and who had one hundred and twenty lands. He had a prince called Haman the foolish who caused the land's problems. The king loved him very much. Just listen what this scoundrel did. He ordered all the people to fall on their knees in front of him whenever he passed in front of them. However, a man disobeyed his command: he thought it went against God. The lord was furious about this and wanted to be rid of his clan. He wished to hang him there and then and gave orders that the gallows be erected. We should praise almighty God who, with great courtesy, prevented it, knowing as He does how to fell arrogance with all the force of His goodness. In response to the pleas of the queen, the king had Haman seized and ordered that he be hanged from the gallows on which the good man was to have been hanged. All this came as a great relief to him: he and his kinsman were released. I have neither heard nor read that there was ever any man who trusted in God and came to grief. I have not heard or seen—and I can say this in all truth, too—that any educated man wished to trust more in himself than in God without subsequently being mocked and coming to realize that he was devoid of sense. This is what happened to the man I have just named, Haman. (10744)

Nicanor[12] raised his hand when he came into the land of the Jews and swore to burn down the temple if he were to return without having defeated his enemies, but he committed perjury, for he was the first in his troop to be killed in the battle. I never hear anyone lament much that he lost the hand with which he had awakened the wrath of God, for it was cut off. Nor was his head spared: it was hacked off, too. I do not grieve much for that. Look, anyone who is so arrogant that he undertakes to inflict great harm on this one and that one should take this as his example, for whatever a man may undertake in ten years a single day can change, if God so wills it. Therefore, no one should undertake too much. (10768)

King Nebuchadnezzar was so rich that there has never been such a powerful king either before or after him. He became an ox and ate grass when out of arrogance he did not know his place.[13] Whoever does not maintain his proper position as a master shall rightly become a servant. Whoever cannot be a man should live out his life as an animal. It was only right that he who had so shamed himself that he did not know his place became an ox. He thought he was god in his own land. His immoderation and his arrogance had driven him so crazy that he wished to put himself on the same level as the One before whom all arrogance must disappear. (10786)

On account of his arrogance, his son, King Balthasar, lost all his kingdom and his honor and his very life: he did not have them any more. Here, if you have been listening properly, you have probably seen the example of how the father became an ox, but the son was also not spared from being thoroughly demeaned, for he lost his honor and his life. No one should take any consolation in saying: "Such and such a man is doing wrong. God will surely not wish to abandon us, that's a fact." To him I will give this reply: those who choose to live unjustly are all lost, know that for certain. God has many in His company and can increase that number if He so desires. He has the skill to create this company for Himself. He who has made the whole world out of nothing has certainly the means today to make angels and people out of stones. Therefore, one should not threaten Him that He will be alone if He loses any of us. What I have written is true, that He loves us out of goodness, for He does not do it out of need. We, however, do not want to love anyone unless we are sure that we shall gain either material things or honor from it. Our Lord, on the other hand, can never have either material things or honor, for everything is subject to Him. Therefore He does not love us out of necessity. However much he loves us, that comes about from His profound goodness, for He does it for no other reason. So if we do not take care, He will allow us to go to hell, and it will do no harm to Him: He will continue to live in comfort. (10832)

The man is cursed and damned who always relies on the following thought: "God will not let us go to hell for any sin, since He suffered martyrdom for our sake." In truth he is deluding himself with this notion. To be sure, the child who goes against his mother's wishes and her intentions is cursed by her. If a child brings suffering on his mother, she will tell him what pain she has suffered on account of him and she will be quick to curse him. Our Lord does likewise: if we break His commandment, He recounts to us the anguish and the death He suffered on our account and that increases our guilt, in that we have lost His favor, since for all our sakes He endured such trials and tribulations. The first man was banished, so we find it written, because he broke God's commandment and yet God had not been martyred. Thus we can see that worse will befall us if we do not do His bidding, for since then He has done very much for our sakes. The person who takes note of this will realize that, given that Adam was driven out because he did not keep one commandment, we can surely be sorely afraid since we have disobeyed even more of them. (10866)

Balthasar did not wish to better himself when he saw what had befallen Nebuchadnezzar, who had been turned into an ox, but had then changed from an ox back into a man. If anyone can grasp it properly, the son came off far worse, for be sure that, if someone does not wish to reform when he sees the examples in front of him, worse will befall him. It is true that the father spent seven years in the form of an ox and yet got his kingdoms back again when he returned to his proper self. His son lost all his kingdoms and his life, that's true. It was only right that he should meet a worse fate, since he did not wish to mend his foolish ways by looking at his father and his misfortune. (10886)

If worse should happen to us because we hear and see that evil happens to evil people and we do not improve ourselves because of that, then we can certainly be sure that great harm will come to us, for we see on a daily basis that he who has lived an improper life fares badly and yet we are so foolish that we behave worse than he does. That can only hurt us more. Our books are full of people who have not lived well and what may have become of them. You can see for yourself, too—you do not need to ask me—for one sees it every day. (10904)

I have noted one example: a lion had fallen into a hole and was lying there as though he were injured. Immediately all the wild animals everywhere were told about this, and they came running there from all sides, from the forest and from the fields. They wanted to know right away whether it was true or false and unadvisedly, prompted by their weak mindedness, came running to where the lion lay. They tended the patient in such a way that they came to grief because of it. They all became his refreshment, for he ate them, that's a fact. The fox elected not to go there, for you have certainly heard that the fox is very cunning. A squirrel said: "Fox, you have come from a long way off. Why do you not see your master, who is lying sick in there?" The fox replied at once: "I see the tracks all leading that way, and they have fared badly in there. I would not be very bright if I wished to enter, since the tracks go in and have not come out again." A man who has a good understanding of things could likewise say: "I see clearly that pride falls. Whoever does evil must go down to hell and never come back again" and should be very careful not to go to where the devil waits with open mouth, just as a lion does all the time. He does no one so much harm as the one who wants to serve him. To be sure, a sheep has the good sense, if a wolf is luring another one away, not to run after it. A man ought to do the same: he should not be eager to run after someone who cannot keep from sinning, for sin will bring him to a place where he must find himself lost and in disgrace. It would be better if he had never been born. (10956)

Now I have said something about what misfortune and what a curse come about as a result of immoderation and arrogance, if someone turns his mind to immoderation. If anyone records the deeds of common folk, as those of the nobility have been recorded, and if one pays as much attention to what they do as one does to the deeds of the lords, then you should know this to be the truth: anyone wanting to get to the facts would find a greater number of common people who have been lost through arrogance and wickedness than one would find among the nobility, for there are more common folk. Nevertheless, I have learned a lesson from something I have seen a lot of during my lifetime: that the people have lived with usury and false counsel, with a lack of chastity and thieving. Let whoever wishes to do so believe that I have seen few such people—this I can say truthfully—who have managed to prevent themselves from coming to a bad end. Know that for a fact. (10984)

At this point I want to let you know, as I have shown, that just as the arrogant man is the one who always rules differently from the way he should, so is the arrogant man certainly the one who does not wish to be subject to the person whom he should be subject to. If someone orders something that he should not order then he is not ruling well, but if someone does not wish to follow the person he ought to follow then he is very arrogant. One should follow without hostility whomsoever God appoints as our ruler. Otherwise He may perhaps give us a man who can make us subject to him by means of wickedness and arrogance, and we would then have to be content with that. That is what He did to the Greeks: in their arrogance they did not want to tolerate their masters, but now they have to be content with anything that is inflicted on them by a stranger who is able to hold them to their own idea of justice. They slew some people out of necessity; others they killed unjustly and with no good reason. They have forfeited the grace of God. No one can tell me that Alexius and Isaac[14] would have done anything that would have cost them their lives, and I have often experienced that anyone who wishes to place himself on the same level as the person whom God has appointed above him is totally deluded and very often becomes a figure of fun on account of our Lord's commandment. (11022)

Aaron's sister was not spared,[15] since she was afflicted with leprosy because she sought to put herself on a level with someone with whom she should not have compared herself. Then those two men Abiram and Dathan were doomed on account of their arrogance, in that they thought they were as good as the man whom God had given to them to have total authority over their lives. They did not wish to obey him and that was how this fate came about. One should carry out the commandment of one's master for the sake of our Lord God, who gave him to us as our master, if we wish to live properly. (11038)

I know that it is written that at some point one gets a wicked master because of one's own misdeeds, and wise people should thus always be conscious of their own sins. If their master is a wicked man, who cannot rule them well, they should not criticize him, since this has come about because of their own sins. I know that, alongside a respectable man, people accept a wicked one who can do nothing honorable. How does that come about? One has merited no better. Thus it is quite right that one should tolerate in humility much that one's master does and carry out his commands, since one owes that to God. One should always be patient: the bad judge is the arrow of God and the good one is God's broom. Anyone who acts against these two is to some extent going against God. Therefore, it is His commandment that anyone who wishes to live in a righteous way should put up with a great deal from both of them. Unfortunately we do not do this, for anyone who perhaps speaks against it thinks himself a good man. Even if his master is a really worthy man, this will not help him at that time. If my master orders me to do something, I immediately say that I want to do something better, not what he wants me to do, and much misfortune befalls us as a result of this. (11074)

Josephus thought he could do better than his master ordered him to do, and this landed him in great trouble: two thousand men were killed. Azarias, his companion, was also too zealous in this respect. Because he broke the command of Judas, God visited misfortune upon him,[16] and the same happens in our own times. The world is full of strife: know that this comes about because one person does not follow the other. We are completely without leadership and because of this our power must vanish too, along with our wealth and our honor. We have no discipline and no guidance. (11090)

God has given us a master who is supposed to govern our lives, and we are criticizing him the whole time for no other reason than hatred and envy. This is the pope, believe me, after God, the head of Christendom. Now know for a fact that the man who, out of arrogance, says that the head of Christendom is not good brings great shame on Christendom. If someone has too long a tongue, I wish to advise him to have it shortened. Indeed, I would rather speak without a tongue than wrestle with my tongue against God and honor. He who unjustly treats his spiritual father badly is using his

tongue in a wicked way, and he will forfeit God's favor. To be sure, I may
have known a man for ten years and do not know whether he is good or bad
and if he then, out of arrogance, says that the pope is a wicked man, look
how I can assert myself. Anyone who does that is wicked, and I'll speak my
mind to him. If someone who never saw him says that he does not like the
pope, and thinks because of that he is superior, that just shows his foolish-
ness. Perhaps he says: "Somebody told me. To be sure, everyone knows all
about him." However, it's likely that the person who told him such things
is a liar. One should not put something forward as the truth unless one has
experienced it oneself. Then he probably says: "I have seen it" but I venture
to declare that one sees a great deal and yet does not really know it. He
probably thinks he (i.e., the pope) is behaving badly and if he could really
see these things, you should believe me when I say that he would think bet-
ter of it. I believe that whatever he (i.e., the pope) does, he believes he is
doing the right and proper thing. No one should think that he is deliber-
ately behaving in a way that will bring him to the devil, for he is supposed
to take us away from him if he behaves rightly and properly. He surely has
enough intelligence not to want to go to where he will be lost: he has more
sense than that. (11148)

Now, assuming that he does something he might have done better, he
probably deceives himself in the process: he is not God, but a human being.
I will not tell you any lies about this: his foolish mind may be deceiving him.
However, if he does it with no evil intention, then know that he is less guilty.
But we do not want this, for whatever he does, we always want to think that
he has applied his evil intention to it. And, assuming that he behaves justly,
we speak disparagingly about it. (11162)

He has sent his preachers throughout that very blessed land where
Christ lived and died and where he suffered great anguish for all our sakes.
In our minds we thought he had done it for his own advantage. Because for
the benefit of the poor he had an offertory box placed in the churches so
that anyone who wished to make a contribution towards the journey could
place it there—for know for a fact that one could hear about more who
were wanting to help than themselves wished to make the journey (see,
he did it entirely for good reasons)—our foolish minds told us that he was
doing it for personal profit. It seemed a good idea to us to think like this. It
seemed complete nonsense to me, for I was there and heard his letter read
out in public because he wanted people to understand it well where people
had collected the money together until it was placed in the service of God.
The pope's emissary read the letter out where many a worthy man was pres-
ent. (11190)

Now how wrongfully has that good fellow treated him when in his blus-
tering he said that the pope wanted to fill his Italian coffers with German

spoils. If he had taken my advice he would not have said these words with which he rendered null and void all the good things he has said, so that people take less notice of them.[17] (11200)

Noble gentlemen and poets and preachers too should be very careful what they say.[18] Whenever a lord says or does anything, he should not race away so fast without first considering how people may take it. The preacher should speak in an easy and meaningful manner, so that people cannot distort what he says—(the wicked spirit tends to teach this)—and so that people can understand him. It is also not becoming for a poet to be a liar, for both he and the preacher should reinforce the truth. A man can do more to damage Christendom with one word than he can benefit it. I believe that all his singing, whether long or short, is not so pleasing to God as this one thing is displeasing to Him, for he has made a fool out of a thousand men to such an extent that they have not heard the word of God and the commandment of the pope. Messengers and messages come to us from both heaven and hell. Wherever we may want to venture, people will receive us well, just as they should. Now tell me, my dear friend, do you and all your nearest and dearest believe that throughout your life the quantity of alms you have given outweighs the extent to which you have gone astray in this world in a short time? In my opinion, if you can understand [what I am getting at], then you must be very much ashamed of it. Indeed, I feel sorry for him, for he has demonstrated good breeding and good sense in many of his excellent poems. Because of that I feel worse about it, for if a man with little understanding makes a mistake in what he says, people take little notice of it, or no notice at all. The situation is different with a wise man, for people listen to whatever he says. Therefore he should be very careful that people do not say that he has gone crazy now. (11250)

Now let's assume that a man does not speak in this way and that what he says is more pleasing than I have said: then he cannot remain without the fear that he is offering bad examples, for people are always quicker to believe the bad than the good, but he who does that is a wretched man. One can always easily change the good with little thought and little skill, but the bad is not so soon changed, because people are reluctant to leave it alone. What people are always unhappy to do, one can turn around with little effort. Know this: people are quick to follow a foolish man who cannot give good advice, but rather gives bad advice. (11268)

That is why there are so many profligates around, that I will say, if anyone is prepared to listen, that they do not give good or bad advice, but only say what people are happy to do. The profligate says to the usurer: "Do not take any notice of what the priests say: if you commit one sin, then go on and commit more. You can do penance just as easily for ten as for one." You should recognize that what he is saying is very foolish. If my squire offends me once I put up with it better than if he did it more often, be sure of that. Moreover, he more easily gains my forgiveness for a little error than for a big one. No matter what wrong a man does, it seems very good to the profligate and he persuades him to do worse still, for he can atone for it later. That way he separates the fools from their souls and their wealth; you should know that he does that. (11292)

You should know for a fact that he who always staunchly defends evil ways and who thinks that everything he likes doing most is good is living the life of a profligate. I have certainly seen a thousand profligates and can say in all truth that I have never seen one who could respond or speak with any authority. A priest should not lower himself to argue with them: they lack instruction and good sense. They advise everyone to do whatever he thinks is to his advantage, and because of that many people follow them in terms of vice and stupidity. Anyone who is inclined to wickedness will be attracted to this without any effort. Likewise I say that every man, the knowledgeable and the ignorant, can perhaps give the advice that people should not undertake God's journey across the sea, for it will be very costly for anyone who wishes to make it. If we knew that there were any advantage to be gained, he who would like to prevent us from traveling there would certainly need to use his wits. People can also surely advise us not to offer assistance in this matter. We detest the taxes that cause our purses to become empty. If one penny were to bring in ten you would see them all pushing in front of one another with their money belts. They would all be shaken out. You see, it is not necessary for us to compose songs about such matters to prevent people from serving God too much, for with our poetry people serve God not much or not at all.[19] It is true that without our encouragement people do not fear God at all as they ought to fear Him if they wished to live in a righteous manner. If we wanted to encourage people to do wrong, since people like to do wrong in any case, we would be strange indeed and thus incur the hatred of God. You should really believe me when I say this. (11346)

Take it from me, German knights! I know very well that your power and your reputation are recognized far and wide, for at all times you have been the most valued company of knights that we have read about in books. Do not now shirk hardship but demonstrate your courage, for we are being attacked. The heathens in their arrogance have taken over our lands. Nor should one forget the grave of God: they are resolved to prevent us from going there. Ready then, noble knights! To be sure, your chivalrous spirit should not tolerate their arrogance. If anyone can judge it sensibly, how could Christianity suffer a greater disgrace than that the land where the Holy Sepulcher is, in which our lord Christ lay, should be in their hands? They have brought much shame upon us. Their excesses and their arrogance have been raised up against God, and now it is His will and His commandment that people should not put up with them. Justice should certainly spur us on to take umbrage at their injustice, and their boasting and their din. Anyone who calls himself a Christian, or is one, should demonstrate that Christ and his own honor are dear to him, and they have denigrated Him. His land has been taken both from Him and from us, for you have heard what miracles He performed there when he walked upon the earth. He chose that land for Himself, for He was born there and was martyred there and died there. There He endured great suffering for our sake. Should then they leave that country without a fight, they who have spread their name and their renown, their praise and their excellence? One should not flinch from hunting after the praise that shall never end. Make no mistake about it: whatever fame one may garner in this world does not last until the Day of Judgment, but one thing will last for ever more and that is virtue and honor. Anyone who can achieve the fame which makes him look a worthy man in this world and still serve God faithfully as well, know that he shall be blessed. Anyone who wishes to achieve that fame should not be terrified of loss, for it is true that anyone who is at all afraid of loss can never attain fame in conflict. In truth, it is completely unnecessary for us to fear it, for we cannot lose anything there, if anyone chooses to judge aright. If we lose a horse here, God will give us a hundred horses in another place. If we lose our worldly goods here, God is indeed so rich that He will see to it that we gain much more in terms of wealth and honor. If a man loses his life in this world, God will preserve his body and his soul elsewhere in all eternity, truly in His Father's kingdom. There one can confidently reveal one's goodness; there one can gain much and lose nothing, if someone so desires. Who could tell me why anyone would deny help and service to Him who at all times helps us and can bestow on us more than we can lose for His sake, if anyone wishes to choose aright? (11434)

At this point you should also hear that if anyone wished to deprive our Lord of His land, we would hazard our lives, our possessions, our wives and children and would defend it with all our strength. We would be cowardly if we were to retain our lives and our possessions, if anyone sees it properly. A landed nobleman would think it very bad—believe this for a fact—if any one of his men were not willing to come to his aid if he was about to lose his land. He would simply be so angry with him that if he did not lose his land after all, he would not let him remain there but would banish him from it. Take this as an example of what God should do to us, who has Himself made us and has given us intelligence and judgment, worldly possessions, honor, body and soul, people, vassals, wives and children, and everything that a man can have. What will He say on the Day of Judgment to those who would not serve Him when by rights they should have done? We should think of His death and His martyrdom and the suffering He was prepared to endure for our sakes. Accordingly, we should not think anything inappropriate that we might do for His sake. That would be virtuous and sensible. (11466)

The great reward that God gives us and the loyalty He has always shown towards us in His goodness should certainly prompt us to want to serve Him if we wish to do the right thing. Truly I wish to say to you that if a stranger were to give us as much and as great a reward as God gives us, we should be happy to support him in his fight. If anyone has any doubt about the reward, let him see how much God has given to us without our serving Him and let him then quickly be assured that God will give us still more if we serve Him well. We had not served Him [at all] when He put into our hands everything one sees in the world: fire, water, and land. Whoever does not wish to trust Him is himself full of mistrust, for He has shown us clearly that we should trust Him. Therefore do not shirk the task you undertake for Him but grieve that the grave, where He lay dead when He had suffered anguish for us, is in heathen keeping. We should always be dismayed that it is not honored as befits its holy nature. (11498)

At this a man who lacks understanding is probably saying: "I do not want to go to too many pains over this, for, if it is God's will, the Holy Sepulcher will be freed. God Himself has the means, the power, and the wisdom to bring that about quickly." I'd like to answer this man like this: "My dear fellow, you want to lead a comfortable life." I have known for many a day that no one can do anything good without God, yet he who displays a willing spirit towards Him is very virtuous. (11512)

I wish to tell you something similar. God could make all the poor people rich if He wanted to. Now tell me: how should anyone show that he is generous if not a single purse is empty? God gave substance to the rich man, when He was creating poverty so that he would have the means to provide what he ought to for His sake, if he wanted to. Generosity would be worthless if there were no poor people. If there were no poor people, the wicked man could convince himself that he had no one to whom he needed to give anything, and thus he must live a bad life in public, as he is wicked with his wicked scheming. He does not need an excuse not to commit his wicked deeds. Similarly a man cannot excuse himself by saying that very soon God can give to Christendom the land where His grave is and that He will do it, if He should. He gave the land to us as the means to enable us to live without leisure and without idleness, know that for the truth. He wishes to put a stop to the conflict we are constantly waging here out of arrogance and wants us to go to that place where we fight without vanity for the sake of God and Christianity. It is true that He has taken from us all our excuses, so that we cannot say anything. If God reproaches us by saying that He suffered death for our sakes and that we absolutely do not wish to endure this suffering for His sake, what do we say to that? God has often put us to the test and, no matter how much He seeks, He finds few who wish to renounce the world. Now He has granted us the grace of achieving for us that to which we most earnestly aspire. If a man is courageous he places nothing as a pastime above chivalry and in doing so often commits a great sin. Now observe the great goodness of God, in that He has turned about that which we do most gladly and desire for the service of the devil so that we can serve Him by doing it. It is a strange man who does not wish to serve God with anything with which he serves the messenger of the devil. We often fight unnecessarily and now He wishes to see if His death can prompt us to accept or deliver any blow for His sake. People are accustomed to strive hard to demonstrate their courage. Let them demonstrate it without vanity, for if anyone wishes to serve God for the sake of fame this will not help him much. Anyone who dissipates his service and his effort for the sake of fame and vanity is giving away gold in exchange for lead and no one should be well disposed to him. (11588)

Now listen to another adage: that same land makes smooth for us the way to heaven and to God. If anyone comes there in response to His commandment and is slain there after he has made his confession, one need not grieve for him, since in that way he goes straight to where God has him in His care. If anyone does not take the roundabout way but loves the straight path that brings him to God, even if he fights against the heathens, he can come there more quickly than by remaining here, and that's the truth. He who wishes to come to God must travel around a lot in this world: the martyrs go straight to God once they have been martyred. (11606)

It was when Christ lay dead upon the Cross that He released us from the devil and his bonds. Afterwards He commanded that people should guard that which He had released with His blood. Since Christ came to our aid by saving us with the Cross, we have bound ourselves tightly with many sins. Now He wishes once more to release us with the Cross and in doing so He intends to slay again the dragon that threatens to swallow us. His love shall force us to eradicate our sins with the Cross on which He was willing to die for the sake of the sins of all of us. Anyone who is designated with the symbol of Christ shall also be crucified by His Cross. He wishes man to crucify himself in this way in order not to indulge his physical being. If any crusader gives in to his anger he will have lost his heart's cross. The Cross of Christ has the special quality that it will tolerate no enmity, no matter in whose heart it may dwell. For our Lord Christ Himself asked on the Cross and at the moment of His death that His Father should forgive the guilt of the people who martyred Him and grant them His grace. The length and breadth of the Cross signify the love and truth which shall be common to God and indeed to all people. Any man who follows His desire in any way will not have crucified his heart. If a man has sewn the symbol of the Cross on his clothing, the outward sign signifies very clearly that he must carry the Cross inside him. If he does not have it inside him, then his coinage is worthless, for the copper is overlaid with gold.[20] Because of his guilt one should treat him the way one treats a fraudster. Which should be called a crusader: the man or the clothing on which he has sewn the Cross? One should stretch oneself out upon the Cross, it is true, in order that one does not do one's own will, if one wishes to emulate the Crucified One who, when He had to suffer the Cross, said humbly and softly to His Father: "Not as I wish, may it be as you wish."[21] The nail of the Passion shall indeed fasten us to the Cross, in order that we have His wounds before our eyes at all times. Anyone who is spiteful or cowardly, or in any other way lacking in virtue, shall extend himself upon the Cross and in that way he can raise himself above evil and cowardice. Let anyone who has made the effort to accumulate savings send them across the sea, in order that he may avoid the charge of avarice, and, assuming that he is ready to sacrifice his life, his cowardice will leave him. (11678)

God has given us the means to depart this life and go to Him in the manner of martyrs. Anyone on this side of the sea who does not receive acclaim for fighting against wickedness will think the heathens' ways are good. They never take issue with their evil desires, and anyone who is inclined to follow them on this side of the sea will not do much harm to them over there. I have often seen the man who dares to say in public that he would gladly martyr himself for the sake of God and yet does not wish to obey His commandment, as he easily could: what a fool he is making of himself the whole time! It has often enough become apparent that we claim to be so saintly that we do not wish to be either penitents or martyrs. If this journey were undertaken for no other reason than that people should see what one was doing there and take a good example from it and allow one to repent one's sins, even then one would be happy to travel there. Moreover, one can better protect oneself from grave sins there than anywhere else, for there one gains heartache, both on the sea and among the heathens, so that one can truly suffer for one's sins. (11708)

If our Lord had not wished people to toil away in order to gain back His gravesite, there would not in the interval since we lost the grave have occurred so much conflict and anger among the Christians. In truth I think that twenty-eight years have passed since we lost it, and it is true that in the meantime there has been nothing but fighting, aggression, enmity, and envy, fear, hatred, and other anguish among Christians.[22] We do not want to fight for the sake of God, so I believe that it has befallen us since then to fight many a battle on account of our enemies. Now the time has certainly come when we shall fight for the sake of our Lord, and anyone who chooses to fight for God overcomes many enemies. (11730)

Noble princes from German lands, your minds and your hands have
fought often back at home, and now whoever wishes to gain the victory
should henceforth fight for the sake of God. It is His wish and His com-
mandment that anyone who wishes to fight for Him shall achieve victory. If
anyone wishes to fight for the enemy and thinks he will do better that way,
know that he is defeated. That is what always happens. (11742)

Those who avenge His shame and His agony with suffering and toil
could be ashamed for so neglecting God, from Whom we derive all our
possessions and all honor. Those who give away their wealth for the sake of
their honor should also be inclined always to give for the sake of Him Who
gave them their possessions. Anyone who is not prepared to give up his
possessions for the sake of Him Who gives him so much is a thief. In truth
he must also give in a shameful manner. If my steward were not willing to
produce my money, when it was a matter of life or death or in some way of
my honor, he would not be able to disgrace me more and would justly be
seen as my thief. How am I supposed to love Him? Know that anyone who
wishes to be wicked when Christ's grave has, or so we read, been held cap-
tive for such a long time is God's thief. The person who has been greedy in
this world shall live generously in the next. One can hoard more while giv-
ing in that world than one can collect elsewhere. One can well go to school
there, if one wishes to guard against greed, for anyone who does not learn
generosity there must always remain a scoundrel. There silver and gold in
abundance shall flow out of the hands of noble princes from German lands.
Whoever gave treasure away in this world for the sake of his honor shall
work all the harder at doing so in the next, for there he will gain wealth and
honor. Anyone who likes comfort should heed my advice and make comfort
for himself there through discomfort, in order that he may live comfortably
forever according to his desire. (11786)

Noble King Frederick:[23] you are noble in mind and spirit and can
achieve so much if you wish to. Now show that you are wise and aspire to
the reward that never ends. To be sure you can do this very well, for true
wisdom is to serve God at all times. (11796)

I know of two members of your dynasty who traveled there with a mighty
force. One was the emperor Frederick, the other surely was your uncle: you
shall be the third to follow after them. As the result of a misfortune the
emperor did not manage to get across the sea; your father got there but
did not complete his mission. You are the third and shall get there and
complete the mission. I have heard that in the number three there is always
perfection. The perfection of God is always associated with three names,
and thus you shall surely know that there will be nothing lacking in it. Since
there is nothing lacking in the number and since you are the third, I have
faith in God that you will fulfill His commandment. Every perfect task has a

beginning and an end. The beginning was given to your grandfather at his birth, and your uncle, know this, continued in the middle. Thus you shall be the ending, if God grants it to you. The end completes the task and you are in truth the third, and the end is the third part: thus go for the salvation of everyone. (11830)

If you have been listening to me properly, I have digressed a little from my theme, and yet not too much. I did it because I had to, and now I will return homewards again, for it is not fitting that I should wish to remain in the open fields and in the forests along with the wild animals. He who leaves his theme somewhere so that he cannot come back to it properly remains elsewhere. If someone can manage to come out of it and then go back in again, I do not call that stupidity. I am saying all sorts of things about immoderation, but I will not leave arrogance without including it too, for they have the same properties. (11848)

Why is arrogance so called?[24] That is well enough known to me: I know it from the way it behaves. No one should aim too high. A man does not have wings that would help him to fly, and so he must fall down hard from his arrogance. The higher someone flies, the harder jolt he receives, for he has a greater fall too. This happens all over the place. (11860)

I may well write that anyone who maintains his arrogance falls in five ways and cannot prevent this happening. Firstly, he falls into guilt; then he falls from God's grace; after that he falls into the depths of hell; also, at some point he falls physically and [even] in terms of honor. Moreover, you shall know for a fact that he must fall into all manner of vices, for he will lose his balance. Note that the first fall brings all the others with it. How one falls into guilt, and how one falls from God's grace, you can observe clearly in the example of the devil. That person will fall from God's favor who, through his arrogance, is always guilty. The guilt leads straight to the fall, believe that as a fact. Then, when he has fallen from God's favor because of his wrongdoing, he falls into the depths of hell. This is what happened to the foe at the moment he fell from heaven, and since then he has never returned there. That was a fall, in truth, that we should greatly fear. Since out of arrogance he fell so hard from heaven into hell, anyone on this earth who is arrogant should certainly live in constant fear. I have provided you with examples from the life of Haman of how one can fall through arrogance in terms of life and honor, and from King Khosrow, who was very arrogant, and from King Balthasar, who lost his life and his honor. Now I shall tell of the fall, and how people, old and young alike, all over the place fall on account of arrogance and through vice. If a man is arrogant he always denigrates what another man does, for he does not think it good. He falls into slandering and ends up becoming vain, for his arrogance causes him to want people to call him virtuous. He succumbs to foolishness, for

he believes it to be the truth that he is the best one there. He is also filled
with envy, for he is always jealous of a decent man. His anger does not leave
him, for often out of arrogance he falls into a rage when people will not do
something for him. He commits acts of violence and injustice, and in his
arrogance says that the crooked is straight and right, and gets into the habit
of procuring many women, so that he can boast of his conquests. (11930)

At the top of the chain of wickedness I placed greed, and after that
arrogance. However, if one thinks about it properly, one can also place arro-
gance at the head of another road. My mind directs me that arrogance
often leads a man into greed, and I will tell you how. Suppose a man is
arrogant: he immediately thinks how he can outdo others, but then when
he sees that his arrogance does not go very well with boasting when he lacks
material things, he becomes greedy for wealth in order to fulfill his arro-
gance. But then he does not remain in this situation, when he later takes
a fall. If he is greedy it upsets him very much if someone acquires more
than he does, and thus he falls deeply into envy. When he has given himself
over to envy, know that he does not stop at that, for he develops anger and
hatred towards those who are better at acquiring wealth. Anger causes him
to consider injustice right and proper. Now he has taken a very bad fall,
but he must surely fall even further. He cannot commit wrong all the time
without going in pursuit of evil cunning and slyness, falsehood, lying, and
perjury. Once he has arrived at perjury, his evil conniving is no help to him
but he must fall through sin into the depths of hell. Know that I am not
telling a lie: you have it painted on the stairway to hell, as I have said, if you
have taken good notice. If you have truly understood it, the first thing there
is arrogance and after that greed. Then know for a fact that beneath that is
envy, and under envy lies anger; under anger there is injustice, which paves
the way forward to perjury. Know this to be the truth: that perjury always
goes right to the depths of hell. The first journey to hell came about as a
result of arrogance. Greed and wealth betrayed the wise mind of Balaam.[25]
Cain killed Abel out of jealousy and since then much misfortune arose from
it.[26] Herod became blind with anger when he slew his own children.[27] The
two who unjustly abused Susanna received their just deserts.[28] The person
who commits perjury completely denies God, that's the truth, just as these
two denied Him and inflicted damage on no one but themselves in the pro-
cess. That is the kinsman of immoderation, and through this vice immod-
eration has the power to drag both men and women to hell. (12002)

Now take note how one should avoid vice. One should always shore up
one's house on the side where it is weaker: people like to attack that side.
Let a worthy man do the same thing. The person who would ward off sin
should at all times defend himself well against the vices which he loved in
his youth, for whenever he wishes to do good the devil immediately pres-

ents them to him and reminds him of his habit. Therefore, he should be
well prepared so that the devil does not attract him in this way. Wicked hab-
its and wicked ways are the devil's rope with which he drags us to damna-
tion. Know that if someone wishes to secure his house well he should lay the
foundations of humility deeply. If there are any cracks in the foundations
the timber frame will be awry and unstable, that's for sure. Anyone who
wishes to build his walls high with virtues should sink the foundations just as
deep. One should also climb high with the same measurements and desire
no more than the timber frame of his virtue. Anyone who has come up on
this structure can at all times avoid vice totally, for one should believe that
no vice can break up the foundation of humility with any hammer blow: this
I venture to say. (12040)

Whoever intends to eschew arrogance should think very hard about
what he was and what he may be. In the process he should also consider
what is to become of him. If he will think deeply about that, he can prob-
ably bring his arrogance down to the level of the mentality of a man. If you
are better than your companion, then quickly remember that someone else
is even better. However, if you are the best of all, then you should consider
that you could still be perfect, and be humble about this in the meantime,
since you could be better than you are. But we do not do this, for no one
recognizes that another person is probably behaving better and becomes
humble as a result. We do notice, however, who is worse and take our exam-
ple from that by saying: "Do you see what that fellow is doing: what harm
does that do?" Know this: people have turned their eyes away, for everyone
prefers to see who is behaving worse in order to take after him and does
not look ahead to see who is behaving better so that they might copy him.
(12070)

One should also bear in mind that our Lord desired to become a man
through His love of us and for the sake of humility. Anyone who looks at this
correctly can certainly humble himself in the right way, as a man should. Be
sure that he should not think himself better than any man. Nor should he
be ashamed that it fell to him to be a man, since our Lord wished to become
a man. The One who determines all things, our Lord, surely possesses all
the virtues in their entirety, yet none seemed better in Him than humility.
Know that His humanity and His poverty demonstrated great humility to
us.[29] (12088)

Anyone who desires to abandon greed should give close consideration
to how quickly wealth comes to an end, and he should think just as quickly
of those of whom we read that they were so wealthy. He should also remem-
ber where their wealth ended up and what use it was to them: that is my
desire and my advice. If avarice has taken hold of his mind, let him throw
his wealth away from him. He should put aside everything that loves avarice,

that is true: that way wickedness will not remain there. I can say this: whoever wishes to take leave of wealth and women should not often look at either of them. It seems to me that anyone who tries to extinguish fire with straw and wipe mud away with mud is playing a trick. Anyone who can do that can do too much. All money-changers are such tricksters, for they believe that with their wealth they can satisfy their greedy minds and they set themselves alight with greed. You should certainly believe for a fact that if they do not change their ways because of this, their avarice and their materialism will lead them yet to hell. I believe I know that better than I know where their wealth would lead them if they really needed wealth. (12124)

Whoever wishes to avoid envy should love the wealth that one divides up with such skill that it always remains whole. Whoever greatly loves worldly goods must be disposed to become passionately envious if another person acquires more than he does, for he will receive all the less if the spoils are divided. If anyone wishes to be subject to God, the wealth which God gives to him is not like that, for it remains completely intact. However much of it he wishes to give away, much of it will still be left. Then there cannot be any envy, since the wealth is lying whole in front of everyone. (12142)

The man who wishes to avoid anger should remember that he has transgressed greatly against God, to Whom he should be subject. At this point he should think: "Since it has come about that our Lord has overlooked much of what I did, I also propose to abandon my anger against him who has done less to me and who is less guilty towards me," and he should always forgive [people]. Know that whoever can control his anger is a good man. He who controls it at all times is waging a fierce battle. Whoever makes his anger subject to him should consider it a great penance. It takes much virtue to master one's anger. (12162)

Whoever wishes to avoid injustice should think hard about how our Lord, Who has so much power and so much authority, wishes to do injustice to no one, and every man must be aware of how He graciously judges our misdeeds. If anyone has ruled the world with injustice, he has not protected himself well, for injustice has ruled him. He should rather be ashamed of this, if he wants to achieve good sense and honor. If someone cannot protect himself, whatever that man gains is absolutely nothing, for he is, after all, a scoundrel. (12180)

If a man wishes to guard against perjury, let him think how grieved he would be if his son wanted to deny him. I know he would have to lament that forever. God is Father and Lord, and anyone who wishes to deny Him is quite out of his mind. Unfortunately, a great many do just that. Know that whoever commits perjury is denying God. By what right and with what intention does he ask Him for anything, since he has denied Him? Alas, what a foolish state of affairs, that a man dare not deny his friends and yet completely denies Him Who holds us in His hand and Who, without ado, can allow us to fall into the depths of hell! One should always fear Him greatly, for were he to forsake us, the person who thinks himself very bold will quickly be dragged off struggling down to hell by a miserable devil. Many a person is so stupid as to wish to take his oath in a deceitful and cunning manner. I will never lose any sleep over that, for anyone who takes an oath with cunning[30] will certainly commit perjury with cunning too. Anyone who dares to swear an unjust oath is also committing perjury. If I swear to kill a man I cannot protect myself through perjuring, irrespective of whether I have lied or spoken the truth. I wish to advise anyone who has sworn malicious oaths not to do something because of that: he can better atone for one thing than for two. (12220)

I'll leave the eighth part at that, and now we shall write the ninth.

BOOK IX

"Let me have a rest, it's high time I did," says my pen. "It's very unfair if someone does not grant his servant rest. Now, the truth is that I have served you the whole of this winter and you haven't let me off writing day and night. You have abused my mouth by tempering and cutting me more than ten times a day. How could I put up with that for so long? Sometimes you make large cuts, then small ones, and have used me to write about both lords and servants. You are doing me a great injustice. When you were cultivating fine ways I was very happy to accompany you, and when you were watching jousts and dancing with knights and ladies I was very glad to be by your side, for—believe me when I say this—when you were wanting to be at court among the people, I thought I was better off with you than anywhere else, you know. Now you have given this up and have abandoned your real purpose and turned your back on it. I have not gained anything from it but having to write all day long. Take this for a fact: I cannot put up with it. You have become a hermit. When you were in school you did not upset me so much. Your gate is barred by day. Tell me, what has happened to you? You do not want to see knights or ladies. The light that you keep burning the whole night through annoys me terribly. If you want to write and compose in a year everything that you ever want to write, then I cannot remain with you. Anyone who relies on poetry must surely become a nothing, for he completely loses himself in his thoughts, and that's the truth." (12270)

Stop moaning and don't complain so much, and listen to what I want to say to you. If I had taken up writing as a pastime, I should not have come so far in four years as I have, unless my mind is playing tricks on me. You know perfectly well that I am speaking the truth: I have completed these eight sections in eight months (and you yourself have spent a lot of time awake in the process) and now I am to write two more. Now you must stay awake for another two months. So you can see that this poem is not composed to while away my time. In truth, I would have had to spend five years on it if I had just been composing for entertainment. I took this on because I had to, because I have noticed that people never behave as they ought to. That is why I have turned my back on what I should otherwise have been doing, for I wish to proclaim here and now what it would bother me very much to keep quiet about. You say that the person who relies on poetry becomes worthless, but if in olden times people had not become "worthless," there would not be today so many good men, as we read in the books. We would also have become worthless if we had not found written down something which we could use as models and from which we could learn a lesson. I have become aware of one thing: namely, that it is true that one does become completely lost in thought while one is writing, so that one can hardly behave properly when one is deeply entrenched in one's thoughts of it. However, when one emerges from this phase and returns to normal, know that a man will behave even better than he did before. If my gate is barred for a while, that should not be too disconcerting, for it is in a corner that one must create a "foot" for the poem, so that afterwards it can run around in the world. I was longing to see knights and ladies, but I think it better to do without them for a while, so that I can well express in words what will benefit all of them. He who has served much and well is not well advised if for the want of a small service the abundant service he has performed will be in vain. Thus I say about your situation: you have won me through your service, but if you are proposing to abandon me now, what you have achieved will be lost. With your assistance I have spoken much about inconstancy, about steadfastness, and moderation. Nor have I neglected immoderation, for I have spoken about that too: it is the sister of inconstancy. Constancy and moderation are sisters: they are the children of one virtue. Justice is the brother of the two of them, and now I should like to speak of that and write exactly what I should say about it. Justice, write about justice within my heart, so that injustice does not prevail on the outside. To be sure, you do not write in ink but what I may write in ink is nothing at all unless you are witnessing it all day long. (12350)

You will probably recall that I said that three lions and half an eagle should never appear on anyone's shield.[1] I have stated that three lions denote pride, which a single one does not. I also said that a demi-eagle signifies the division of honor, since a complete eagle is meant in truth to denote honor. For this reason there should indeed be an eagle in the heart of a gentleman, since, by rights, he should certainly follow the eagle. It is good if in his mind he has the heart of a lion. If he protects himself effectively from arrogance his buoyant spirits should do no harm. The difference between high spirits and arrogance, if anyone observes it, is this: high spirits certainly dare to do what they should, whereas the arrogant man wishes to do a great deal unjustly. (12374)

Justice is everywhere where all things display moderation, balance, proportion.[2] No one can thrive without justice. In fact, even a thief cannot exist without justice, and he complains bitterly if his companion intends to do him an injustice in dividing up the spoils. What he gains by injustice he wishes to share according to justice. Anyone who has ever committed an injustice will even so wish to have justice meted out to him. (12384)

The lion is accustomed to having a dog attached to him, for if at any time he commits a wrong, the dog is beaten.[3] That way he is trained to do what he should. A gentleman should do likewise. He should not transgress boldly against God when he sees the suffering that befalls a bad man. He should take another man as his example. Know that if someone can properly follow the lion in this matter, it will do him good. He should know that our Lord holds him firmly in His power; how much more firmly might he hold someone who is subject to him? Therefore, it is truly my advice that he should fear God, particularly before His court, for he cannot avoid standing before God. Then it will not go well with him if he has not judged well, for he will fare accordingly. (12410)

If I had to select a master, know that I would take the one who feared and honored God. The person who does not rely on God for his power oppresses the poor people greatly. Whoever fears God shall succeed. The fear of God shall inform these things, namely, that one should honor one's father and one's mother, and instruct one's underlings, and should also resolve to love one's fellowmen and fulfill God's commandment, so that there is no transgression against God, and live peacefully with one's countrymen. Know that he should, by rights, have pity on the poor if he is capable of fearing God (12428).

He should dispense equal justice to both rich and poor. Because of this, I said that it would be a good thing if he had the courage of a whole eagle in his body. If anyone were to drop half an eagle down from a tower, it would not have the strength to get back again and yet a whole eagle can fly enormously high, that's the truth. If someone has odd feet, know that he must lean to one side, and anyone who has to fly with one wing cannot fly well: know that he flies lower on the side where he has no wing. A lord must have the wings of his heart complete, in order not to fly towards his judgment with an unbalanced verdict. Let the peasant and the servant and the lord all have justice. A master should behave so evenhandedly that the poor man and the rich man both have their rights: then, in truth, he is behaving well. (12454)

A decent man of noble birth should, neither out of pity nor of anger, act or move in such a way that anyone can discover his intention. It is not good when a person betrays what he is thinking on his face and particularly in a court of law, for there one should not show whether one is angry or compassionate: that is the purpose of the court. (12464)

The poor man should not be disadvantaged by his poverty in a court of law, nor should the rich man's wealth help him, if anyone wants to judge aright. But unfortunately that may not happen, I can say that for a fact. Whenever a noble man is wishing to pass judgment, there are so many circumstances that force him to abandon justice and act unjustly. In such an instance, he is lacking the wings which should raise him up evenly at court and let him down again. I have often observed that he falls like a demi-eagle to one side. It is true that if someone has a broken wing he always leans sideways. (12482)

Compassion, fear, love and hate, promises, gifts, envy, and foolishness, these things completely break the pen of the law, that's true. Out of fear a wicked master often leaves justice right out of his judgment. Similarly, to be honest, compassion, foolishness, envy, gifts, commandment, love, and hate also bring it about that a man completely loses his sense of justice. A noble man often does something that he ought better not to do out of foolishness because of gifts, love, or hatred. Also he often thinks he is behaving well when, out of pity, he permits a wicked man to leave the court without justice having been done to him. However, I do not wish to applaud this. (12500)

It is right that one should have compassion and I think that is very good, but on no account should compassion compromise the process of the court. If someone does not intend to make amends and if he has done many bad things, he should be separated from other people, that is true. It is better, this is also true, to lose a part of something rather than the whole of it. If a farmer were to have a sheep which was going to eat up all his other sheep, he would not allow it to live, that's for sure, and a master who wishes to judge according to justice should do likewise. He should not forgive the man who will probably kill three men yet he should not be happy to get rid of him, for a shepherd cannot choose the death of a sheep without being sad about it: know that for the truth. (12522)

If I were to be shot in the hand with a poisoned arrow, immediately you would know that I would want the hand taken off, if I knew that the poison would spread to my heart, as often happens. You can believe me when I say that, however sorry I might be about the hand, I would still rather lose it than choose to die. This is just what a lord should do if he wishes to judge in a just manner: however wicked a man is, he should receive compassion in the course of the trial and yet the court should not let him off. The humanity of the man he has wronged should show him compassion, but his wolf's demeanor should ensure that the judge judges properly. If he has pity he should pass judgment speedily, but if he does not have pity then his judgment is not sound. The judge who does what he has to do with compassion and still does not neglect justice has the right idea. Know that he has God's favor, since he does what he does for the sake of justice and for no other reason. However, know that anyone who laughs while he is passing judgment is judging quite differently from the way he should. Then again, if anyone has a good time when he sees another man dying, God will not pay any attention to *his* suffering. (12558)

The judge should take great care not to become angry in court, in order that he should wish for or desire no other sentence than a just one. Anyone who allows anger to inform a verdict is doing great harm to justice, and it should not be called justice at all: it can better be called revenge. Anyone who practices revenge in a court of law is a complete villain and is doing what he should not do, since he is not really passing judgment in the name of justice. One should avoid stupidity and idleness, so that one never does less than one should, if one wishes to pass proper judgment out of justice. (12574)

Know that anyone who wants to make his land peaceful should find out who is harboring thieves—this would be good sense—and pass judgment on him. If there is no one harboring him, the cunning of the thief is useless, since he cannot survive without him. Anyone who behaves like this should rightly be the lord of a land, if in other respects he is good. (12584)

By these examples I have said how fear and stupidity and bribery and bias can render a judge foolish, so that he will not judge according to justice and leans too much to one side. If someone does not avoid them in a court, his judgment is worthless. Know for a fact that he who eschews fear and stupidity completely when he is passing judgment must have the heart of a lion. He who takes care that bribery and a favorable bias do not affect his thoughts while he is doing this must have the eyes of an eagle. The eagle's gaze does not flinch because of the sunlight, for he certainly looks into it without averting his eyes. The judge should do likewise: the light of partiality should not so influence his view of justice that he chooses to neglect justice, for that would not be right. He should view bribery in such a way that he can discern what is right or wrong: in that case he has the sight of an eagle. Know that the heart of the lion and the eyes of the eagle ensure that the wings of the judge are not broken in the court of law. Anyone who overlooks fear and partiality and bribery always has the good sense to ignore promises, hatred, and envy. Thus his wings will not be broken in the court of law. (12622)

At this point I wish to tell you that justice is meant to have two wings: spiritual justice and worldly justice. If it does not have these two wings, then be assured that justice will always be subjected to injustice. As long as worldly judgment did not deviate from spiritual judgment, justice was good and upright throughout the world. Ever since the one has given way to the other, justice has become foolish and weak and necessarily took a fall. Since then, excommunication does not instill fear. How does that come about? In fact one is more favorably disposed towards it. Whoever is excommunicated now is always more highly honored. In fact, the lords do not put the fear of God into such a fellow because, with their secular court, they always ought to be struggling to see how they might convince him that spiritual judgment is not totally worthless. (12646)

But how has it come about that we see so many heretics? These people have little or no fear of any ecclesiastical court. They should be judged by worldly criteria and be forced to it by spiritual means. At this point a man who cannot understand the matter properly is probably saying that one should not force anyone to believe what is right and good. "We leave even the Jews alone, if they do not wish to be Christians," he says. I would like to answer him: if my child did not want to live according to my wishes, as he ought to, I would admonish him and give him a good thrashing. On the other hand, if your child did not wish to live according to the rules, as he ought to do, I should not want to take it upon myself to beat him: it would be better for you to do that. The Church ought to act in the same way: it should certainly exercise control over its own children and allow the children of other people to be subject to their fathers. How should she exercise any authority over the Jews? They will not adhere to it. She should compel the heretics, since they were certainly her children. When a man is baptized he is a child of the Church forever. If later he wishes to separate from her, then believe me that he should be compelled to do what is right and good, and here there should be worldly judgment, if the spiritual judgment does no good. (12682)

Lombardy would be blessed if it had the lord of Austria, who can boil heretics alive.[4] He invented a splendid dish: he does not want the devil to break his fangs right away when he eats them, and so he had them nicely boiled and roasted. If secular and spiritual courts do not support one another, then justice will collapse completely. Believe me, that is the truth. (12694)

Wickedness, animosity, anger, and envy bring it about in our time that the secular court does not support the ecclesiastical court, and, as a result, justice fares very badly, since it must give way to injustice. Envy derives from great evil, for know for a fact that a man who envies another man believes himself diminished thereby. Anger often comes from greed, for a man becomes angry and distressed if another man acquires more in the way of material possessions: it upsets him very much. Look, these things generate hatred among people, know that to be a fact. (12710)

There is always envy and anger to be found among priests and laymen. Each one of them believes that the other is better off. The priest sees that the knight has a beautiful lady and can go out enjoying himself whenever he wants to, and derives lots of pleasure all the time from jousting. Because of this priests often become envious. On the other hand, the comfortable life of the priests often causes the knights envy, too, and greed makes the priest angry because he is very put out if an uneducated man acquires more wealth than he does. Then he says angrily that he has wasted all his effort and asks why he bothered to study. Greed causes him to think this way. Then, on the other hand, the layman is angry and says he has lost out, no matter how much he may serve his lord. "The priest earns more in a day than I do in ten years. All my service has been completely in vain." (Thus whatever he does is supposedly in vain.) "The priest acquires possessions for nothing." Look how such anger and such envy always promote great animosity among them. You can well believe me when I say that, because of that, justice has become injustice and the crooked has become straight, since secular and ecclesiastical courts do not support one another.[5] Note that this creates envy, anger, and hatred among those who, if they had a mind to, should cultivate spiritual and secular law. (12750)

The priests and laymen have become so blind in their hostility that they have begun to act like women. I have often noted that they rail against one another, and, to be sure, this arises from a feeble mind. He who can scream and shout and behave in such a way that his envy becomes apparent does not display the demeanor of a courtly gentleman. Know that it derives from a feeble mind. (12760)

If a man wishes to chastise another man, he should first think hard what he is like himself and should thus guard against criticizing something that he can clearly identify in himself. Every man would be really courtly if he were so good and so well-mannered that he recognized his own lack of courtesy, his decadence, and his inconstancy as well as he recognized the disposition of another man. That man is full of flaws but he is so lacking in insight and only observes the behavior of another man and says that it is not good. Let whoever observes the lechery of another man also notice his own sloth. Or, if he is not lazy, let him at the same time be aware of his anger or his drunkenness, his nastiness or his greed, his unchaste ways or his arrogance. It is right that he should do this. It strikes me as good that, if anyone wants to accuse another person and say that he is doing lots of bad things, he should think what he does himself and improve on it. Anyone who accuses another man of anger is wasting his accusation if he himself is arrogant, for arrogance does the same thing. If anyone accuses another man of drunkenness, then know for a fact that if he himself is not chaste he is always close to it (i.e., drunkenness) himself. Drunkenness, lack of chastity, anger, arrogance: the one often behaves like the other, for these four vices are all children of insanity. If anyone, man or woman, can observe the negative qualities of another person and not notice his own, he must come to hear about it. (12804)

If it pleases you, I wish to say further that the person who wields spiritual jurisdiction should not dispense secular law,[6] and he who judges from a secular perspective should not make spiritual judgments, unless he is authorized to occupy both offices. No layman should ever preside over an ecclesiastical court nor pass ecclesiastical judgment, or he will easily land in trouble. I'll tell you what once happened to 250 men who had taken upon themselves to serve God as priests were supposed to serve Him. They said: "We are as virtuous as Aaron who serves Him." At that time Aaron was the bishop of these lords who, out of jealousy, wished to be on the same level as Aaron, whom God had certainly chosen. The two hundred and fifty men put on their white habits. The Bible has informed us that each man took his censer and departed as they went forth to serve God in a way other than the way they should have. I have learned from the Bible that, when they had arrived in front of the altar, they were, in truth, set on fire and immolated, so that there was nothing left of them. That should put so much fear into us that no mortal man should assume a spiritual function. If he believes he could perform that better than the priest, then know for a fact that this is not recommended for him, and let him now take as an example what misfortune befell the 250 men.[7] (12849)

If it happens that a bishop is a duke, he should always have his judge who, on a daily basis, metes out worldly justice to his people. A lord must not be idle but should travel throughout the land with his court. He should find out what this one or the other is up to, and should, this is true, make him pay for his actions. This displays the true bearing of a lord. One thing you ought to know for sure, his eyes and his heart should be broader than his lands. His land should be in his hands, for he must suppress the wicked people and draw the virtuous towards him. (12866)

If a lord does not have the power in his court that he should have by rights if people are to be subject to him, then he should behave as the eagle does: believe this as a fact. When the eagle becomes old, he flies so high at that time that, in truth, the sun burns up his wings. Then he goes away from the sun and drops down into a spring and thus renews himself by becoming new and joyful and happy. A lord should do likewise: as soon as he cannot control his people and his land properly, he should turn upwards towards God in humility, with prayer and goodness, in order that He may help him to rule well and do what he ought to do. Once he has done this, he must descend again to [perform his daily] tasks, and immediately rule his land properly. He must not lose heart, no matter what people do or say to him, for things will turn out well. If he has the courage to dare to gain from this, he will accomplish what he should. The fear of God arises out of love, and anyone who fears Him has the advantage that all manner of things fear Him, and anyone who does not fear the power of God must constantly fear everything that is in the world. (12904)

Whoever neglects his legal judgment out of fear has no trust in God, for no one can withstand anyone who wishes to proceed righteously. Whoever wishes to follow God and justice should not be unduly afraid that his enemy has great strength. If, on account of that, he neglects his duty, he has not shown proper respect towards God Who must be more powerful still. As I have already heard, he who wishes to do his duty in all humility according to God, as he ought to do, is never overcome. On the other hand, one can make a bad thing out of one's duty through arrogance. (12920)

Judas Maccabeus often defeated an enormous army with a few men—so I have heard in the scriptures—and yet in the end he was slain, for he wished to gain the reputation of never retreating before his enemies.[8] Know for sure that if vanity accompanies duty, it does great harm to the latter. Whoever fights for the sake of justice and not for fame cannot be defeated. Jonathan and his companion one day swiftly put a mighty army to flight.[9] They were all unable to defend themselves. It is still written today how Gideon overcame a huge army with a handful of men. Despite its size, the army could not defend itself.[10] Whoever wishes to search in books will find much written about those who could not be resisted while they were resolved to adhere to justice. Whom, then, should the man fear to whom God has granted wealth and honor, unless he does not rule his land as he ought to do and does not judge in a just manner? Know that he should fear no one. However, if he has acted against God, he must fear his underlings in any case, for he can easily slip up. (12954)

At this point I want to advise you that whoever has acted against God should take the lion as his model. Now let it please you to observe how the lion behaves: the lion can sense exactly when someone is hunting him and then he completely wipes out his tracks with his tail, and that is a fact.[11] That way he wants to ensure that the huntsman cannot find him. A lord should do the same. He should completely erase his sins—that's my advice—with confession and good deeds. If, through his own fault, his countrymen do anything against him, let him first of all be inclined to atone in the eyes of God: then he will overcome them. When the lion wants to take revenge and is not as angry as he would like to be, he first inflicts pain on himself with his tail. That's what a lord should do. He should first chastise himself thoroughly and then approach the man who has done him wrong. He should act like the eagle, which shatters its beak when it wants to renew it. This has happened a lot. A lord who wishes to conduct himself well according to justice should do likewise: with his good deeds he should break up whatever useless tools he has. That way he will really renew the beak with which he is to lead his people to justice and to God, whenever he fulfills His commandments. (12992)

Let me tell you more about this: a master should learn that he should not be rash, for a person seldom does good without due thought. Whoever likes to act without thinking often regrets it, but whoever does what he does with circumspection rarely regrets his action. I'll demonstrate with three examples that one should be prepared to take to heart. First of all, a man does not see what another man with him sees; second, one person should admit it to the other; third, if it goes wrong for him, all those who advised him to do it criticize him. (13008)

It is true that the lion sleeps for three whole days after his birth.[12] After the third period of daylight, his father wakes him up as a lord should, and at his leisure he should observe three pieces of advice, if he is sensible. First, that he should take to heart the good advice that he is given; second, that he should distinguish who has given him the better advice; third, that he should quickly think what he wants to do now. When he has done that, it seems to me a good idea that he should quickly do whatever he ought to do. According to the advice, justice should swiftly alert the lord to action, just as the lion is woken up after a period of three days. Now—know this—I propose to explain better to you the three things that one should accept as advice. One should listen very hard when the advice is being given to what the poor man and the rich man, the young man and the old man, wish to say, without distinguishing between them. And one should simply admonish them to say exactly what they are thinking. It is a fact that the poor man often gives good advice when the rich man has none to offer, if one were to ask him for it. It is not a question of wealth. If anyone understands it properly, the sense is absolutely in the intention. Thus the poor man and the rich man may be exactly alike when it comes to the sense of their advice. In truth I want to tell you this: it often happens quite a lot that a man has great sense, if you can call it sense, when it comes to making a profit, and yet has very little sense when he is called upon to give advice. See here: a lord will send a long distance for that man to advise him and overlook a poor man close at hand who can advise him well. And I want to say similarly: that an old man who should have sense is often a child in terms of sense, whereas you should know that some young people are very wise. (13063)

Let anyone who wishes to track down honor and renown observe precisely what the young man, the poor man, the rich man, and the old man wish to say, and then let him think long and hard who has spoken better. It makes sense that he should do this. He should register the advice of everyone, and when he has done that he must see which advice he can say is the

best and choose one or the other, if he thinks it good. I think he is right to
do this. A lord should not reveal too quickly which advice he proposes to fol-
low: as long as he does not reveal it, he remains in command of that advice.
Once he reveals the advice he intends to take, he has placed himself and
his intention in the control of that advice and must be subject to it. A lord
should seek advice from someone who has tried it out: that way he will find
out better without harm to himself, rather than by trying it out. If he does
not wish to hear what this one and that one has to say, then you shall know
that his mind can perceive all the less. If a man is ashamed to inquire what
one or the other wishes to say, then be sure that he will be more ashamed of
himself when he acts. I would rather be ashamed of asking on one occasion
for advice than simply speaking and acting [without advice]. (13100)

A young man who is willing to take note of all kinds of things can learn
more in a year than an old man who has succumbed to idleness has learnt
in his whole life, that is a fact. If he listens to what he is taught, a poor man
can also learn more than a rich man who has set his mind on gaining profit.
Therefore, one should listen to them all, and separate the wise men from
the fools. To be sure, it is true that a lord should put all his countrymen
to the test, for take note that a precious plant can often be suffocated by a
thornbush, so that one can see the thorn and has completely lost the plant.
The ignorant rich man will force out a poor wise man, so that one misses
him completely and overlooks him, that's a fact. Therefore it is my wish and
my advice, too, that one should seek out the little plant and then just as
quickly cut down the nasty thorns: that is good and sensible. It is good that
a master should identify a rich man to see who can advise him well: it makes
sense that he should do that. One does not wish to hear a poor wise man if
one is in the company of rich fools. One does not look for a man when one
sees a wooden picture decorated in gold and precious stones. They all push
their way forward, but someone who has tried this out will not find much
advice there. A wise lord should encourage the man who advises him, for if
he is meant to give advice when he is afraid, he will never give good advice.
The man who speaks according to what his master wants very seldom gives
any advice, and anyone who gives advice according to the disposition of a
wicked lord casts him into the flames of hell. (13148)

One should not be hasty with one's advice, unless there is a pressing
need for it. It is a good policy to allow the person one asks to think it
over. Know that one can work out advice better at one's leisure than by
rushing things, but when you have come across some good advice at your
leisure and have thought what you should do, then do it very quickly.
Each has its own special nature: lengthy consideration and swift action.
Therefore, one should do quickly whatever one wishes to do according to
advice, for the advice which is good today may easily become poor advice

at another time. What might be good to do today is better avoided tomorrow. (13168)

Whenever a lord is asking for advice, he should for the time being neglect other things and other matters. The person advising should not take any notice of what his lord wishes to hear: he should advise him in accordance with what he thinks will be best for him. A lord should be wary about unsolicited advice, unless he has already recognized the loyalty of the man. May he protect himself from feeling regret later! A counselor should also be careful, whenever anyone asks him a question, that he does not reply on the spot, if there is another, wiser man present, for it is good breeding and honor to respect one's master. One should allow a man to speak his mind, that is a good idea, and should not be too quick to answer in the presence of his companions. The counselors should not argue among themselves when one of them gives good advice. (13192)

If someone does as I have said, then know for a fact that he upholds his court of law which is nothing without sound advice. There is more I would like to tell you. One should follow this guideline, namely, that anyone who wishes to judge well according to justice should judge without seeking fame in the process. The court should be based on justice, and if it were to exist for any other reason, it would not properly be called a court. Every man should know that a court that is based on patronage and friendship cannot have the validity of a court. And, again, if it is convened for the sake of fame, it cannot be called a court. It does not warrant the name court unless it is based on justice. For this reason, those who are intimately bound up with the court should take great care not to lose their good judgment for the sake of fame. Whoever surrenders his good life to boasting has sacrificed the most for the least. Know that whenever one behaves better and judges better one should preserve that which has been well done from blemish. A blemish certainly looks bad on fine wool: likewise, boasting does not accord well with the good action of any man. One should also resolve not to judge for the sake of gain, for he who hangs a thief for the sake of material possessions is behaving very unjustly. The thief has had his just deserts, but I can say for a fact that he who gives someone his just deserts without justice is perpetrating great injustice. Justice must abandon the name of justice unless justice is done to justice. He who judges otherwise than he should is certainly turning justice into injustice. (13236)

I want to offer another piece of advice: a master should not issue a lot of threats. Because the clap of thunder comes after the flash of lightning, one is not without fear once one has seen the lightning. If the thunder always rolled at the same time as the lightning was flashing, one would be even more afraid than one is. Know this: however loud the sound of the thunder might be, if it were not accompanied by a lightning strike, one would not be very much frightened, or not frightened at all. Know that it is the same with a master who wants to issue threats yet does not do much. If it comes about that a master threatens and does nothing, his threats have the effect that people feel more secure. The threats of the man who threatens all the time without acting make me feel safe, for by threatening he draws attention to things which he will not dare to carry out. (13260)

Here you should hear a cautionary tale and take it as an example, too. The long-eared Baldwin was once [cavorting] on the green grass. He ran about and jumped for joy, and after that he started singing so loudly that the forest resounded. His playing about and the noise he made were so loud and so terrible that they upset the wild animals. From the beginning, the wild animals everywhere were frightened by the din. Then the lion came trotting up and began to console them all. He said: "It is my wish and my command that a swift messenger should run as quick as a flash and find out for us who is making this noise. If we cannot live peacefully, then we must go away and protect ourselves from him. That is my advice. He might very well be my master."[13] Without delay he had the wolf brought to him and spoke thoughtfully to him, saying: "Wolf: I know that you are bold and wise. At the moment we have great need of your cunning and your boldness, for you must be the messenger of all of us. My dear friend: find out what creature that can be, and quickly let us know whether we can go on living here with him." "Oh dear, what a terrible voice he has," said the wolf. "I can say for a fact that you won't see me again." All the assembled animals began to plead earnestly with him to undertake this, that's the truth, and he set out on his journey with trepidation. Now hear what the wolf said when he saw Baldwin: "They have sent me here thinking I'm a fool. He could strike me dead with those ears. Alas, what danger I'm in! From his voice I might have known that he was the devil. Shall I flee or not? I know for a fact that, if he sees me, I am certainly dead. Then I shall never be able to get away from him. However, I'll keep close to the forest, and then if, as is likely, he attacks me, I can quickly flee into the undergrowth. I am scared stiff of his gaze." Baldwin looked at him, and the wolf started up: thanks to his father's teaching he did not flee at top speed, for he had taught him never to flee unless he saw that he was being chased, or he would be a complete coward. When the wolf saw that Baldwin was not speaking, he approached him very quietly, in his usual way. He was standing very close to him. "I must see what this is," said the wolf. When he saw that he was still not speaking, he went gently forward and bit him from behind, that's a fact, with great trepidation and leapt a good spear's length away from him. If Baldwin had had the sense to turn towards him the wolf would certainly have run away from him in cowardly fashion, but he did not do that, and so the wolf turned to the scoundrel and bit him all over, both front and back. You can well believe that he was not afraid of him after that, nor does he ever fear him. He said: "From now on I shall not care, whatever racket there may be. I will not pay attention as long as no one does anything to me." When the wolf told the wild animals what had happened, anyone there could have seen that the wolf was welcome to them. After that [even] the rabbit did not fear the villain Baldwin. Certainly no brave man can compare himself to Baldwin. Anyone who chooses to make a lot of threats in his court without doing anything is not judging well in the process, for he is like Baldwin. Anyone who is like Baldwin is all bluster, and anyone who comes to know what he is like will fear him less and less. A lord should be very careful that he should not issue his threats too forcefully from the start, so that it does not happen to him as it did to Baldwin when the frightened wolf saw him, for that way, to be honest, he will lose his honor. When people do not fear him, he has to be a scoundrel. He should always be happy, and, whatever he has to do, he should only issue a mild threat. That is my desire and my advice. He applies the correct pressure which one should fear after a threat has been made. The person who is threatening all the time is not someone whom one needs to fear much. (13386)

   If you have heeded my example, you should have taken to heart that one should oppose injustice from the outset. Whoever does not do that has the spirit of a Baldwin. Since the wolf ate Baldwin, it has become apparent to us that he never leaves anyone alone if he has the upper hand.[14] The same befalls a bad man: if one does not from the start protect oneself from the injustice that he perpetrates, then he will acquire such a reckless disposition that he will never let anyone live while he is in control. The wolf and the bad man are alike in this: that no injury ever occurs because of them unless people do not stand up to them. Thus it has become clear to us that Baldwin is like the man who threatens all the time, when he has absolutely no need to do so, and when he really needs to do so, he does not dare to make a move. (13412)

   I want to give another piece of advice: one should not be too quick to believe everything one hears. I very often hear people complaining about something that does not warrant complaint. If someone is always inclined to believe all that people complain about, he will hear lots of unnecessary complaints. If anyone has heard a complaint, he will do better to have the sense and the wisdom to look into it properly before he believes it, for know that anyone who is willing to believe [something] at once is behaving very wrongly. Also, take into account that the same man can make the straight crooked and the crooked straight. Indeed there are three kinds of wrongs: the first, that a man acts without knowledge, the second with certainty, the third, that he does not prevent something, for if injustice befalls someone and someone will not help him, that man is doing himself much wrong. (13436)

The first wrong—that one acts without knowledge—stems from a fool-ish mind, and often from rashness, and most often of all from laziness. Know, too, that it often also emanates from great anger and hostility. Know that sometimes it often comes about from love. It also derives from foolish-ness if a man cannot work out sensibly to what extent he should believe a story, and whom he should truly believe. That goes along with rashness, for it is great stupidity if someone straightaway believes someone who has not proved it properly. And know for a fact that in that case it derives from idleness that someone does not wish to protect himself and believes before he has experienced [something]. That same injustice often stems from anger which is innate in a man, in that a matter seems so unjust to him that he cannot wait until it is made known to him and wants to pass judgment straightaway. Injustice often derives from hostility, for—know this—one often believes straightaway that one of one's enemies has committed some injustice. It also often stems from affection, for, even if a man is known to be a thief, the person who loves him sincerely will always believe him. On this point I wish to offer a piece of advice: that if a lord has inadvertently com-mitted an injustice against a man, he should behave as though he had not noticed and put it right without delay. Why do I offer such advice? Because people will certainly become overconfident if someone pleads with them. If one has hit a child one should not cuddle it too quickly. (13480)

I have said what I think about someone who inadvertently commits an injustice, for whatever reason. Now I must not neglect to talk about the nature of the man who intentionally commits a wrong. He often does it out of greed, out of fear, or out of vanity. Sometimes, too, he does it out of hostility or envy. He does it because of a greedy disposition: if he is pas-sionate about acquiring the wealth of another man, then out of greed he inflicts both injustice and harm upon him. This injustice stems from fear. Very often a villain will think: "That man is too powerful and has too much. If I do not inflict some injustice upon him he will become so powerful and so wealthy that he will be a match for me and then I shall be completely deprived of honor, that's a fact." Then whatever injustice he inflicts upon him derives from his cowardly disposition. It can also often be attributed to vanity that someone inflicts injustice and harm upon someone who has not warranted it, for he wants to ensure straightaway that people understand what he is capable of. Know that all the time people are committing injus-tice out of enmity and envy. (13512)

I'll tell you how the third thing—that one does not prevent something happening—comes about. It often occurs as a result of idleness and because people want to avoid the trouble and not use up any effort. Much injustice comes from this. Certainly out of enmity people also allow things to be done that should not be done, because they are afraid of gaining enemies. There is not much sense behind that. It often happens that one does not stand up against injustice because one has other things to do. It seems to me unwise that because of one's own affairs, because of idleness, or because of enmity, because of the cost or the effort, people are allowed to inflict injustice and suffering on their neighbors. That all comes from a feeble spirit. I do not say this in order that someone should subject himself to the court if he does not have one at his disposal. One could help a man with advice and in other ways if one wanted to do what one should do. Know that, if anyone does not wish to assist justice, he sins just as much as someone who deserts his father, for anyone who has the strength is certainly obliged to help everyone to attain justice. One must not neglect justice. If someone sees a house burning by the side of his own house he is more inclined to take care that the same does not happen to him too. One should indeed know for a fact that the man who inflicts injustice on one man is actually threatening another. Anyone who does not understand this is a fool. (13552)

Now I have expounded to you according to my thoughts and my beliefs what is right and what is wrong, and I have told you in the process how a lord should judge who wishes to judge in a just manner. Now may God grant that we pursue justice in such a way that the path which is meant to lead to heaven is made straight for us. Then everything will have been well done. (13562)

Here the ninth part shall be at an end, and I shall not neglect the tenth.

BOOK X

Dear pen, you should not become bored, because what I want to write will soon be done. Justice has often urged me, after writing about her, to write about that virtue which in youth and in old age can by rights both retain and bestow. Every generous man possesses it. That same virtue is called generosity and it is an adornment of youth and the very crown of old age. It makes the other virtues beautiful and radiant. It is true that it is the actual mirror of virtues. Justice embraces generosity: generosity is, in fact, the child of justice. By its very nature, justice can occasion each man to have what he ought to have, and generosity also bestows in abundance according to justice. Notice that justice always gives each man what is rightfully his, but know also that generosity does not always dispense fairly in accordance with justice. (13588)

Certainly one can justly desire that one should be recompensed, whether to a great or small extent. The one is the companion of the other inasmuch as one man should be compensated for whatever has been taken from another man, that's a fact. Generosity does not make them all equal.

It gives little to this one and much to that, each according to his worth: that is the way of generosity. (13598)

Know that whatever one gives justly one must give at all times, unless one is wishing to commit an injustice. Thus that which one gives out of generosity and not out of obligation is justly given. Generosity only ever gives what is in its possession, but sometimes justice gives what is not in its possession. If a man has something by unjust means, justice should not allow him to keep it but should then give it to a person who justly had it at some point or by rights ought to have it. That is only right and proper. (13614)

Justice gives and takes, whereas you should know that generosity is inclined only towards giving. It does not take, that's a fact. Generosity gives out of a full heart both small and great wealth. Justice can give in a court of law whatever one does not justly possess. (13622)

Justice bestows both joy and sorrow, whereas know for a fact that generosity always bestows that which gives a man pleasure. Justice demands that one must pay compensation; generosity demands that one give in abundance. Justice desires to have nothing unjustly, whereas the nature of generosity is that it always gives of itself willingly and happily. (13632)

Generosity gives more than justice does, and it is also easy to understand that justice gives something that generosity never gives, for justice also gives a judgment, whereas generosity always gives something material. (13638)

If it were not for justice and the law, one man would not live side by side with another, for one would do the other an injustice. Thus their friendship would be unstable too, and there would not be any generosity. Therefore, understand that it always comes about as a result of justice that one man lives alongside another and it should come about as a result of generosity that one man lives happily alongside another. Know that even if justice has forced us to live alongside one another, we would be doing so with great animosity, if it were not for generosity. Whatever justice ought to do, generosity certainly enhances it, for generosity follows after justice. Now I have explained clearly to you why, after writing about justice, I must certainly write about generosity, for they have a lot to do with one another, if anyone can understand that properly. (13660)

If it were deemed to be a good idea, then I should gladly tell you in full why I have left the material about generosity to the end. That way the radiance of the greatest virtues shall shine forth. That is what I believe and desire. A person should demonstrate many virtues to another person before he gives him anything, and then when it comes about that he likes him very much or that he must part from him, then in truth he should far exceed in terms of generosity whatever virtues he has demonstrated: that is my counsel and the counsel of good breeding. (13676)

Virtues are completely worthless if they are not adorned with generosity. Nor does the generosity of a person who in other respects is not virtuous carry the weight of generosity, for, as I have said, the other virtues must take precedence and generosity come along behind, and that is the proper order of the group. That is a quality which so far I have not mentioned with respect to generosity, for I must talk about it later, since it goes so well at the end. (13688)

It is right that the company of maidens should leave the chamber ahead of their mistress. Likewise, it also very fitting that generosity is seen bringing up the rear, for it is the mistress of the virtues. Generosity is indeed the mistress of virtue, and anyone who possesses it in his youth considers it to be the truth in childhood and old age. (13698)

If someone forces himself to be virtuous for the sake of fame, this rarely lasts beyond his youth. If anyone likes to give gifts for the sake of fame, his generosity is exhausted by the time he reaches old age, for by then he is lacking fame. It is often apparent that, if that same person is generous for the sake of gain, he is not inclined to be generous once he has gained it. If his mind inclines him towards generosity and he does not force himself to it for the sake of fame, and if in addition he has the [good] sense not to be generous [merely] for the sake of gain, then be sure that he is generous at all times, in his youth and in old age. (13714)

If someone's generosity comes from his heart, then know that he will have it just the same in youth and in old age. No other virtue is like this. If a man is constant, then he is far more constant by the time he reaches old age. I have read and heard that a person in his youth never exercises complete constancy. Whoever is temperate in his youth will have that same virtue to a greater extent when he is old: that happens all the time. However, believe me, anyone who is generous in his youth has such a virtue that he cannot have it to a greater degree when he is old, for it is true that he has it to the full, whether he be young or old. Anyone who in his old age likes to give out of true generosity would not have thought it fair to hang on to anything when he was young. I tell you that, because generosity of all kinds is the same at all stages, I like it better than any virtue. (13742)

If a virtue is always to be found fully in one heart, that virtue is perfectly true to its name, and that's a fact. If a vice is always complete and getting bigger, then truly that is called a vice, too, and it leads to disgrace in youth and in old age. That is certainly the case with greed, about which I have said a great deal. (13752)

No glutton is so boorish that, if someone gives him enough, he does not hunger all the less. On the other hand, we have become well aware that whenever greed is given a lot of good things, it immediately hungers after even more. Fire and the greedy man are similar in that nothing satisfies them. Fire burns, while avarice manages to contaminate what is good. My heart and my mind tell me that fire and the greedy man should never be parted, for fire must consume everything that avarice wanted to gather together and contaminate. Avarice collects all kinds of things: its coldness is compelling. The power of fire always consumes everything. Generosity is so tempered that its coldness cannot contaminate, nor does its heat damage it so that it casts it away completely. It is too finely tempered. (13776)

I wish to tell you a little more—and you should not get fed up with this—about avarice, for know that one can better understand the goodness and value of generosity by comparing it with the evil of avarice. You should all take note that avarice increases every year. No one is so laden with vice in his youth that he does not become more greedy when he emerges from his childhood. (13788)

Avarice is derived from a cold nature, and because of that its strength increases when the man becomes old, for at that stage he is colder. Old age brings great avarice with it, and it is the nature of coldness to dominate. Know, therefore, that the avaricious man who is colder is even more avaricious. If a man is not constant in his youth, it often comes to pass that in his old age God grants him constancy. The same is true of immoderation, and I am not excluding licentiousness from this category. Anyone who, in his childhood, is given to immoderate and unchaste behavior very often turns his back on that when he becomes old and behaves in a better way. It is a different matter with avarice. The person who is greedy in his youth must always remain so, for avarice does not take leave of him. He has to be a complete scoundrel. His avarice does not leave him, and take this to heart: the older he gets the greedier he becomes. From this you must really understand that avarice must be considered a nasty vice. Anyone who has it in his youth can rest assured that he will have it in his old age. (13820)

Now take note how it comes about that one cannot cast aside avarice, whether in youth or in old age, as easily as other vices. It is the nature of avarice that it makes people think they are perfect: in the other cases people do not believe that they are perfect. You must already have heard this: however arrogant and however immoderate, however quick-tempered, jealous, and inconstant someone may be, he still cannot think that he can thereby acquire enough in material terms. The greedy man is so uncouth that he thinks he can gain much wealth through greed and cannot imagine that the wealth which avarice can achieve for him will not be sufficient. Thus he must keep on striving for it and is never satisfied during his lifetime. Now hear why no amount of wealth can satisfy a greedy disposition. The heart of man is so noble that it is the seat of God, but if someone's greed and rapacity, vice and malevolence drive God from his heart, then he cannot attain any wealth that would be so great or so noble that it might fill the seat of God. Anyone who believes he can fill with wealth the place where God should sit wants to fill the world with something completely useless, for it is true that, unless God Himself is there, the world is small and paltry compared to God, and His seat, whatever may be seated on it, is barren, unless He Himself is upon it. Anyone who wishes to fill his greedy heart with possessions will torment himself far too much and make his heart barren, and in that way he will be worse off for having wealth. His heart would not be so empty if God, Whom he drives away with his rapacity, were closer to him. You know for sure that the heart of anyone who drives Him away will remain all the emptier, and the emptier the heart is, the more he strives for wealth, for whatever is empty in the world always exerts a pull towards it and wishes to become full. One can very well note that if anyone looks into a barrel, the wine does not flow straight out unless there is an opening somewhere else. It will spurt out, for whatever wine runs out of the barrel, air must first go in, know that to be a fact. A greedy heart can attract a great deal, but, since God does not wish to enter it, it must remain empty. However, if God Himself were there, all good things would be there, too. Alas, alas for the greedy heart, for it never acquires enough and it must always cause itself grief that it ever considered filling itself up through greed, for it can never accomplish that. Now you have certainly heard why a person hardly abandons greed once he has truly acquired it. (13894)

Side by side with the wickedness of greed stands the nobility of generosity, for it is always the opposite of it in all respects. Whatever greed can take hold of, the generous man rightly dispenses. Whatever greed wickedly hoards, generosity distributes sensibly. A man who knows how to dispense in a just manner becomes very much valued for his generosity, and the one who does not wish to dispense according to justice very little valued on account of his avarice. Generosity wins us more friends than any other virtue, for its teaching causes a person to overlook it if a man does not possess in full the virtues that he ought to have: generosity can certainly do that. Thus, avarice wins many enemies for us, if you can understand that. Even if a man is virtuous in other respects, his virtues do not have the power to make people speak well of him, if he is lacking the generosity that he ought to have. (13918)

Observe the great wickedness associated with avarice and the great nobility associated with generosity. No one is keen to hold on to his wealth unless he is contented in his heart that people say that he likes to give. That happens all the time. No one is so greedy that he is not always glad when people say that he is generous. From this you can know as well that generosity is a pure virtue and one ought to love it always. (13930)

Because generosity fulfills virtue and is also an enhancement to youth, I have left it to the last to speak of it. It certainly deserves to be accorded special mention by me, and I am glad to do this, you can certainly believe that. (13938)

It seems to me that it has been clearly demonstrated why one ought, quite rightly, to speak about generosity after having spoken about justice. I have also made it quite clear why one ought to speak about generosity last. In what follows I shall tell you more about what generosity is and whether someone who does not possess anything can still be generous. Accordingly, I wish to say how someone who really wishes to give justly ought to give. (13950)

Generosity is a laudable virtue and has its roots in a noble spirit. Now tell me what generosity might be. It is the reflection of a noble spirit. Giving is not in itself generosity, but know that it comes about as a result of generosity if someone enjoys giving. Gifts are always the sign, whether true or false, of generosity. If someone gives purely out of a generous spirit, then in truth the gifts represent generosity and goodness. However, if one gives for any other reason, then those gifts are not the true signs of generosity, for they represent generosity in a false way. To be sure, if I were to see far in the distance a coat of arms that I recognized, I should think and immediately say that the knight whom I had seen with these emblems was there, and yet the situation might be quite different: for the man who is actually there might have stolen them or acquired them elsewhere by some other means. That has often happened, too. So you should know that a gift is not always a sign of generosity, for if a man gives for the sake of fame, then his fame has actually stolen the sign of generosity. Please believe that to be the truth. (13982)

Now you have certainly gathered that a gift should not be called generosity, and yet it comes about as a result of generosity. Why is the man who has nothing to give not deemed to be generous? That is because of our foolish way of looking at things, for we only value what we are more likely to see clearly. People do not notice what is in the heart. It is because of greed that people notice how much is given and refuse to notice the spirit with which it is given, which is what one should look at first of all. (13996)

If a man is born generous but is poor, he has completely lost the seal on his letters. Then, quite truthfully, it comes about that people do not believe [what is in] the letter when they do not see the seal. If I were to send a letter and did not wish to place a seal on it, then it is very likely that people would say it was not mine, and the same thing happens to the generous man who has nothing to give. If people do not see his gifts they will not say of him that he is a generous man, however much he is actually in a position to give. (14012)

Does a scribe write anything when he has no ink? He is thoroughly accomplished in his art, yet it is true he does not write anything, and that is a fact. Sometimes it is the same with the generous man who does not give anything. Even though a scribe has fine parchment and however swiftly his pen passes back and forth on the parchment, nevertheless he does not know how to write anything, if there is no ink in the pen. If a man's purse is empty, no matter how much he would like to be generous, he can shake nothing out of it, however long he may try to do so. (14028)

The man who has the virtue and the mind to give if he possessed anything is no less virtuous than the man who has demonstrated his abundant generosity far and wide with gifts, because he has the wherewithal to give. Whoever wishes to redeem his pledge has redeemed it well if he has the desire and the mind to do so, but if he does not do it, if urgent matters lead him astray, be sure that this does not bother him. (14040)

It is true that what the sun does above the clouds is exactly what the heart of a generous man who has never had great wealth also does. It must be very dark down here below when the clouds block the rays of the sun, but it is true that up above there is plenty of light. The sun is always shining on whatever is above the clouds. Generosity behaves in the same way in the spirit of a generous man. It lights up his whole heart, and yet cannot, true enough, shine forth from that man's spirit. The clouds are poverty, which remove the light completely, so that it cannot shine forth as it should. (14058)

If you have understood me correctly, then I have reached the point where I should tell you how a man may be generous. It upsets me and I get angry over the fact that we have lost the name of generosity and call something generosity that might better be called vice. We call someone generous when he gives away what he is always taking by robbery and by evil means. You can be certain that greed causes us not to distinguish better what is generosity and what not. If anyone sees and takes note that a man is giving a lot away, and does not want to pay attention to where it has come from, he is not actually recognizing his generosity, for greed has poked out the eyes of common sense, that's a fact, so that he cannot see at all what one should see when it comes to generosity. He can see well enough what someone is always giving him, and he does not care where it has come from. (14086)

There's a plant, the name of which I do not know in German, that, if a sheep happens to eat it, it dies, and yet the sheep craves that plant, and its sweetness causes it to die.[1] The same thing happens to us: we cannot recognize that there is no generosity in a gift if someone gives us something taken from somewhere else. The sweetness of the gift prompts us to overlook a person's giving us something that he takes wrongfully from all over the place. We say that the man who can give to us like this is a generous man. That is the nature of greed, and in this way we deceive him and ourselves. I can say quite truthfully that a sheep does not know what is going to hap-

pen to it on account of the little weed, and a man cannot really think that a
man who is always taking what he proposes to give away for the sake of fame
is not generous. He considers many vices to be generosity. If the man who
does not give is bad, then he who is taking all the time is worse still. How can
such a man be generous? The objects of generosity are poor people, whom
today we have turned into the objects of avarice, for we rarely take, if you
will comprehend this, from anyone but the poor who can do nothing about
it: that is sheer vindictiveness.[2] (14122)

Generosity and injustice are never in one another's company, for gen-
erosity is the child of justice. Therefore, that man is truly an ox who follows
the advice of generosity that injustice has given something to him. I can
say for a fact that generosity cannot bear to witness something being taken
unjustly. It always sickens it. How could a man live with the fact that he
wished to give away out of a sense of generosity what he had taken unjustly?
I have heard of that. If a man likes to give gifts so that, at another time,
someone bestows something on him, and if he wishes to take even more,
then there is much greed behind his gift-giving. Know for sure that such a
gift derives from greed. If someone gives like that, then that gift does not
come from generosity. (14144)

I despise it and it makes me angry that someone who cannot under-
stand what a generous man is should believe that he has generosity born
in him. The person who is always giving out of vanity thinks he is a gener-
ous man. If someone wishes to give to me like this I shall never thank him
much, for truly he has given out of vanity. I am happy to think a man good,
but let the lady on whose account he has done this thank him, if she wishes
to do so. I shall never thank him much for it. However, one should always
thank the man who gives out of generosity. (14160)

Every man should watch where his gift will do most good. One should
always observe who the man is to whom one is giving [something], so that
one always gives according to who the man is. To be sure, one should cer-
tainly give exotic things to the rich man and always give to the poor man
what is good and useful. Anyone who does not distinguish people gives in
a totally unconsidered manner. Where there is a lack of discrimination,
generosity is not present, for vice is always a long way away from virtue.
(14176)

If someone wishes to give sensibly, let him give neither too little nor
too much. The man who has given correctly has measured his gift in terms
of his means. It is true that the man who squanders all his possessions is
robbing himself, and I think that he who has robbed himself will not leave
mine (i.e., my possessions) alone. The man who gives according to his
means always gives properly. If a man wishes to give more, he will, of neces-
sity, help himself to much in an unjust way. He must swear false oaths and

lie and rob and deceive. The person who has acquired something unjustly has left generosity behind him, for virtue does not do injury: harm comes about from vice. (14194)

One should give in such a way that the person from whom one has taken it does not become unhappy about the gift. That is the desire and counsel of generosity. Generosity does not set out to harm anyone: it bestows much joy without sorrow. Generosity inflicts harm on no one. Generosity is completely devoid of avarice, and anyone who is greedy for material things cannot have a generous disposition. (14204)

At this point I wish to inform you that a lord and an ordinary man must adapt their expenditure to their possessions in an unequal way. For if a knight chooses to use up an entire year's pay in one year, that is not very much, whereas if a prince wishes to do that I am not so happy about it, for every lord should place something in his coffer every year. He should do this because if, for the sake of the honor and the reputation of the land, he were to become involved in a war, it would be neither chivalrous nor good if he were to take more from his friend than his enemy did. One thing that the lords like to maintain is a full treasury, but they do not maintain other things, for if they consume resources on account of the honor of the land and their own honor, they want to be given more and bring great suffering on their people, by supporting their [own] greed. However much I may criticize the lords, I criticize still more those who praise this. It has reached the point where people praise their whole lifestyle. If a lord is greedy and lacking in renown, people say: "Master, you are wise to have been able to keep a hold on your wealth." Thus, his avarice is known far and wide, even if he himself does not recognize it. Look how the scoundrel is making a fool of him. If he wastes everything he has, people say: "You have a generous disposition." By means of such deception, people pull the wool over their eyes so that they can neither live nor die, save nor give away. Many a man thinks he is very respectable, who would truly recognize that he was not, if people were to say openly to the lords what they say behind their backs. It is the greatest nonsense that they practice, believing people say to their faces what they say behind their backs. Indeed, that brings them into the trap whereby the lords often believe that foolishness is generosity and avarice wisdom. Take note how this happens, for now I must abandon this subject and begin the third rule. (14258)

Anyone who wishes to dispense gifts appropriately should not delay too much. Know that anyone who allows himself to be petitioned too long has actually sold what he then gives to a man. One always pays a high price for what one must buy with shame, know that for sure. If someone wishes to give quickly he gives a lot with small things, for he saves the other man from embarrassment and the fear that he is begging. The person who gives large gifts is giving little when he takes his time about giving. Take note of this: the man who lets another man ask him for something for a long time has long nurtured the desire to give him nothing. One should not thank him too much. Know that if a man gives and gives quickly, he has given twice over. Believe me, if a man has to be forced with much begging to give, he is not giving out of generosity. If someone is constantly asked for something, he is making his life a bit easier by giving and has not given out of generosity, for if he were to be left alone he would rather people never begged him [for anything]. The generous man who gives appropriately does not act in this manner, for he seeks out both whom he should give to and what he should give him. I never thank anyone who gives with anger and ill grace. The man who acts that way has not given out of generosity. Know that if a man gives joyfully, he gives enough, whether he gives little or much. A good heart always makes small gifts pleasing and good, whereas a poor spirit makes large gifts so displeasing that they cannot be compared with the small ones. If a man is so malevolent that he is always seeking to protest his objections in advance,[3] and is inclined to complain about his troubles and how much he is expected to give, he is not refusing graciously. A man is useless when it comes to generosity if he makes a face when he is giving. Be sure of that: he would do better not to give at all. If someone gives what he gives with trepidation and always grudgingly, then he is a very cowardly man and just as bad as the one who refuses. (14316)

Whenever one is giving one should see to it that one's eyes and one's mouth convey the impression that one is clearly doing it gladly. Know that he is giving appropriately who always gives in such a manner that, along with the material things, he gives both his heart and his goodwill. Only a real scoundrel thinks about payment when he is supposed to be giving something. He certainly cannot give appropriately. If he cannot give in a suitable fashion, he is not a generous man. Indeed, he is simply a merchant who is giving for the sake of profit. (14332)

Let anyone who proposes to give out of generosity not pay too much attention to recompense. The nature of generosity is that it gives, while greed always takes. Generosity takes when it wishes to pay back more, or at least as much. Generosity takes in order that it may give back more and does not follow the wicked practice of giving [simply] when it can take. Know for a fact that this does not happen. Generosity always gives and accepts without malice that there is no repayment. The man is a complete scoundrel who abandons his generosity because someone has not paid him back. A man cannot demonstrate his greed more effectively—know this—than by complaining that no one gives him anything and that he is giving all the time, for that way he makes everyone aware that he gives only for the sake of gain. (14354)

No generous man—I certainly dare to give this advice—should abandon his generosity because the man to whom he has given a great deal perhaps does not thank him. That is truly the way of generosity. If one were not meant to bring up one's children, and if one should, out of cowardice, not test the sea and the wind, because they often inflict harm upon us, then we would be complete cowards. I wish to say the same thing to you: that even if a bad man were ungrateful for what I had done for him, I should not abandon my generosity because of it, unless I were a scoundrel. It belongs to the free spirit that one loses and [yet] acts justly. Generosity would not be a virtue if what happens did not happen, and it was never deceived. It is very often lied to and even so it must have complete faith when it is to give something. Whoever wishes to practice generosity must lose many of his gifts, in order that he may give at a time when it is right to do so. Yet the man loses nothing at all if he looks at it correctly and sees it aright. In a rugged, unpleasant field the generous man can sow a seed which can bring forth fruit abundantly in the heart of him who is happy to act in a generous manner. If I give to an ungrateful man I do not lose my seed, for the gift provides me with virtue. Therefore, let people give at all times those things that are external to the body,[4] [for] those of us who distribute our wealth in a just fashion will always acquire virtue in our hearts. If a man does not wish to give, he is always just as guilty as he who does not say thank you when someone gives him something, for it is true that the stingy man actually produces the ungrateful man. (14402)

Furthermore, I also wish to say and reveal to you why a man is sometimes ungrateful. If a man makes a promise and delays for a long time and does not give something to someone and leaves him hanging about in hope, then truly that man becomes completely ungrateful. Hope is not sweet if the promise comes along dragging its feet. It would be better to do without the hope. Now believe this: it causes much hurt if someone has to hang about hoping. If someone is left hanging on hope for a long time, he also neglects many of his own affairs. A scoundrel who makes a promise and does not give, or if he gives does so too late, pays no attention to this. Do you know who is so inclined? If a man is ignoble and at some point is accorded honor, know that this is occasioned by his ignoble spirit. Every day he says "tomorrow," for he wants the other man to pay with anxiety for what he gives him, and so he causes him anxiety all the time. For this same scoundrel does not want to give him anything for nothing when he gives him hope and keeps him waiting. With that trick he is seeing to it that he is always serving him. He also does it because he wants people to see that he can do much that he thinks good. His feeble mind takes pleasure in this. Many a man is accustomed to doing this, so that someone else will ask him for something, and he is inclined to let him beg for a long time without giving anything. Another man may be so wicked that he does it just to make the other man so wretched that he never asks him for much, for the pain of anguish is such that it never leaves his heart. I can certainly say in truth that for whatever reason he does it he ensures that a man is always ungrateful for his gift. If a man does not give the whole of what he has promised, then certainly he compromises truth and mingles truth with deceit, and makes the man to whom he once made the promise an ungrateful man. Anyone who moans all the time that he gave or gives makes those to whom he gave totally ungrateful, that's a fact. (14466)

As soon as a man has given he should forget that he has done so. However, he who receives should remember his whole life through that the man did something good for him. The one who gives must keep silent: the one who receives must always proclaim it. The generous man should not think that he has given anything, unless the man to whom he has given a lot chooses to remind him. (14478)

If a man is generous he should always give in such a way that he thinks he is receiving. That way he can never give in a better way, for he cannot fault his gift at all, no matter what happens. (14484)

If anyone gives a generous man anything, let him receive it as though he has never given anything himself: that is certainly entirely in keeping with generosity. Let him not think: "I gave him more," for if he did he would have completely changed the honor of generosity into a business transaction, believe that for a fact. A decent man should consider good whatever someone gives him out of the goodness of his heart. Let him always consider abundant whatever his poor friend gives him. One should certainly thank effusively for a modest gift the man to whom one has given a great deal: that is the very essence of generosity. If someone does not thank another because he gave him more, this stems from other bad traits. The truth is: he is a merchant through and through. A generous man should not refuse if someone wants to give him something, for if a man is dear to me I am always happy to be in his debt, and pay back more to him: that is the lesson taught by generosity. If my enemy gives me something, then I am not so happy to receive it from him, for I should not be glad to give to someone whom I did not trust implicitly. If a wicked man were to give something to me I should be very reluctant to take it, for I should not wish to be in his debt. Know that it never does any good for someone to be indebted to someone to whom he never likes to be in debt. However, if a man owes his friend something, this gladdens his heart, for he is always happy to give to him without any sense of obligation. If a man is respectable, he must always be our friend as long as he lives, thanks to the things we might give him. (14528)

One should be glad to be indebted to someone to whom one enjoys giving: that is my desire and the advice of generosity. One should receive gladly and without hesitation from the person to whom one wishes to give back more: that is precisely the counsel of generosity. Since my friend trusts me implicitly, know that I should not falter were I to be the custodian of his possessions. What he gives to me is in my safekeeping as long as I am going to repay him in full and more besides, that's true. On this point I wish to offer a piece of advice: one should not be too hasty to repay what one has accepted, for that way one gets out of debt.[5] Know that he who always repays promptly is not happy to be in debt. If someone takes something and then immediately gives it back, he thinks he has been conducting a business transaction. Know that the man who gives and takes back so promptly has made a sale. If one wishes to behave correctly one should avoid both courses of action. (14552)

A generous man should be minded to follow the example of the fertile field, which does not yield anything immediately but yields abundantly in its own good time. A decent man, who can give in a correct manner, should do likewise. He should bide his time well, whether he is paying back or giving. If a man is generous he waits for the [right] time and the [right] place to repay or give away. That pleases me greatly. (14564)

If he has not the means to repay, then let him give his rich spirit. If he has nothing more to give, then, like the ploughed field, let him have the experience and the virtue and the good sense to be happy to pay back less. Some people are inclined, if they lack the means to repay, to avoid the person who has given to them. Know this to be the truth: this stems from great cowardice, and I can see very clearly that they do not know what generosity is, for generosity asks nothing of them. Anyone who behaves like this is a scoundrel. If anyone shows me a willing spirit, then I accept that as great riches, and if [those people] were to do likewise they would not need to hide away. (14584)

There is more that I wish to tell you. The man who gives publicly to a man when he ought to give to him in secret will make him very ungrateful. (14588)

At this point you ought to know that some gifts one should bestow publicly, in front of people, and others clandestinely. One should give openly that which brings honor to a man's life. One should certainly bestow courtly gifts publicly. If something brings honor to the person who receives, then the person who is to give it should give openly. That is certainly the right way to do things. If someone wishes to give courtly presents—falcons or hunting dogs perhaps—he should be open when he gives them, for this is always a matter for rejoicing. Anything that assists [in ameliorating] poverty—pennies or similar things—one should give secretly: it does not bring honor, but it does help people with their lives. (14608)

One should never give anything that is shameful to a man or that can cause him harm. If anyone gives wine to a drunkard or water to a man with a fever, or a fish bone to a child, or a sword to a madman, then he has treated them all badly. If one judges it correctly, that person has taken away more from all of them than he has given. (14618)

Anyone who adorns his life with generosity should not give superfluous gifts. Anyone who gives weapons to women is not giving as he ought to give. (14622)

One ought to be happy to give gifts that last and have a long life, for the friendship which prompts them should [also] last a long time. (14626)

A book is meant to last a long time. Therefore, I wish to bestow it on those whose friendship I greatly wish to have, if God will grant it to me. To anyone who is virtuous, or wishes to become so, I give my book out of friendship, in order that with it he may give directions to his fine manners. With good deeds he should also improve on what he has read in my book: let him be urged to do this. The person who is not endowed with courtesy and fine manners should not wander around with it. No advice has the power to make virtuous someone who is not possessed of virtue. One can beat on water forever without its bursting into flames, for fire is not in its nature. However cold a stone may be, one can still with skill derive fire from it, because it is contained inside it. If a man has some sense, then, however slow he may be to do good deeds, one can nevertheless, through instruction, bring him to virtue and goodness. Know this to be true: the tinder sets the fire alight, but no one should believe that it can make fire itself. Similarly, teaching can wake up the senses and yet cannot make them [in the first place]. Thus teaching is nothing to fools. Whoever passes on advice to a fool is doing him an injustice, for he cannot cope with teaching. Whenever anyone withholds it from a wise man, he is doing him an injustice, for he is depriving him of what is his. No man, whether out of recklessness or affection, should give to his sweetheart, or his master, or his lady, or his friend this book of mine to look at unless it is apparent to him that that person is virtuous. People can give my book to the man who is accustomed to live in such a way that I would not begrudge it to him, for I would not want anyone to have it, nor would I give it to anyone save him who, with his good life and his good deeds, fulfills what he has read. (14680)

My book is called the "The Italian Guest," for I am a guest to the German language and will never get any further with it than I have so far. Now go on your way, Italian guest, and be very careful for my sake that you do not find lodging with any scoundrel, but, if you do come upon one, don't sit down, for you should see to it that you get away from there quickly, for a decent man should take a look at you in peace and quiet. Sit on his lap: make that your fief.[6] Brave knights and virtuous ladies and wise priests should look at you. If a scoundrel grabs hold of you, have no fear that he will dare to look at you for long. I can assure you that he will see something in you that will cause him extraordinary pain in his heart. Then he will toss you into some trunk, and there you will remain, my dear book, until you fall into the hands of someone who will recognize you better and will often read you and always treat you well. (14708)

Now be warned, Italian guest, that when you take hold of a noble branch you do not allow yourself to pluck a nasty thorn from it. It's a waste of time to say the Lord's Prayer all day long to the wolf, for he will never say anything but "lamb," and the same is true of a wicked man. No matter what anyone says to him, in truth it goes in one ear and out of the other. How could good sense exist where there is no reflection on the matter? Know that a scoundrel cannot force his thoughts to go from useless things to good ones. Know that one cannot fill a sack that is full of holes until it is mended. The same always happens to the man who has pierced himself with wicked thoughts, with false counsel, with evil deeds, and with sin. Then at no time can any good words remain in his intentions and his heart unless our Lord God wishes by His commandment to close up the holes through which they escape. Otherwise there is no help for him. Therefore, my book, you should remain with him who wishes to have you inscribed in his heart and his mind. Anyone who is so steadfast and so virtuous and so imbued with constancy that you could not fall out of him, that is the person you are meant to improve with your instruction. Thus, he will improve you too, for the good man must perform even better deeds than you teach, be sure of that. (14748)

At this point I will bring you to a close. May God grant that we live eternally for the sake of the three holy Beings: Father, Son, Holy Spirit. Amen.

NOTES

Notes to Thomasin von Zirclaria's Prose Foreword

1. The majority of manuscripts of *Der Welsche Gast* include this summary of the work in prose. The lines do no more than set out the content of Thomasin's work, in ten sections which follow the same divisions. Like the copious illustrations which accompany most of the manuscripts, this contributes a further feature which marks out *Der Welsche Gast* as a unique work in its time and in the literature of medieval German.

In the interest of completeness we include it here in our translation. The lines supply clear guidance through a lengthy and complicated work, and while we would not necessarily subscribe to Jacob Grimm's view of them as "ein anziehendes Prosadenkmal" ('a charming piece of prose'), we felt, like him, that they deserved to be placed at the front of the work, where they could fulfill a useful practical purpose, rather than languishing, as in Rückert's edition, among the *Lesarten* at the back. (Cf. von Kries, *Thomasin von Zerclaere*, vol. 1, p. 12, note 25.) Like Rückert, but unlike von Kries, we have made no attempt to number the lines. Von Kries's decision to organize the prose introduction into 610 lines and to begin the translation of Thomasin's first book with the number 611 has been particularly criticized for the confusion that it can cause readers attempting to identify lines in Rückert's edition.

2. Thomasin demonstrates a penchant for polysyndeton and we have retained his repetition of the conjunction "und" in our translation to provide an adequate reflection of his style. He will, however, tend to omit the conjunction from time to time at the beginning of a new clause. Here, as well, we have adhered to his format.

3. Assuming that the reference here is to more than simply the outer trappings of chivalry, this is a rather startling declaration by Thomasin. Given the lament of his pen in Book IX that life was more enjoyable when his master spent his time at court with the knights and ladies (12239–43), it might be conjectured that Thomasin had grown cynical with the life of a courtier and turned from a *vita activa* to a *vita contemplativa*.

4. Section II is missing in Rückert; the lines have been added here from the von Kries edition. The Roman numeral II appears to have been manually altered to III in the Rückert edition.

5. The Roman numeral V is missing in Rückert's edition at this point.

6. Thomasin uses the singular "er," which we have amended to the plural form for consistency.

7. We have followed von Kries here and supplied an adjective which is clearly missing in Rückert's edition.

8. The number VIII is missing in Rückert's edition.

NOTES TO PREFACE TO BOOK I

1. We are quite likely dealing here with the topos of "affected modesty." While Thomasin may not lay claim to being the greatest stylist in Middle High German, he is certainly proficient in the language, to which over fifteen thousand lines of text provide eloquent testimony.

2. Gawain and Kay are two of the recurrent figures in the Arthurian romance. Gawain (OF Gauvain; MHG Gawan or Gawein) is a frequent character, traditionally the exemplary knight and a favorite with successive narrators. Kay (OF Keu; MHG Kei) is Arthur's seneschal and often presented as a somewhat ambiguous figure, upholding the standards of the court but depicted as personally negative. In Chrétien's *Yvain* (c. 1180), on which Hartmann von Aue based his *Iwein* (c. 1205), Keu (Kei) berates the courteous Calogrenant (Kalogreant) and is in turn reprimanded by the queen, who assures him that his insults are valued by the virtuous, since he reserves his approval for the malevolent. This episode, which would undoubtedly have been familiar to Thomasin's audience, may well be the basis for the extended comment here. If he is admired by Gawain, the mockery of Kay will not offend him.

3. This does not necessarily include his own earlier contributions in Italian to the subject, and he does claim in verses 109ff. that it is no vice to incorporate into his work what another hand has written. Thomasin may simply be reassuring his readers at this point that the core of what he has to offer in his book is original, even if he did present it earlier to an Italian audience in his native tongue. See introduction, p. 3.

NOTES TO BOOK I

1. Precisely what Thomasin means by this phrase is not clear. Lexer includes it among his examples under *zûn/zoun*, but with no explanation. Perhaps Thomasin has in mind a young nobleman given to a somewhat profligate life who, after a night of debauchery and self-indulgence, falls asleep in an inebriated state under a hedge, in other words, an individual who could certainly profit from Thomasin's words of advice.

2. We have slightly expanded the original here, in order to clarify the nature of the boasting.

3. The word used is "hort" which means 'treasure,' 'treasury' (as in the "Nibelungenhort," which is an enormous mass of gold). Literally: "that is the treasury of good breeding."

4. A fine pair of legs was an attribute in a handsome knight, and the suggestion

here is probably that it is ill manners for a knight to keep looking (admiringly) at his legs while out riding. (Cf. Joachim Bumke, *Courtly Culture: Literature and Society in the High Middle Ages*, trans. Thomas Dunlap [Woodstock: Overlook Press, 2000], p. 146: "Masculine beauty manifested itself most conspicuously in the legs and what covered them. The 'knightly' or 'imperial' legs of the courtly knight were often praised by the poets.")

5. Waving his arms about might give the impression that he was going to attack the other man.

6. The fabulous beauty of Helen of Troy was well known, but Thomasin is emphasizing the negative aspects of her story, her responsibility for the Trojan War. A little later (821–36), he uses her as an example of great beauty coupled with a lack of good sense, stressing the terrible outcome of this combination. The unidentified woman who first read the story (776–78) was misguided, he says, in her interpretation of the role of Helen. We are indebted to Michael Curschmann for the suggestion that the reference could be to Dido, who has the story of Helen of Troy painted in her palace.

7. In accordance with MS A, we have read "daz guote" in 788 and translated it as the subject of "gît."

8. Thomasin presents the women as crowing over the misfortunes of another woman and deluding themselves into believing that they will not get similarly caught out.

9. At this juncture, Thomasin demonstrates a thoroughly orthodox stance with respect to the relationship between the sexes in the High Middle Ages. It also accords with the belief that vices such as boasting and falsity are more repugnant in a woman than in a man.

10. One of a number of instances in *Der Welsche Gast* when Thomasin expresses a point of view that contrasts with the prevailing one of his age, namely, that the outer is necessarily a reflection of the inner. This extended discussion of the discrepancy between outward beauty and inner goodness is reminiscent of an important passage at the beginning of Wolfram von Eschenbach's *Parzival* (c. 1200–1210), in which Wolfram, too, makes clear his intention to praise a woman for her inward integrity, regardless of her appearance (2, 25–3, 24). Wolfram condemns the falsity that may lie beneath external beauty and rejects the false praise it may seem to invite. Thomasin, too, plays with the idea of falsity (959–72), and he uses the comparison of precious substances (gold and silver) and inferior gilded copper, where Wolfram makes his point by referring to a piece of glass set in gold, and a precious ruby in a brass surrounding.

11. These names of women who, as Thomasin says, may not all be queens but would qualify as such as far as their fine minds are concerned (1039–40) would all be familiar to the educated medieval audience, coming as they do from contemporary literature and from classical sources. Andromache: wife of Hector and mother of Astyanax, from whom she was separated and who was killed by order of the Greeks in the *Trojan Women* by Euripides. In the *Iliad* she is presented as the example of devoted wife and mother. Enite: the devoted, submissive wife of Erec in the work of Hartmann von Aue, based on the romance by Chrétien de Troyes. Her obedience to her husband is coupled with steadfast courage through a series

of ordeals. Penelope: the wife of Odysseus, renowned for her patience in awaiting his return from his prolonged journeying, and her resourcefulness in handling her many suitors. Oenone: the mythological nymph of Mount Ida, beloved of Paris but deserted by him in favor of Helen. It was to Oenone that he turned, though too late, when he was wounded by the arrow of Philoctetes in the course of the Trojan War. Galiena: a figure from legend, the (heathen) wife of Charlemagne. She was unjustly accused of adultery. Blanscheflur: several possibilities offer themselves here. The mother of Tristan bore this name, and she is remembered, in the version of Gott-fried von Strassburg (c. 1210) for her overwhelming grief when she believes her beloved Riwalin to be dead and subsequently when, now her husband, he perishes in battle. Because the name is coupled here with that of Galiena, Rückert rejects this as the likely source, however, and postulates a figure from Carolingian legend. The story of the young lovers Flore and Blanscheflur, as told in Middle High Ger-man by Konrad Fleck, is far too late to come into question, though the engaging tale of two people devoted unto death was familiar much earlier in both French and German. Likewise, the name, while not in Wolfram's version, exists in Chrétien's story of Perceval, where Blanschefleur is the *bel ami* of the young hero, though lack-ing the particular attributes recalled in Thomasin's list: the manuscripts are quite unclear here, and Rückert declares himself at a loss to supply a name, though he plays with the idea of Sigune (the first cousin whom Parzival comes across on four significant occasions in Wolfram's poem and who is notable for her grief-stricken devotion to her dead knight) and Itonje, also in Wolfram's *Parzival*, the sister of Gawan and beloved of Gramoflanz. Friedrich Ranke and Friedrich Neumann both favor Lavinia, wife of Aeneas. Sordamor: the wife of Alexander, named in 1050, and the mother of Cligès, who is named at 1042. Wolfram names her twice as Surdamur in *Parzival*, only in passing (586, 27 and 712, 8), but positively on each occasion. The fact that she is the sister of Gawan lends weight to the suggestion that the missing name, with which hers is coupled, is indeed Itonje.

12. In the parallel passage to the preceding lines, Thomasin directs the atten-tion of young men to the heroes of medieval literature. The names have close links in many cases with the women characters just named. Gawein: see note 2 of the preface to Book I above. Cligès: son of Alexander and Sordamor, and the central figure in the romance by Chrétien de Troyes (mid-twelfth century). Erec and Iwein: central characters in the poems of Hartmann von Aue, again based on Chrétien de Troyes. King Arthur and Charlemagne are juxtaposed here, as examples of heroism. King Arthur is the focus of the romances of Chrétien de Troyes, and, in German, of Hartmann von Aue and Wolfram von Eschenbach. Charlemagne, the eighth-century king of the Franks renowned for his military exploits but also as a propaga-tor of culture, was lauded in Old French literature, notably in the *Chanson de Roland*, which found its way into Germany in the *Rolandslied* (c. 1170) of Pfaffe Konrad. Alexander is commemorated in German literature in the later thirteenth century, but already to Thomasin's audience he would represent an outstanding example of heroism, though probably also with the accompanying admonishment to virtue and self-control. Likewise, he offers as models Tristan, recalling perhaps his courtly excellence rather than his involvement in a duplicitous love affair, Segramors, whom Wolfram had presented as a dashing knight at Arthur's court and Kalogreant,

notable in Hartmann's *Iwein*, following Chrétien's *Yvain*, as a gentlemanly exponent of knightly virtue.

13. Key: see preface to Book I, note 2 above. Thomasin refers to him here as the antithesis of these other models of courtly behavior and sees the very name of Kay as a generic term denoting dishonor and disgrace. The specific episode to which he refers occurs in Book VI of Wolfram's *Parzival*, where, in a joust with Parzival, Kei breaks his arm and his leg and is borne back to Arthur's encampment. Unabashed, he challenges Gawan to joust with Parzival; although Gawan does not do this, he meets Parzival, brings him to the Arthurian assembly, and thus unintentionally sets him on the path towards the Grail, to which Thomasin refers in his oblique comment at 1076–78.

14. The word "schrift" is any piece of writing, although at its subsequent occurrence in 1103 we have taken it to mean specifically the Bible, given the association with a priest.

15. Thomasin's remarks on the significance of illustrations for the uneducated found reinforcement in the copious use of illustrations in the majority of manuscripts of *Der Welsche Gast*. See introduction, pp. 5–6.

16. We have viewed 1163–65 as a unit, followed by 1166–68 as an independent second cluster. Rückert has a comma at the end of 1165 that we are altering to a period, while changing the period at the end of 1166 to a comma. Associating 1166 with 1163–65 makes no sense to us. What would prompt Thomasin to consider refraining from saying a lot of things had those things *not* been irksome to young people? The amending of the punctuation seems quite justified here. We are at variance with Eva Willms, who translates: "Ich habe mein Ziel aus den Augen verloren und viel von dem gesagt, was ich nicht gesagt hätte, wäre es den jungen Leuten sonst nicht langweilig geworden" ('and have said much which I would not have said if otherwise it would not have become boring to the young people').

17. As far as we know, this book is no longer extant, if it ever existed, though one wonders why Thomasin should be making a false claim. See introduction, and 1554 and 1684.

NOTES TO BOOK II

1. Thomasin is, of course, making the point that people have rather skewed priorities with respect to what is important in life.

2. See Willms, *Thomasin von Zerklaere*, pp. 178–79, for a full discussion of 2215–2422.

3. Which book this is remains unclear. On this occasion, it is almost certainly not the Bible.

4. Verses 2225–28 bear some similarity to the explanation given to Parzival by Cundrie in Book XV of Wolfram's poem: Speaking of the seven planets, she says: "die sint des firmamentes zoum, / sie enthalden sine snelheit: / ir kriec gein sime loufte ie streit" (782, 14–16). Hatto translates: "these planets are the bridle of the firmament, checking its onrush; their contrariness ever ran counter to its momentum" (Wolfram von Eschenbach, *Parzival*, trans. A. T. Hatto [Harmondsworth: Penguin,

1980], p. 388). Central to all that Thomasin says here is his belief that the constancy of the universe is in sharp contrast to the inconstancy of man.

5. Verses 2259–60: according to K. F. W. Wander, *Deutsches Sprichwörter-Lexikon*, this is the first occurrence of a proverb which occurs later frequently and in varying forms. See also Willms, *Thomasin von Zerklaere*, p. 180.

6. The concept of the four elements which together compose, in differing mixtures, all living things is central to medieval thinking. Earth, water, air, and fire stand in constant opposition to one another.

7. On the practice of bloodletting for medicinal purposes in the Middle Ages, see Auty et al., eds., *Lexikon des Mittelalters*, pp. 150ff.

8. Verses 2435–76: Thomasin was writing in a period of great unrest, not least in his native Italy. Although he seems to be attributing this to the fall of the Roman Empire, he is also thinking of the specific conflicts which were raging in his own time. Some of these were political and economic in origin, between growing and increasingly powerful cities, but there was also the threat throughout Europe to the stability of the Church from the Cathars and the Waldensians, among other sects, the "heretics" to whom Thomasin refers in 2472. Verses 2437–38 refer to the clash between the citizens of Rome and those of Viterbo, just north of Rome, a conflict which raged for the best part of a decade and in which Innocent III became involved, before a compromise was achieved. Verona was the object of repeated attacks in the middle of the first decade of the thirteenth century (2447–49) and Brescia, Vicenza, and Ferrara were likewise ravaged by warring factions. As Thomasin remarks, these named cities are just some among the many which fell victim to conflict generated, as he sees it, by malice and disloyalty. When he goes on to speak of Provence and Spain, he is referring to the impact of the so-called Albigensian Crusade, the attempt condoned by Innocent III to assert the authority of the Church, even at the expense of persecution and devastation. However, when he speaks of how loyalty and truth have been abused and put to flight, he is looking not so much at the effect of the "crusade" as at the reason it came into existence in the first place.

9. Thomasin, familiar with the (spoken) German language of his district, employs the popular term "Kerlinge" to describe the French. See Rückert's note on 2468 (*Der Wälsche Gast*, p. 55).

10. The two kings are John of England ("John Lackland") and Philipp August of France. John had attacked France with great force in 1214, in a vain attempt to recover lands lost to Philipp ten years earlier. (The disastrous and costly campaign was, in fact, the impetus to the uprising of the barons which led to Magna Carta, though this consequence is not significant in the context of Thomasin's work.)

11. Willms notes that this is one of the first literary occurrences of the word "ketzer" to describe heretics. See her note, *Thomasin von Zerklaere*, p. 181.

12. We have not tried to express the irony in this line, where Thomasin actually says of the heathens and apostate Christians that "they adorned them in evil fashion."

13. Apulia was the designation for Sicily, restored in 1194 to the empire by Henry VI, who was proclaimed Rex Sicilie, and since then the focus of conflict, particularly during the minority of his son Frederick II and the regency of the latter's mother Constance. It became a bargaining point between Frederick and Innocent

III, when he agreed that he would renounce the kingdom of Sicily in favor of his eldest son Henry once he had himself been crowned emperor, a promise he reneged on, though he was left with the task of sorting out the chaos which prevailed in that part of his kingdom and to some extent neglected other areas which required his urgent attention. Even at the time he is writing, Thomasin has every reason to see Apulia as a place where loyalty and truth are not at home.

14. Pilgrims on their way through Tuscany were frequently ambushed and robbed. Monte Fiascone was a stronghold protected by papal guards.

15. Thomasin is thinking, no doubt, both of the strife among the cities, which resulted in "fire, war, and pillage," but also of the activities of the "heretics" and the opposition to them by the forces of the Church. See note 8 above.

16. Thomasin responds to the very idea that there might be loyalty in the German lands with this generalized comment. Willms interprets his reticence as "schonende Parteinahme" (*Thomasin von Zerklaere*, p. 181: "a protective taking of sides"), but it could be the opposite, a kind of contemptuous dismissiveness.

17. Queen Gertrude, the first wife of King Andreas II of Hungary, was killed in 1213 by a Hungarian count, in the course of a rebellion of noblemen protesting at what they saw as her German roots. (She was the daughter of Margrave Berthold IV of Merano.)

Notes to Book III

1. The salamander is a lizardlike creature popularly credited in mythology with being able to withstand fire. Wolfram von Eschenbach mentions it several times, particularly in *Parzival*, where he refers to the silk woven by the salamander into a precious material which bears the same name and is likewise proof against fire: 735, 25; 757, 4; 790, 22; 812, 21. Cf. *Willehalm* 366, 4, and 366, 9, where the apparel and trappings of King Tybalt are made of pure white salamander. Wolfram's only mention of the salamander in his *Titurel* comes when Sigune is describing the power of the love of Schionatulander which enflames her, "as the mountain Agremuntin does the salamander" (121, 4). Clearly, Thomasin's audience would be aware of the inseparability of the salamander and fire, hence his apposite reference here.

2. In 2624–38, which speak of the order of nature, there seems to be an echo of Walther von der Vogelweide in his *Reichston* trilogy where he contrasts the discontent and disorder of human beings with the fact that, in the animal kingdom, each creature is assigned its proper place and accepts this.

3. We note a marked discrepancy here between our understanding of these verses and that of Eva Willms. The difference stems from our differing interpretations of the noun "werunge" (2684) and the verb "wern." Willms interprets these in terms of defense against attack, whereas we see them as relating to payment of debts, linking more closely with the preceding references to the poor man and the rich man. Thus Willms translates: "Greift man mich an, bekümmert mich, da das Abwehrgerät nicht bereitsteht. Soll dagegen ich angreifen, ist mir arg, da ich nichts habe, womit ich kämpfen kann" ('If someone attacks me, it bothers me that I have nothing available with which to defend myself. If on the other hand I am to do the attacking, it grieves me that I have nothing to fight with'). See *Thomasin von Zerklaere*, p. 68.

4. Throughout these lines Thomasin is playing with the two distinct meanings of "guot": good/goodness and wealth/possessions. We have tried as far as possible to express this double entendre.

5. Thomasin's formulation in 3001–2 is reminiscent of what we find in the *Strassburger Alexanderlied* of Pfaffe Lamprecht (ca. 1170), 2614–15: "zimberen begunder dā / eine burg unde eine stat" = 'there he began to build a castle and a city.' While we can only conjecture that Thomasin was familiar with the earlier work, it may be more than coincidence that later in this book he turns his attention to Alexander and his conquests.

6. Our translation of 3077–81 is predicated upon a revision of Rückert's punctuation. We have read 3079 with a period after "herr" and 3080 with a comma after "henden." We remain perplexed over the exact meaning of "zwischen henden," but feel that the translation we have offered with the revised punctuation goes some way towards supporting our rendering of the phrase. Regrettably, Rückert offers no commentary on these verses in his notes.

7. The roles of cupbearer and steward were an important aspect of the ceremony of courtly banquets, dispensing drink and food in a formal manner. Sometimes the offices were filled by individuals of considerable nobility themselves, and the decision as to who should occupy these functions lay with the lord. (Cf. Bumke, *Courtly Culture*, pp. 187–89.) Thus Thomasin sees this as a part of the fantasizing of the foolish man who deludes himself that he has enormous power. Cf. 3282–84.

8. Alexander was a popular heroic figure of the Middle Ages, but central to the depiction of him in literature was the ambivalence seen in his character, his courage, and powers of leadership, side by side with his overweening ambition and his frustration at not being able to fulfill all his desires. Thus, 3376.

9. Julius Caesar (100 B.C.–44 B.C.), Roman statesman of enormous power who assumed the title "Dictator for Life" but was assassinated at the height of his power.

10. In the *Iliad*, Hector was the eldest son of King Priam. He led the Trojan forces during the siege of Troy but, following his death at the hand of Achilles, he was dragged by him around the city.

11. The old queen of Troy is Hecuba, wife of King Priam, reduced to slavery after the fall of the city.

12. Anchises, father of Aeneas by the union with the goddess Aphrodite. As punishment for boasting of this union, he was struck by the thunderbolt of Zeus. He was carried out of the burning city of Troy—the fire in which he suffered terribly (3405)—and accompanied Aeneas on his wanderings but died at sea (3406).

13. Hannibal, great leader of the Carthaginians and a sworn enemy of Rome in the Second Punic War (218 B.C.–213 B.C.). Thomasin's reference is to the defeats that he inflicted on the Roman armies, and thus his success in undermining the power of Rome. What he does not add is that Hannibal himself eventually succumbed to that power when, rather than surrender, he took poison. His emphasis is on the humiliation of the famously superior Romans.

14. The reference is almost certainly to Otto IV, whose recent defeat at the Battle of Bouvines (1214) would be very much in the mind of Thomasin and his audience. See 10470–552 below, and note.

15. Rückert (*Der Wälsche Gast*, p. 561) points out that this anecdote is told, not

of Alexander, king of Macedonia ("Alexander the Great," 356 B.C.–323 B.C.), but of Alexander of Pherae (assassinated in 358 B.C.). The two seem to have become conflated in Thomasin's version.

16. This sudden and somewhat unexpected reference to King Arthur seems to be saying that if his widespread reputation is based on a falsehood, then the numerous tales told of him are also untrue.

17. Rückert (*Der Wälsche Gast*, p. 561) refers to an episode in the life of Alexander related by Seneca which Thomasin uses here to illustrate his point about the discrepancy between reality and the reputation bestowed by those who seek to flatter people in authority.

18. The scribes do not seem to have had any trouble with the noun "croiraere," which is recorded elsewhere in the literature of the day (see Lexer, *Mittelhochdeutsches Handwörterbuch*) and fits in with the French terminology of chivalry. Our translation 'heralds' is not ideal, but is perhaps more easily understood and more appropriate to the context than 'criers.'

19. There is a slight echo in this formulation of the words of Hartmann von Aue at the beginning of his *Iwein* "swer an rehte güete / wendet sîn gemüete / dem volget saelde und êre."

20. The juxtaposition of joy and sorrow is a recurrent theme of medieval German literature, expressed in the *Nibelungenlied*, for example, and in Hartmann von Aue's *Der arme Heinrich*, and a central concept in Gottfried's *Tristan*. Cf. also 3989–90 and 4105–8.

21. The issue of surveillance ("huote") had recently been treated at length by Gottfried von Strassburg in his *Tristan* (c. 1210), where he, too, condemns the practice by which a man exercises scrutiny over the behavior of his wife but actually is at fault himself. Gottfried goes much further than Thomasin, however, maintaining that it is in a woman's nature to do what she has been forbidden to do, although he has praise for the woman who can overcome her nature, suggesting, in a somewhat unexpected turn to medieval orthodoxy, that such a person is 'only in name a woman, but in spirit a man' ("diu ist niwan mit namen ein wîp / und ist ein man mit muote" [17978–79]). An ambivalent attitude to the practice is expressed also in the songs of Friedrich von Husen over twenty years earlier.

NOTES TO BOOK IV

1. Thomasin uses the word "vâlant" rather than the more common and less colorful "tiuvel" to convey the impression of a larger-than-life, demonic being. Cf. its occurrence in the *Nibelungenlied, Kudrun, König Rother*.

2. We supply the period which is obviously missing at the end of 4520 in Rückert's edition.

3. Verses 4737–46: Although the reign of King David is often idealized, it was, in fact, fraught with tensions, and David's own behavior sometimes reprehensible. The specific events referred to here probably concern David's adultery with Bathsheba, his responsibility for the death of her husband Uriah, and his marriage with her (II Samuel 12). David repented, but God punished him by taking the child of the union. Many years later, when David's authority was waning and his people dis-

content, his son Absalom rebelled against his father, having promised that he would set right any grievances. In the course of the final battle of the ensuing conflict, Absalom was caught in the branches of a tree and slain by a group of David's own men, though against his instructions. The sins to which Thomasin refers here are both his revolt against his father and his much earlier killing of his brother Amnon in revenge for his raping of his half-sister Tamar (II Samuel 13). This complex series of events no doubt accounts for Thomasin's judgment that Absalom was slain on account of his sins and because he did not exercise justice for the sake of justice. In Hartmann von Aue's *Der arme Heinrich*, Absalom is cited as an example of hubris, meriting retribution from God (85–89).

4. Verses 4785–94: The whole of the book of Job tells of a righteous man who does not abandon his faith in God, despite the many sufferings inflicted upon him by God, acting through Satan, who is depicted in the Old Testament not as a figure of evil in opposition to God, but as a part of the divine court, acting only with the permission of God (Job 1:6ff.). It is this latter factor that Thomasin seems to be stressing here, showing that, by allowing Satan to tempt Job, God fulfills His own purpose of demonstrating the goodness of the man. Equally, the book of Job culminates in Job's own recognition of the supremacy of God. Job as the epitome of the patient, suffering man is a familiar example in medieval literature: see, again, *Der arme Heinrich* (128–32).

5. Verses 4795–4805: This passage represents Thomasin's only precise reference to a source, the *Moralia* of Gregory the Great (c. 540–604). Thomasin doubtless knew this work well, since it was one of the most popular theological primers of the Middle Ages, and here he translates almost verbatim from the Latin.

6. According to some traditions, St. Paul was beheaded in Rome c. 64 A.D., executed on the authority of Nero.

7. See note 4, above.

8. Genesis 4:8.

9. See Luke 8:2, where it is said that Jesus drove seven devils out of Mary called Magdalene.

10. The reference is presumably to the death of Judas by his own hand (Matthew 27:5).

11. See Exodus 4–14, when Pharaoh (Rameses III) is adamant that he will not let the Israelites go and remains resistant to all pressures until the tenth and final plague, the death of the firstborn of the Egyptians, persuades him of the power of God.

12. The book of Jonah tells how the prophet Jonah is sent by God to Nineveh to announce its destruction, as punishment for its sins. Reluctant at first, he goes there, after God shows His mercy by saving him from "a great fish"; warned by Jonah of impending disaster to their city, the people of Nineveh repent of their sins and mend their ways and God does not exact retribution.

13. Shadrach, Meshach, and Abed-nego are three Jewish boys taken by King Nebuchadnezzar after the siege of Jerusalem and brought up, along with their friend Daniel, at the court of Babylon. When they refuse to worship the golden idol set up by the king, he has them thrown into the fiery furnace, but they survive, much to the amazement of the king, who recognizes the power of their God and promotes them within his land (Daniel 3).

14. We are grateful to Michael Curschmann for having pointed to the parable of poor Lazarus and the rich man (Luke 16:19–31): This beggar of the same name waits for the crumbs that fall from the rich man's table. When he dies, angels take him to heaven, while the rich man is tormented in hell. Abraham reminds him that he received only good things in life, while Lazarus endured only bad things.

15. Daniel 6 tells of Daniel's own ordeal at the hands of Darius, successor to Nebuchadnezzar. When he disobeys the king's order that all prayers should be addressed to him, Daniel is thrown into the lions' pit but he survives, saved by the angel of God. The scribes, "weniger bibelfest als Thomasin," as Rückert puts it ('less sure of their Bible' [*Der Wälsche Gast*, p. 565]), were defeated by Thomasin's use of the Latin word 'lacus' for "pit" or "hollow" and made various proposals for alternative readings and paraphrases.

16. Genesis 39 tells of the attempted seduction of Joseph by the wife of Potiphar, his Egyptian employer and the head of the royal guard. Although he resists her repeated attempts to lure him, he is wrongfully imprisoned as a consequence of her accusations but subsequently rises to power under Pharaoh.

17. Verse 5278: See note 8, above. Thomasin reiterates that Abel has the better fate, despite his death at the hand of his brother, since this brings him to "the place where he is very glad to be" (5189–93).

18. The adjective "unmære" has two possible meanings, denoting either positive unpleasantness or indifference. On this occasion we opt for the latter.

19. Verses 5418–20: We have taken some liberties with Rückert's edition here, changing the comma at the end of 5418 to a period, and adding a question mark at the end of 5420. This is, admittedly, only one way of interpreting the meaning.

20. Thomasin echoes here some of the sentiments expressed by the maiden in Hartmann von Aue's *Der arme Heinrich*, who is also eager to leave this world so that she may enjoy the delights of heaven.

21. The sickness to which Thomasin is referring is a spiritual one, but the implied reference to leprosy, that great scourge of the Middle Ages, which separated the sufferer from the rest of the community, will not escape his audience.

NOTES TO BOOK V

1. An explanatory note is called for here. Verse 5707 "Bereitschaft" is understood by Lexer in his *Mittelhochdeutsches Taschenwörterbuch* (p. 15) as "zubereitung, ausrüstung, verpflegung, gerätschaft; bares geld; erfordernis" (in the appendix, p. 357). None of these terms would appear to fit the context. We understand Thomasin's term in the theological sense of *dispositio*. While Thomasin states in verse 5708 that "bereitschaft," as the fifth element, always generates evil, he is much less uniform about its function when he defines what constitutes "bereitschaft," namely, "adel, maht, gelust, name, richtuom, hêrschaft" (5743–46). Note also 5752, although Thomasin returns to a unilateral identification of these six categories with "übel" in 5775. Given that all six can be used to do good or evil, depending on the individual who possesses them, we have opted for the term "tools," in the sense that any of these attributes could be used as a tool for good or evil. In 5919, these "tools" are

referred to by Thomasin as "des tiuvels haken" ('the devil's hooks') and "haken" occurs several times in the subsequent passages.

2. Numbers 25:7–13 tells how Phinehas, son of Eleazar, son of Aaron the priest, received from God His covenant of peace, "because he was jealous for his God, and made an atonement for the children of Israel."

3. Verses 6058–69: The Old Testament does not supply evidence of the specific virtues attributed by Thomasin to the familiar biblical figures, and he seems to be making a general point: that these virtues are requisite in those who aspire to come to God, and that God Himself possesses them all to a far greater extent than each of them does (6080–95). His audience, undoubtedly familiar with the Bible, may have had difficulty relating the individual virtues to the events known in each case, yet they would certainly have grasped his overall purpose.

4. Nimrod is named in the Table of Nations (Genesis 10) as the son of Cush and the great-grandson of Noah, cf. also I Chronicles 1:10. Micah 5:6 names Assyria as the land of Nimrod. These references do not account for Thomasin's comment, however, and there is some doubt whether Nimrod was an actual historical figure. More relevant is the fact that Jewish legends about King Herod—which may have influenced Matthew's account—have astrologers predicting his birth by the appearance of a huge star: when they report this to King Nimrod, he slaughters seventy thousand children (J. R. Porter, *The New Illustrated Companion to the Bible* [London: Duncan Baird Publishers, 1995], p. 204). How Thomasin would have come by this concept is unclear, but it accords with his view here that Nimrod was destined for hell through his evil deeds.

5. The reference to Cain is much more obvious. Cf. 5191–93.

6. I Kings 5 and 6 tell of the magnificent and costly temple built by King Solomon in honor of God. Mark 12:42-44 and Luke 21:2–4 relate the story of the widow who, despite her poverty, contributes her mite to the treasury. Thomasin links the two, in order to make his point that God takes account of the intention and rewards accordingly, rather than measuring the size of the gift. Rückert makes much of the fact that the Bible does not link the two stories and that they must be linked in legend, but it is also possible that Thomasin takes two unconnected, familiar, biblical stories and juxtaposes them. We have ventured to underline this latter possibility by translating the conjunction "dô" in 6189 as "whereas," although it most often suggests a temporal idea ("when").

7. St. Peter, the fisherman (Matthew 4:18–20), received the keys of the kingdom of heaven from Jesus (Matthew 16:18).

8. The emperor Flavius Claudius Julianus (332–63), the son of the half-brother of Constantine the Great, proclaimed himself a pagan, hence his nickname "Julian the Apostate." Though not linked with the persecution of Christians, he revived pagan cults, which probably accounts for Thomasin's assigning him to hell.

9. The link with the previous note is clear: the emperor Constantine (c. 274–337) is notable both for his enormous power and wealth and for his protection of Christians following his victory over Maxentius in 312, an event which he attributed to the Christian God. By his Edict of Milan (313), he assured toleration of Christians throughout the Roman Empire and was himself sincerely committed to the faith he had espoused. The city of Constantinople was founded by him (324) as a Christian

>` a

city, on the site of Byzantium. His remarkable achievements in political and cultural spheres earned him the title "Constantine the Great." The Italian scholar Boninus Mombritius (1424–c. 1500) relates this anecdote (6226–31) in his *Sanctuarium seu vitae sanctorum*, a collection of 334 legends of the saints (c. 1480). Mombritius also translated the writings of Eusebius, bishop of Caesarea (c. 263–339), a close contemporary of Constantine and greatly devoted to him, whose works included a life of the emperor and numerous references to documents no longer extant. It is entirely possible, therefore, that Thomasin was familiar with such sources and that they belonged to commonly held knowledge among the theologically educated of his day.

10. Thomasin highlights his despondence at the apparent absence of virtuous people by this lament for the central heroes of Arthurian romance and for King Arthur himself. The message would be very clear to an audience conversant with the tales of Chrétien de Troyes, and, in German, of Hartmann von Aue and Wolfram von Eschenbach. Yet his final comment here shows that, for him, these are the representatives of courtly values, which could still be revived by others.

11. Echoing his previous lament for the absence of the Arthurian heroes, Thomasin lists these famous Greek philosophers. (See his longer list at 8937ff. with our detailed note.) His lament that Aristotle is no longer alive is linked with the implied lament that, even if he were, there is no king comparable to Alexander (the Great) to promote him. Aristotle was originally the tutor of the young Alexander, but later in his career the king was his significant and dedicated patron, aiding him when he established his school of philosophy in Athens and the great library there.

12. "I have seen servants upon horseback and princes walking as servants upon the earth" (Eccelesiastes 10:7).

13. The sense seems to indicate that the period at the end of verse 6782 in Rückert's edition is an error, and we have ignored it.

NOTES TO BOOK VI

1. Genesis 37–50. Cf. note to 5276 above.

2. Verses 6887–94 presumably represent Thomasin's understanding of Exodus 2:11–14.

3. I Samuel 16:11–13.

4. I Samuel 21–II Samuel 5.

5. We have taken "bî dînen ougen" to be some kind of exclamation, along the lines of the (Shakespearian) "gadzooks!"

6. Around twenty years later, another German didactic poet, who called himself Freidank, evoked the same fable: "so der gouch daz êrste loup gesiht, / so getar er sichs gesaten niht, / er fürhtet, daz ez ime zerinne" ('when the cuckoo sees the first leaves [in spring] he dare not sate himself for fear that he might run out of them') (H. E. Bezzenberger, ed., *Fridankes Bescheidenheit* [1872, rpt. Aalen: Otto Zeller, 1962], p. 147, 88, 3–5; cf. Gerd Dicke and Klaus Grubmüller, *Die Fabeln des Mittelalters und der frühen Neuzeit. Ein Katalog der deutschen Versionen und ihrer lateinischen Entsprechungen*, Münstersche Mittelalter-Schriften, 60 [Munich: Wilhelm Fink, 1987], no. 366).

7. MHG "gouch" = 'cuckoo' and 'fool,' and the audience is likely to have enjoyed the double meaning.

8. Verses 7363–64: We can unfortunately not imitate the play on "guot" = 'wealth' and "guot" = 'goodness,' which will not have escaped Thomasin's audience.

9. We have chosen to follow Rückert in the matter of capitalization, bearing in mind that the personification of abstracts is common medieval practice. It must be said, however, that Rückert is not altogether consistent in his practice.

10. This sounds like a reference to Exodus 20:5, which speaks of the sins of the fathers as being visited upon the children.

11. See I Samuel 2 and 3. The old priest Eli, into whose care the boy Samuel is placed for his training in the service of God, has watched the blasphemous behavior of his sons without restraining them. As a result, God places a judgment on his household. The sons are slain, Eli dies of a broken neck when he falls on hearing of the defeat of the Israelites by the Philistines and the loss of the Ark of the Lord, and Samuel assumes the role of judge over Israel. Thomasin uses this example to demonstrate the responsibility that a man has in the eyes of God for the behavior of those under him.

NOTES TO BOOK VII

1. In these lines which speak of the authority of man over the creatures of the natural world, there is an echo of Walther von der Vogelweide in the *Spruch* of his "Reichston trilogy" beginning "Ich horte ein wazzer diezen" (= Lachmann 8, 28ff.). Although the thought is quite different, since Walther is speaking of the order that prevails in the animal kingdom, in contrast to the chaos in the human world, the language of Thomasin recalls Walther's formulation: "ich sach swaz in der welte was, / velt walt loup ror unde gras. / Swaz kriuchet unde fliuget / und bein zer erde biuget." See *Die Lieder Walthers von der Vogelweide*, ed. Friedrich Maurer, vol. 1: *Die religiösen und die politischen Lieder*, 2nd ed., ed. Friedrich Maurer, Altdeutsche Bibliothek 43 (Tübingen: Niemeyer, 1960), pp. 20–21.

2. We are using an idiom here, to indicate an enormous length of time, rather than rendering the expression more literally as "until the Day of Atonement."

3. We have elected to use the plural pronoun to refer to "intellect and common sense," although Thomasin employs the neuter singular in 8594 and 8596 ("wirz"/"erz") and a genitive singular in 8599 ("sîn").

4. The man is making a song and dance, pretending it is a matter of principle, whereas actually he is only concerned for his own interests.

5. The comma at the end of 8734 seems to be a mistake in Rückert's edition, and we have disregarded it.

6. In the interest of clarity, we translate these terms into English, while retaining a capital letter to convey the sense of a personified abstract.

7. We have deviated from the original syntax here and ignored the imperative "sage mir," in order to arrive at what we hope is an acceptable English reading of a rather tricky passage.

8. In the medieval European university, the seven liberal arts aimed to educate a person and develop his intellectual capacities. Grammar, Logic (also identified as

Dialectics, see 8916), and Rhetoric constituted the trivium, and Geometry, Arithmetic, Music, and Astronomy the quadrivium.

9. Not all of the names which follow are readily identifiable, and Thomasin is sometimes quite free with his attribution of expertise to specific names. However, the list reflects his broad acquaintance with ancient scholarship.

Donatus: fl. mid-fourth century, a famous teacher in Rome, one of whose pupils became St. Jerome.

Priscian: fl. c. 500, best known of all Latin grammarians, author of the influential *Institutiones grammaticae*. He taught in Constantinople.

Aristarchus (of Samothrace): c. 217–145 B.C. A Greek critic and grammarian, pupil of Aristophanes of Byzantium. Cicero and Horace valued him very highly.

Aristotle: Probably the most famous of the philosophers named by Thomasin, 384–322 B.C. A prolific writer of enormous range, although Thomasin points specifically to Dialectics. Cf. 6409 and 6414, where Thomasin laments him as one of the great people no longer alive.

Boethius: c. 470/475–524. Roman scholar, Christian philosopher and statesman, author of the famous *De consolatione philosophiae.*

Zeno (of Elea): c. 495–430 B.C. Greek philosopher and mathematician to whom Aristotle attributed the invention of Dialectics. Thomasin juxataposes his name to that of Aristotle in 6409, see above.

Porphirius: otherwise Porphyry, 233–301, one of the chief exponents of Neoplatonism. Among his works is a "History of Philosophy" and a life of Pythagorus.

Tullius: Thus does Thomasin refer to the great Roman orator and statesman, Cicero (Marcus Tullius, 106–43 B.C.).

Quintilian: c. 35–post 96 A.D. Latin teacher and writer whose *Institutio oratoria* is a major contribution to educational theory and literary criticism.

Sidonius: probably Gaius Sollius Apollinaris Modestus, 430–c. 483, who became bishop of Auvergne. Not generally highly valued as a literary figure, although he wrote poems and epigrams and was honored by the emperor Avitus with a statue in the library of Trajan, some of his writings, among them a number of letters, are interesting for the information they provide of life in Gaul at that time. His lament for the decline in interest in literature may have appealed to Thomas, who may, however, have had in mind an earlier member of the family, likewise called Sidonius, who was known as a Christian writer.

Crisippus: probably the Greek philosopher Chrysippus of Soli, c. 280–c. 206 B.C., who completed and systematized the Stoic doctrine.

Gregorius: Thomasin is presumably referring to St. Gregory (the Great), during whose reign as pope (590–640) the liturgical music of the Church was collected and codified, hence "Gregorian Chant."

Timotheus: 447–357 B.C., a poet and musician of Miletus, known as a composer and also said to have introduced some significant technical innovations into music.

Millejus: Could this perhaps be Melissus of Samos, the Greek philosopher, fl. fifth century B.C.? Or is Rückert correct in linking the name with the immediately preceding Timotheus and identifying it as a place-name "Miletus" (see above)? The occurrence of "Micalus" in the manuscripts is no easier to justify than either of these conjectures.

Thales: of Miletus, Iona, a sixth-century B.C. Greek philosopher, remembered for his cosmology based on water as the essence of all matter. No extant works but inclusion of his name in canon of the Seven Wise Men led to his idealization and to the attribution of many acts and sayings to him. This would certainly account for Thomasin's inclusion of him in his list, and his juxtaposition to Euclid.

Euclydes: fl. c. 300 B.C. in Alexandria. Most prominent mathematician of Greco-Roman antiquity, best known for his treatise on geometry, the *Elements*.

Albumazar: 787–886, the leading astrologer of the Muslim world.

Ptolomeus: Almost certainly, Claudius Ptolemaeus (fl. 127–45 A.D.), originator of the notion of the "Ptolemaeic system," which holds that the Earth is the center of the universe. His book, *The Mathematical Collection*, became known as *The Great Astronomer*, a work of immense scope and significance, enshrining the findings of Greek astronomy.

Atlas: In Homer, he supports the pillars that hold heaven and earth apart.

10. In particular, as Thomasin has already pointed out, Alexander was a significant patron of Aristotle, who had been his tutor. Cf. 6409–17 and note.

11. This is presumably another reference to Ptolemeus the Astronomer referred to in 8957, although the implied link with Alexander suggests that it could be a later member of the dynasty that assumed power in Egypt after the death of Alexander. The obvious candidate would be Ptolemy I, but then it is not clear why Thomasin should speak of him as "gelêrt."

12. Neptanebus (or, as Rückert suggests, Nectanebus, though without the support of the manuscripts) may correspond to Nectanebo II (fourth century B.C.), the last of the native Egyptian kings. Though history is clear that Alexander was the son of Philip of Macedonia, romantic legend links his mother, Olympias, with the last pharaoh, enjoying the notion of clandestine Egyptian origins. It is just possible that a further complication has crept into Thomasin's work, since Olympias herself was the daughter of King Neoptolemus of Epirus. Neither possibility explains why Thomasin should be using him as an outstanding example of learning, in the same breath as Ptolemeus, although Nectanebo was reputed to be a magician and in that respect could be deemed to have "grôzen sin."

13. I Kings 3 relates how Solomon asks God specifically for a wise mind. The book of Proverbs is traditionally ascribed to Solomon, though it is questionable how much of it emanates from him.

14. II Samuel and the opening of I Kings present a generally idealized picture of David, in which wisdom is implied rather than explicit.

15. Verses 9223–24: The Three Wise Men who bring their gifts to the infant Jesus are not named in the Gospels, but by the eighth century they had acquired the names by which they are traditionally known.

16. Thomasin's view of Julius Caesar is again an idealized one, not altogether endorsed by historical accounts, but he uses him, as he did at 3378, as a familiar example.

17. "Würre" in 9239 is the past subjunctive of "werren," which can mean a number of things: "upset," "dismay," "take amiss," or, as we have chosen here, actively "prevent."

18. Verse 9368: We have not been able to determine the precise passage that Thomasin is referring to. The sentiment expressed in 9368 does, however, echo what one can find expressed within the book of Proverbs (cf. 1:28-29: "Then they call me, but I answer not; they seek me, but find me not; / Because they hated knowledge, and chose not the fear of the Lord").

19. We are using the modern concept of "good news" to describe God's message.

20. Regrettably, we do not know who the "wise man" was to whom Thomasin is referring.

21. A punctuation mark, preferably a period, is needed at the end of 9723 to maintain the sense.

22. The rather odd phrase "ân durft" in 9780 seems to have puzzled some of the scribes, who have emended it to "ân nôt." However, Lexer does include other occurrences of the phrase and the actual meaning is clear enough.

NOTES TO BOOK VIII

1. This line has the ring of a proverb, but it is difficult to assign it to a particular source. Rückert's suggestion that it bears comparison with Ecclesiasticus 7:14, which exhorts "never . . . repeat yourself when you pray" (p. 587) is not altogether convincing, although it is reasonable to conclude, as he does, that Thomasin has adapted a biblical assertion to the exigencies of rhyme and meter.

2. Thomasin clearly refers to the dead in the plural in 10243, but uses the singular masculine, accusative pronoun with "er" ("ern") in 10245. We have corrected his inconsistency and used the plural throughout this section.

3. Verses 10425–70: The whole of this passage maintains the image of the decoration on shields and other knightly accoutrements.

4. See introduction, p. 11.

5. Verses 10470ff.: In order to demonstrate his point about arrogance and reliance on worldly power, Thomasin refers at some length to a contemporary situation with which he and his audience would have been very familiar: the conflict for the imperial throne between Philipp of Swabia and Otto of Brunswick, and the subsequent replacement of Otto by Frederick II. The rise and fall of their respective fortunes had already been the subject of a number of *Sprüche* by Walther von der Vogelweide, and some of the same material is treated here. Otto had been crowned in Rome in 1209 (10473) and Thomasin associates himself with this event in a rare biographical detail (10475–77). However, by the time Thomasin is writing, Otto has suffered severe defeat (10472) at the Battle of Bouvines in 1214, an event which put an end to his aspirations and led to the reign of Frederick II. To exemplify what he sees as the arrogance of Otto, and to underline his own close awareness of earlier events, Thomasin points to the composition of his chosen emblem, which contained three lions and a demi-eagle, as Walther von der Vogelweide had already mentioned in his song addressed to Otto (Lachmann 12,18ff.), probably three or four years earlier. Characteristically, Thomasin

deplores Otto's choice of emblem in terms of a violation of moderation: three lions are too many, and half an eagle is not enough to ensure proper flight. Thus his failure was ensured from the start, and, moreover, it was a twofold failure, since Otto had earlier been rejected in favor of Philipp, despite the support he enjoyed at that time (1198–1201). Even after Philipp's death in 1208, Otto had not succeeded in maintaining his position.

6. Verses 10569–74: Thomasin is continuing his immediately preceding discussion of the fall of Otto and the rise of Frederick II. The child Frederick had been a minor at the time of the death of his father, Henry VI, in 1197, hence his reference to "our child" (10570). "Apulia" is Thomasin's designation for Frederick's kingdom of Sicily, which had been threatened in 1210 by Otto at a time when Frederick was in conflict with the barons. However, Otto had been forced to retreat and had then gone to Germany, where he was elected king in 1212, before having himself crowned emperor in Aachen in 1215. Thomasin sees the success of Frederick as the work of God, while the decline in Otto's fortunes is attributed to his human weaknesses of arrogance and faithlessness.

7. Verses 10585–91: Thomasin sees Frederick's Sicilian kingdom as having been "disrupted" on two occasions, both as a result of internal treachery: the first time was the revolt while Frederick was still an infant, and the second the attempted seizure of it by Otto in 1210, at the instigation of a faction of the Sicilian nobility.

8. For suggestions about the identity of these seven Greek emperors, to whom should be given the designation "saint," see the long note in Rückert's edition (pp. 589–90). The precise list is unclear, and some names occur twice, but it is possible to calculate between five and seven candidates, all of whom came to a violent end.

9. Andronicus I was killed at the instigation of Isaac II in 1185. He was massacred by a street mob.

10. Khosrow II, king of Persia, extended the Sasanian territories in the late sixth and early seventh centuries, taking northern Mesopotamia, Syria, Palestine, Egypt, and Anatolia. His armies were defeated by Heraclius (cf. 10687) in 623–24, and he himself was condemned to death, having seen his son Mardanshah murdered (10693). Thomasin's condemnation of him for arrogance doubtless relates to his thirst for power and his enormous wealth. He reveled in extravagant and excessive display, but his influence in social and economic terms was limited and in many respects negative. Although his own attitude to Christianity was in general benevolent and he was himself married to a Christian woman, the regime over which he presided was brutal towards Christians, which probably accounts for Thomasin's assessment at 10693–95.

11. In the book of Esther, Ahasuerus is the mighty king "who reigned over a hundred and twenty-seven [sic] provinces" (10705). Favorite at his court is Haman, depicted as a scheming villain, who plots against the Jews and is ultimately executed himself on the gallows he had erected for Mordecai, father of Queen Esther, and his fellow Jews.

12. I Maccabees 7 relates how Nicanor, commander of the army of King Demetrius, swore to burn down the temple ("münster" [10748]) if his enemies did not surrender to him, but he was defeated and his failure construed as blasphemy. When he is the first to fall in the ensuing battle, his armies take flight, and his body

is desecrated: his head is cut off and the hand which swore a false oath is displayed for all to see.

13. Daniel 5:21 tells of the humiliation of King Nebuchadnezzar, and 5:22 goes on to say that his son, Balthasar (Belshazzar), did not learn from the example of his father but was likewise arrogant and suffered as a result.

14. In speaking of people who have been ill-treated and even slain by those who were actually beneath them, Thomasin refers to the case of the two Byzantine emperors, Isaac II Angelus and his son who became, briefly, Alexius IV. Isaac had been imprisoned and blinded by his brother, Alexius III. They were both imprisoned in 1195 but escaped and began a famous long journey to join Philipp of Swabia and his wife, their daughter/sister in Germany. They succeeded in persuading Philipp to divert the Fourth Crusade to Constantinople, in order to reinstate Alexius and his father as co-emperors. The plan succeeded up to a point but left them with a debt to the West which they could not repay, while Constantinople was ravaged and pillaged by the crusaders. A national revolt ensued and, after only a year (1203–4) they were deposed by Alexius Ducus, who became Alexius V and had Alexius IV strangled. Isaac died in prison a few days later.

15. Numbers 12 relates how Miriam, sister of Aaron, was afflicted with a terrible disease because she railed against God for singling out Moses for a special position. Abiram and Dathan also revolted against the authority of Moses (Numbers 16).

16. Verses 11075ff.: I Maccabees 5:55–62 tells of the fate of Josephus and Azarias, two of the commanders in the Maccabean force against the Gentiles, who used the absence of Judas and Jonathan, the actual leaders, to try to assert their own authority by attacking the town of Jamnia. The attempt proved disastrous, with massive losses on the Israelite side; the two men whose arrogance had caused the catastrophe were pursued to the frontier of Judaea and excluded from future conflict: "they were not of the family to whom it was granted to bring deliverance to Israel." The example suits Thomasin's purpose well, for the context is his disapproval of those who question the leadership of others and undermine their authority, and the passage immediately following concerns the prevailing criticism of the pope.

17. The "good fellow" referred to here with obvious irony is Walther von der Vogelweide who, in a famous *Spruch* (= Lachmann 34, 4ff.) had attacked Pope Innocent III for placing collecting chests in churches in order to extract money from the Germans to pay for excessive feasting among the clergy. Thomasin's own disapproval of this accusation is evident, and, as he implies, he was certainly not alone in turning against Walther for speaking in this high and mighty way against the papacy. In the adjacent *Spruch*, an unrepentant Walther addresses the chest itself ("hêr Stoc"), whose contents, he maintains, will not be used for their intended purpose of financing a crusade.

18. Thomasin continues his condemnation of Walther with his exhortation to noble gentlemen and poets and preachers to be very careful what they say. Clearly the normally restrained Thomasin, who rarely goes so far as to attack a contemporary, is incensed at Walther's outright attack on the head of Christendom, the appointee of God Himself. The message of Thomasin, however, is clear, even if he does not name this renowned contemporary: Walther has damaged his reputation in the eyes of God by this unjust attack on His representative on earth. Thomasin

will not have been alone in his disapproval. For a full discussion of Thomasin's literary relationship with Walther, see Karl Kurt Klein, "Zum dichterischen Spätwerk Walthers von der Vogelweide. Der Streit mit Thomasin von Zerclaere," *Innsbrucker Beiträge zur Kulturwissenschaft* 6 (Germanistische Abhandlungen) (1959): 63–91.

19. The phrase "ân unserm getiht" presents some problems. We have read the preposition as "an," assuming the idiom "dienen an" (to serve through, by means of) and it seems likely that there is an error here in the edition. There seems no justification, however, for scribe G's emendation of the noun to "geriht."

20. Verses 11649–51: cf. 939–64 and note. Walther von der Vogelweide uses the word "übergulde," though to describe an abstract idea (= Lachmann 8, 17).

21. Luke 22:42.

22. See introduction, p. 2.

23. Verses 11787ff.: Thomasin addresses Frederick II in very positive terms, reminding him of what he can achieve and of the exploits of his predecessors. His grandfather was Frederick I ("Barbarossa"), who had perished by drowning in 1190, before he could accomplish his mission of leading the Third Crusade (11803–4); his uncle, the eldest son of Barbarossa, had taken over the leadership of the campaign but died in 1192. Thus it is for Frederick, the grandson and the nephew, to take up the challenge. (In the event, although he vowed to do so and made several attempts, it was not until 1227 that he departed on the long-postponed crusade, but was struck down by a severe illness which claimed the lives of many of his companions and afflicted him severely enough for him to postpone his journey until 1228. When he resumed it, it was against the order of the new pope, Gregory IX, who had already excommunicated him for breaking his oath. Undeterred, Frederick proceeded on his journey to the Holy Land, where he negotiated for himself the title of king of Jerusalem. These later events, including the death of Frederick in 1250, lie far beyond the scope of Thomasin's work, of course.)

24. Thomasin is playing with the Middle High German word "hôhvart" (literally 'going high'). Unfortunately, we cannot emulate him in our translation.

25. Numbers 22–24.

26. Genesis 4:8.

27. Verses 11991–92: The notoriously ruthless Herod the Great is associated above all with the massacre of the innocents as related by St. Matthew, but Thomasin no doubt has in mind Herod's much earlier slaying of his two sons and their mother, Mariamne, in a jealous rage.

28. The apocryphal Daniel and Susanna (also known as Susanna and the Elders) tells of the false accusations laid on Susanna by the vindictive elders, who see to it that she arrives at the point of execution but are then themselves put to death.

29. Thomasin demonstrates here his familiarity with kenotic theology, the kenotic (humbling) experience of Christ that is described in Philippians 2:5ff., particularly 2:8, which constitutes an integral part of the Catholic Eucharist: "With the mingling of water and wine we come to share the divinity of Christ who humbled Himself to share our humanity."

30. In the closing lines of this book, Thomasin is playing with the pronoun "swer" and the verb "swern," or, in 12217, the past participle "gesworn." Although not noticeably a feature of his style, it is a favorite with his contemporaries, particularly Gottfried von Strassburg.

NOTES TO BOOK IX

1. Note what Thomasin says about Otto's emblem at 10471ff.

2. The word "zal" means literally "number," but we have taken it to mean "proportion," more in line with the preceding words.

3. Rückert observes that it is a familiar idea in the Middle Ages that a tamed lion may be chastised vicariously by having a dog attached to it.

4. Verses 12683–84: The reference is to Leopold VI of Austria, the foremost ruler of the House of Babenberg, who ruled from 1198 to1230, his reign thus coinciding with the papacy of Innocent III (1198–1216). Leopold was a great supporter of the monasteries and himself founded a Cistercian monastery at Lilienfeld (c. 1206). Like Innocent III, he took rigorous action against the "heretics" (the Cathari and the Waldenses) in a period when church and state united to attack doctrines which struck at the roots of orthodox Christianity, with penalties ranging from excommunication to active persecution and execution. This no doubt is the point of Thomasin's assertion here that secular and spiritual courts must support one another if justice is not to be placed in jeopardy (12691–94). Leopold enjoyed a reputation as a firm adherent of the Church, which earned him the nickname "pater clericorum," but Thomasin's picture of him is a much harsher one, of the persecutor of the heretics. His vision of Leopold burning heretics alive leads to the grotesque play on the word "geriht" in 12686, which means both 'culinary dish' and 'judgment' or 'court of law.'

5. Thomasin appears to be grinding a personal axe here and in ensuing passages, or at least joining in the medieval debate about the sometimes arbitrary power of the ecclesiastical courts. These courts, which existed side by side with the secular courts, had a wide range of powers, with their jurisdiction over strictly spiritual matters extending into more worldly issues such as disputes over property and criminal actions. A great many people not obviously connected with the Church were able to claim the protection of these courts.

6. The word "geriht" can refer both to the abstract ('judgment') and the actual court of law, and we use both here, according to the context.

7. Verses 12818–48: The reference is to the rebellion of the 250 princes against the rule of Moses and Aaron in Numbers 16. The "misfortune" that befell them was that they were killed in the fire sent by God.

8. Verses 12921–27: I Maccabees 9 tells of the death of Judas Maccabeus after many triumphs, when he has gone into a final conflict with the Syrians against the advice of his companions, declaring that he has no intention of fleeing: "If our time is come, let us die for our fellow-countrymen, and leave no stain on our honor."

9. Verses 12933–36: The reference is to I Samuel 14, where Jonathan, son of Saul, and his armor-bearer (his "companion" here) face the host of the Philistines alone and "the multitude melted away" (I Samuel 14:16).

10. Verses 12937–40: Judges 7 and 8 relate how Gideon, with a mere three hundred men, put the vast army of the Midianites to flight.

11. See below, note 12.

12. Verses 13009ff.: The *Physiologus* taught that lion cubs were born dead and woke up only on the third day when their father came and snorted them into life.

Wolfram von Eschenbach includes a version of the idea in both *Parzival* (738, 19–20) and *Willehalm* (40, 5–7), and Thomasin himself had doubtless derived from the same source his information that the lion obliterates his tracks with his tail when he knows he is being pursued (12958–62).

13. The lion appears to be suggesting that Baldwin could very well be more powerful than himself.

14. Verses 13392–93: Thomasin has hitherto used Baldwin as a personal name, but in these two lines he seems to imply that it is (also) a generic term. We have taken a liberty with the text by transposing the indefinite article in 13393 and inserting it in 13392 in order to achieve the same effect. It should be noted that Thomasin is the only known source for this fable of the boisterous donkey.

NOTES TO BOOK X

1. It is well known that certain plants, notably clover, can prove fatal if eaten by cows or sheep.

2. The term "widerslac" in 14122 has presented a few problems. According to Lexer, it could mean "wiederholter schlag; das widerstehn; rückschlag, gegenteil, abwehr (beim fechten); widerschein," none of which appear to fit the current context. We have rendered the term as "vindictiveness," fully aware that this may not be precisely what Thomasin intended. We have also considered that he may have understood "widerslac" as "Gegenteil" ("opposite"), in the sense of 'this is the opposite of what one ought to be doing,' but our preference here is for a word that underscores the rather nasty measures meted out to the poor.

3. See Rückert's note on the form "vüresagen," which he adopts in line with MS A, though adding an extra syllable to preserve the meter: ("vür sagen" = 'to pronounce, speak out'). The man is constantly anticipating how he can find pretexts not to give. Some problems have arisen because of the proximity in 14308 and 14316 of the past participle "verseit," leading other scribes (S and D) to substitute "versagen" (= 'to refuse') here.

4. Rückert inserts a period after 14392. We suggest, however, that it makes much better sense to view this verse in conjunction with 14393–96.

5. Verses 14541ff.: it appears that Thomasin is quite happy with lending and borrowing between friends, but dislikes the idea of a more formal, business relationship, which he believes to be compounded if the debt is repaid too promptly.

6. Thomasin somewhat humorously uses the term "lehen," which describes a piece of territory held within feudal law.

Medieval German Texts in Bilingual Editions

Sovereignty and Salvation in the Vernacular, 1050–1150
  introduction, translations, and notes by James A. Schultz

Ava's New Testament Narratives: "When the Old Law Passed Away"
  introduction, translation, and notes by James A. Rushing, Jr.

History as Literature: German World Chronicles
of the Thirteenth Century in Verse
  introduction, translation, and notes by R. Graeme Dunphy

Der Welsche Gast (The Italian Guest)
  Thomasin von Zirclaria, translated with introduction and notes by
  Marion Gibbs and Winder McConnell

Typeset in 10/12 ITC New Baskerville and Adobe Woodtype Ornaments 2
Designed by Linda K. Judy
Composed by Tom Krol
Manufactured by Cushing-Malloy, Inc.

Medieval Institute Publications
College of Arts and Sciences
Western Michigan University
1903 W. Michigan Avenue
Kalamazoo, MI 49008-5432
http://www.wmich.edu/medieval/mip

 WESTERN MICHIGAN UNIVERSITY